Bits to Bitcoin

Bits to Bitcoin

How Our Digital Stuff Works

Mark Stuart Day

with illustrations by C. A. Jennings

The MIT Press
Cambridge, Massachusetts
London, England

This book was set in Stone Serif by Westchester Publishing Services. Printed and bound in the United States of America.

Excerpt from *The Wizard of Oz* granted courtesy of Warner Bros. Entertainment Inc.

Library of Congress Cataloging-in-Publication Data

Names: Day, Mark Stuart, author. | Jennings, C. A., illustrator.
Title: Bits to bitcoin : how our digital stuff works / Mark Stuart Day ; illustrated by C.A. Jennings.
Description: Cambridge, MA : MIT Press, [2018] | Includes index.
Identifiers: LCCN 2017046504 | ISBN 9780262037938 (pbk. : alk. paper)
Subjects: LCSH: Computer science--Popular works.
Classification: LCC QA76 .D3333327 2018 | DDC 004--dc23 LC record available at https://lccn.loc.gov/2017046504

10 9 8 7 6 5 4 3 2 1

OZ: Pay no attention to that man behind the curtain! The great Oz has spoken!

Dorothy (*pulling back curtain*): Who are you?

Man: Oh... I... I am the great and powerful... Wizard of Oz.

Dorothy: You are? I don't believe you.

Man: Well, I'm afraid it's true. There's no other wizard except me.

—From *The Wizard of Oz* (1939)

Contents

Preface

As a high school student in the late 1970s, I wrote an article for the school newspaper explaining what a personal computer could do. Among its other virtues, it could store recipes. That wasn't wrong—it just doesn't seem like the first thing you'd choose to say about a modern computer.

Back in those days, it was easy to perceive that something important was happening, but we couldn't quite see all the way to today's capabilities. Since we now have an abundance of devices and services using computers and communications, there is no longer any need to argue for the value of computers. Indeed, the challenge now is getting people to disconnect from their mobile phones, tablets, music players, and laptops long enough to discuss the merits of something else.

Alongside the evolution of computers from bizarre novelty to ubiquitous necessity, there's been a substantial amount of discovery and invention. In roughly the same way that it was once useful to explain what computers were, I think it's now useful to explain something about the larger context of computer systems and infrastructure.

In everyday life, plumbing is tremendously important but little noticed until it goes wrong—and likewise computational infrastructure. You most likely don't care much about the pipes in your house unless one of them springs a leak or otherwise fails, in which case you develop a strong need for someone to fix it immediately (and are willing to pay them well to do so). Being a "computational plumber" is likewise a good but generally unglamorous life. I have had the good fortune to examine a cross-section of the world's major organizations, where I have seen some of the good, bad, and ugly of what they do with their infrastructure.

It is strange to observe that it is easier for a nonspecialist to learn what physicists know about special relativity than to learn what computer scientists know about coordinating processes—even though almost nothing of daily life has any connection to special relativity, while almost all of our daily activities involve some amount of coordination among processes. I've seen that there is too little awareness of the "big ideas" of computer science in places like the *New York Review of Books* or National Public Radio, where they could and should be relevant.

Accordingly, this book explains computer systems to people whose intellectual interests are firmly rooted elsewhere—particularly in the humanities. Although my own university education has all been in engineering, I am a supporter of both liberal arts and informed citizens. I see knowledge as crucial for our intellectual and political freedom, as well as the realization of our human potential.

The book deliberately avoids programming. My empirical observation is that there are intelligent, educated people who simply don't like programming. I think this claim is readily verifiable and quite understandable: programming is actually quite a strange activity, but those of us who have learned to program tend to forget its strangeness. An unwillingness or lack of interest in programming strikes me as comparable to a lack of interest in opera: it does imply that some arguably important knowledge and experience will remain out of reach, but does not imply that the "non–opera person" needs remedial help.

How can we structure an exploration of computer science ideas where programming is not used? The goal is not to provide a complete introduction for future professionals, but rather to hit highlights for the curious. My organizing principle is analogous to a zoo. There are some collected specimens, and I will both describe the individual "animals" and point out some of the connections among them.

Zoos are out of fashion today. Better to see animals in their natural habitat, or failing that to see them in sprawling parks that better simulate their natural habitat. Certainly if we have a choice, it seems wise to prefer a presentation that is less artificial, less constrained, more like the real world of the animals on display. And yet the old-fashioned zoo with its caged animals played an important educational role of showing real animals from far corners of the world, and starting to create a consciousness of their significance. The zoo was an important bridge between the animals in the wild and a broader human appreciation of their importance.

My zoo contains some technical issues that may well be unfamiliar even to people who are computer professionals. Writing the book was an interesting learning experience, as I repeatedly challenged myself to explain what really matters, and why it matters, without falling back on some version of the generic accepted curriculum for computer science. Some readers may gain helpful insights from reading the book, while some readers may be deeply annoyed. It's even possible that the same reader may have both kinds of experiences.

As with any zoo, reasonable people can find fault with the completeness or coherence of the collection I present. As with any zookeeper, I will explain my choices by pointing to a combination of intent and circumstances. A notable influence is the magisterial textbook *Principles of Computer Systems Design* by my colleagues Jerry Saltzer and Frans Kaashoek. Indeed, you can think of this book as the nonprofessional's gloss on what professionals learn from that text. If you are interested in pursuing these topics further, it's an excellent resource.

Completing a tour of this zoo doesn't make anyone into a professional programmer, or even necessarily give a complete introduction to any of the topics—just as a visit to an animal zoo doesn't make anyone into a zoologist, or even provide a complete view of any single animal. But in both cases we can get an appreciation of some of the individual characteristics and also start to form an impression of the wonders of the interconnected world that contains such individuals.

Acknowledgments

Many people have supported me in this work. Some have provided helpful work environments (at Riverbed, Dropbox, and MIT). Some have commented on chapters or the whole manuscript. Some have provided expertise and guidance at crucial points. Thanks to you all!

In alphabetical order: Aditya Agarwal, the Authors Guild, Hari Balakrishnan, Azer Bestavros, Elly Day, F. G. Day, Jefferson Day, Jonathan Day, Malcom Day, Marjorie Day, Michael Day, Minh-Anh Day, Grub Street Launch Lab 2014 participants, John Guttag, Craig Jennings, Walter Jonas, Frans Kaashoek, Dina Katabi, Jerry Kennelly, Katrina LaCurts, Blanco Lam, Butler Lampson, Marie Lee, Ricky Lin, Barbara Liskov, Kathy Loh, Sam Madden, Jim Miller, Nchinda Nchinda, Jessica Papin, Laura Paquette, Karen Sollins, and Jim Hoai Tran.

Special thanks to my fabulous wife Thu-Hằng Trần, who has now survived two seemingly endless writing projects with me—my doctoral dissertation in the mid-'90s, and now this book. I rarely say enough to her about her support and how much I value her. I hope that this acknowledgment helps to make up for that. *Anh vẫn còn yêu mình*, y'know?

1 Introduction

There is an important kind of infrastructure in the modern world that is not well known simply because it's relatively new. You may well be familiar with other kinds of infrastructure. For example:

• Transportation infrastructure supports how people and goods move around. It consists of roads, bridges, tunnels, rail lines, airports, warehouses, and the like.
• Electrical infrastructure supports how electricity is generated and delivered. It consists of generating plants, transformers, distribution lines, meters, and the like.
• Water and sewage infrastructure supports how water and waste are handled. It consists of dams, reservoirs, aqueducts, pipes, treatment plants, and the like.

Anyone born after World War II takes all those kinds of infrastructure for granted. In contrast, this book explains some important aspects of the newest "plumbing" or "machinery" that underpins the modern world: what is usually called computational infrastructure. This infrastructure consists of elements that will seem to future generations as ordinary as roads, electricity, and running water, but at the moment they're still developing and changing.

Even though you may not have a direct interest in the building or analysis of infrastructure, you have a stake in understanding it—both its capabilities and its limits. You have likely had some experience with devices and services that involve computers of some kind. You probably own a mobile phone, tablet, or laptop, for instance. You are probably comfortable doing online searches or looking on a social network to see what's happening with friends. But you may be a bit fuzzy about how any of that really works. This book explains the ingredients that make it all possible.

Software, processes, computations—these are some of the conventional terms for the most important "stuff" in this domain. Regardless of the words we use, software has an intriguing dual nature. On one hand, software is something real that can affect the world directly; on the other hand, in some ways software is just the shadows cast by computational engines as they run. As other writers have observed, programming is more like the casting of magic spells than like writing literature or building machines. The effects of programs can take place without the participation of a reader, in contrast to the nature of literature; but the material of a program is more like the words of a novelist than like the physical materials of other engineering disciplines.

This book is divided into four parts:

• The first part introduces the world of a single process. That world is both surprisingly powerful and surprisingly limited, even when we assume that its computational machinery always works correctly.

• The second part builds on the first to look at what happens in a world with more than one process, and particularly what happens when those processes interact with each other. Processes interacting with each other are less capable in some ways and more capable in other ways than might be expected. By the end of the second part, we can outline a simple version of how browsing works on the web.

• The third part complicates the multiprocess world by considering processes and machinery that sometimes fail. Various cunning inventions nevertheless allow these interacting processes to surpass the limits of their underlying machinery.

• The final part takes up issues about processes that are attacking each other or defending themselves: how to keep secrets, whether to trust or not, and how to prevent cheating. By the end of the final part, we can explain the mechanisms that allow the Bitcoin system to accurately record money transfers in spite of attackers.

Now it's time to actually begin the tour instead of just talking about it. An old saying is that a journey of a thousand miles begins with a single step. Our journey starts in the next chapter by thinking about a single step.

I Single Process

2 Steps

More than a hundred years ago, artists such as Georges Seurat and Paul Signac began to experiment with using small dots of pure color to create an image. The descendants of this technique—television and digital displays of all kinds—are now so common that it's hard to remember that there was a time when people never looked at visual representations made of little dots.

In modern technical terminology, we refer to those dots as *pixels* (a contraction of "picture element"). Now that such fields of pixels are used widely for all sorts of purposes, many people have experienced the related phenomenon of *pixelation*, when some limitation of the display system makes the pixels weirdly big and blocky, rendering some or all of the image "chunky." Those moments reveal the underlying representation of the image as a collection of discrete pieces rather than the continuous smooth image we might prefer to see. An interesting philosophical question is this: what if the world itself were actually made of very small discrete pieces? How would our experiences be different, and would we be able to tell?

The term *digital* is commonly heard as a description of various kinds of computer or media systems with these "stepped" or "chunky" characteristics. The meaning of "digital" is an important foundation for our upcoming explorations of computation. We can rephrase our philosophical question about a world made of small pieces by asking, What does it mean to be digital? Whatever "digital" is, it underpins all the systems we examine later in this book. Its properties will accordingly constrain what those systems can be.

Our fingers are also called our *digits*, and they give their name to whatever is called digital. Counting on fingers is probably everyone's first experience of a digital system. We teach children to count integers "1, 2, 3..." holding up one, then two, then three fingers. When we're choosing to count fingers, we have a shared understanding that fingers only "count" when they are clearly "up" or clearly "down."

Despite that convention, your hand is perfectly capable of adopting intermediate positions. If we ask a question about what number is represented by such an intermediate position, the usual answer is something like "I don't know" or "nothing." In terms of the integer-counting scheme we learn on our fingers, we can produce only integer-valued answers—it doesn't "make sense" to answer with "2½" or "2.16."

Another kind of digital system in everyday life is a stair. A stair divides the vertical space between two levels into several distinct levels. It's useful to contrast a stair with a simple ramp that leads between the same two levels. On a ramp we can take small moves horizontally—in fact, those moves can be as small as we choose—and for each small change in horizontal distance there is a corresponding small change in vertical distance (and vice versa). That's different from what happens on a stair. There, a small change in one direction doesn't always produce a small change in the other direction. In particular, the edge of a stair step produces a sharp difference in vertical distance for only a small change in horizontal distance.

Let's assume for a moment that the stair and the ramp have the same slope (see figure 2.1). In the real world, such matching slopes almost never happen: such an alignment means that either the ramp is dangerously steep or the stair is frustratingly shallow. But it's useful for our purposes, because we are just trying to understand the characteristics of each.

There are three common ways of relating the stair to the ramp (see figure 2.2). One possibility is that the stair is just below the ramp, so that the "outermost" parts of the treads coincide with the ramp.

The opposite possibility is that the stair is just above the ramp, so that the "innermost" parts of the treads coincide with the ramp. And a third

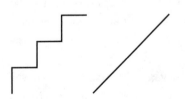

Figure 2.1
A stair and a ramp with the same slope.

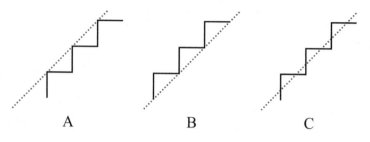

Figure 2.2
Different relationships between ramp and stair.

possibility is halfway between the first two approaches, which makes it so that the center of each tread coincides with the ramp.

We'll choose to talk about the first structure, because the associated physical experiences and intuitions are a little easier to explain. But it's important to observe that it doesn't actually matter which structure is used: we'll be talking about the nature and size of the gaps between stair and ramp. No matter how we align the stair and the ramp, those gaps still have the same total size.

When the stair and ramp have the same slope but the ramp is aligned with the outermost part of the treads, most positions on the ramp are slightly above the corresponding vertically aligned position on the flat part of the stair. If we put a foot anywhere onto the ramp, it rests solidly on the ramp; if we put a foot into the exact same position while using the stair, the foot does not rest solidly on anything—instead, it falls a short distance to the lower position on the step, where it does rest solidly. If we believed that we were walking up a smooth ramp, these repeated drops down to the stairs could be quite jarring. We would experience them as errors, lumpiness, or roughness in the "ramp-ness" that we were expecting. Most people have had the experience of momentary disorientation or discomfort when they miss a step of a stair; this "missing the ramp" would likely feel quite similar, but with the added problem of repeating.

We can reduce the gap between the "ramp experience" and the "stair experience" by making the stairs smaller (see figure 2.3).

Very, very small stairs are indistinguishable from a ramp. In fact, if we look at any real physical ramp in microscopic detail, we'll find that it's not anything like a perfectly straight line connecting the two levels. Instead, it is a bumpy collection of level changes of varying slopes and heights. However,

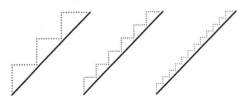

Figure 2.3
Making steps smaller.

that microscopic bumpiness doesn't matter for our typical uses of the ramp; we can simply treat it as though it were smooth.

In general, a system can have steps or it can be smoothly varying. The technical term for a stepped system is *digital,* and the technical term for a smooth unstepped system is *analog*. Sometimes analog and digital aspects can be found together in the same system. The crucial insight is that digital and analog are simply *models*. When it is useful to notice and work with discrete separated levels (like the stairs) we call that system "digital." When it is useful to ignore lumpiness and sharp changes in favor of having as many intermediate levels as might ever be needed—like the ramp—we call that system "analog." But just as we can choose to see a stair as a bumpy ramp or to see a ramp as if it has microscopic steps, there is no way in which any system is "really digital" or "really analog."

Our focus in the remainder of the book will be on systems that are digital in two distinct ways. Computation is about "doing," and it's also about "stuff." Usually we are concerned about their combination, "doing something with stuff," but it's useful at the beginning to separate these. In the rest of this chapter, we focus on "stuff"—what a computer scientist would refer to as digital data. In the next chapter, we focus on "doing"—what a computer scientist would refer to as processes.

Bits

What is digital data? All of our "stuff" is represented as a collection of *bits*. Each bit is valued either 0 or 1, like a switch that is either off or on. There are no other, intermediate values: just 0 or 1, but lots of them! Once we have a "single step" from 0 to 1 and back to 0, we can combine those to build as elaborate a stair as we want. We'll see a little later that we can use these simple building blocks to represent all kinds of bizarre wiggly curves.

Before we do that, it's worth asking, What's good about digital? Why is it interesting or useful to build systems around digital data?

If we need to store or transmit data, we typically care about reliability (we consider reliability more carefully later in chapter 16). If we are storing or transmitting something important, then we want to be sure that we get out exactly what we put in. We don't want to lose anything, and we don't want any distortions. That's true regardless of whether we're talking about a voice, a written message, a photograph, or a movie, and it's true whether we're talking about sending those to another person or storing them so we can retrieve them later.

A digital system is attractive because typically it's easier to achieve a given level of reliability with a digital system than with an analog system. That's not to say that a digital system is necessarily easier to build, but that it's easier to get good results with a digital system.

Noise

The enemy to be defeated in any kind of storage or transmission system is noise. Noise in this sense is not loud or distracting sound—instead, it's low-level "fuzz" that creeps into every stage of transmission or storage. This kind of noise is hard to eliminate entirely, since it often arises from thermal processes—that is, the random vibrations of the molecules in any physical material, including the atmosphere.

In an analog system, it is hard to distinguish added noise from a small fluctuation in the signal. After all, the signal (like an audio recording) may well have some small fluctuations in its original form, which ideally should be captured and retained. So we can't simply declare that all small fluctuations in the signal are noise and should be eliminated.

In figure 2.4, we have a complex "wiggly" analog signal at the left and some lower-intensity noise being added in the middle. The resulting signal

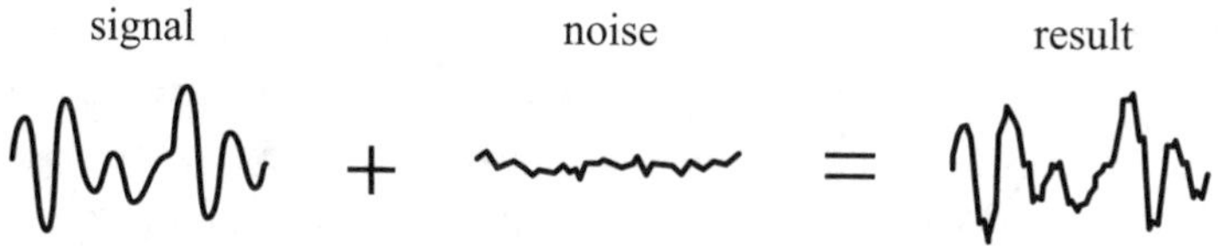

signal   noise   result

Figure 2.4
Noise added into an analog signal is hard to separate out.

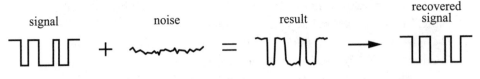

Figure 2.5
Noise added into a digital signal is easier to separate out.

is subtly distorted compared to the original: if you look closely, you can see it's not the exact same shape. Unfortunately, when we look at only the result, it's not obvious which of the small wiggles are noise—some of them were in the original signal. It's not clear how we can improve the result to get rid of the noise and recover the original signal.

In contrast, figure 2.5 shows a digital signal and the same low-intensity noise as in the previous analog example. The result is again a distorted signal, but now we know that the digital signal consists of only the "high" and "low" values, and any wiggles are just noise. We can filter out the wiggles and recover the original digital signal in a way that wasn't possible with the analog signal.

A digital system can be built so that small fluctuations in the signal are not meaningful—the transitions from 0 to 1 or from 1 to 0 can be much larger than the small changes caused by noise processes. Accordingly, the system can successfully extract a clean, noise-free signal by successfully mapping each slightly distorted element back to its original bit value.

Is Computation Physical?

In the world of computation, if we're given a bit pattern in some particular physical form, what matters is the bit pattern, not the physical form. We might draw an analogy to a knot, which is another kind of pattern. If we take a particular knot—for example, a so-called square knot—it doesn't matter if it's tied in a thin cord or a thick rope, it's still a square knot. It likewise doesn't matter if the material is nylon, polyester, or hemp, or what the color is—the knot is the same knot regardless. In fact, if we have a single rope that is made up of different colors, thicknesses, and/or materials joined seamlessly end to end, we can take a single knot and slide it along that rope. It's really the same knot, even though it's composed of different materials at different times.

Likewise, we can see that a page of text (like a page of this book) is the same in its information properties if we photocopy the page onto a different color paper, or a different thickness of paper, or even if we copy the page by hand-painting letters on a wall. Other aspects of the text will change—how easy it is to read, how easy it is to carry—but there is a kind of "textness" that is shared by all the different versions, a kind of Platonic form that we can discern behind the surface variations.

A bit pattern is the *same* bit pattern whether it's represented as fluctuations in magnetization, charge in a semiconductor, black marks printed as a barcode on paper, or a sequence of blinking lights. The physical characteristics of the storage and computing mechanisms can have a large impact in terms of the possible speeds, capacities, and reliability, but "bits are bits"— there's nothing about a "magnetic bit" (for example) that makes it better or worse than any other bit.

Thus, what matters in computation is not physical, but that doesn't mean that computation is imaginary or fantasy. Computation is real, and tangible realizations of computation are physical—but what matters about computation is not physical. The nonphysical character of computation is challenging for people who equate "real" with "physical." Entertainingly, computation resembles magic, something that is itself distinct from the "ordinary stuff" of the world but that nonetheless has the ability to affect the world.

Weighing Programs

In one joke about the nonphysical nature of computation, we see a NASA technician in the early days of the space program trying to calculate the total weight of the rocket to be launched. He goes to the leader of the programming team and asks for the weight of the programs.

"Nothing," replies the programmer.

"No, I really need you to tell me the weight of the programs or else I won't have an accurate total," says the technician.

"I told you, it's nothing!" the programmer insists.

Feeling like he is being brushed off, the technician goes to fetch one of the large decks of punched cards that were used for programming in those days. He drops the heavy box in the programmer's lap.

"There's a program, and it weighs more than nothing!" the technician proclaims.

The programmer quietly replies, "No, the program is the *holes*."

Analog/Digital Conversion

If we're starting with some smoothly varying analog data, it might seem that we have to stick with a smoothly varying analog representation—but actually, we can migrate between the analog and digital worlds. The key is the observation we made about small stairs starting to resemble a ramp: we can make a digital representation resemble an analog representation by making the steps small enough. That same principle applies not only to ramps but also to any analog shape. Better yet, the connection between digital and analog can be cast in terms of rules: we can work out how small we have to make the steps so that we can represent a given set of analog data.

Let's assume that the data of interest is the sound of some music that is being played. Physically, that sound consists of complex sequences of air pressure changes. If we could see the music as it goes through the air, we'd see the air behaving a little bit like ocean waves. Analog techniques like magnetic recording and phonographs produce copies of those complex waves in different media—magnetic particles on tape or grooves in vinyl. A version of the sound waves is actually visible if we look closely at the grooves on a record.

So we can make an analog representation by effectively copying the shapes in a different analog medium. Our challenge is to somehow represent the waves as a series of steps instead. Two handy pieces of engineering knowledge are relevant to our quest to represent the sound in digital form.

Our first handy piece of knowledge is that any complicated back-and-forth wave shape can be approximated by a sum of *sine waves*. Figure 2.6 is a picture of a sine wave. Although all sine waves have a similar shape, they can differ in their frequency (how close together the peaks are) and their amplitude (how tall the peaks are). A single sine wave on its own sounds like a pure tone—at a single pitch and without any complexity to the sound.

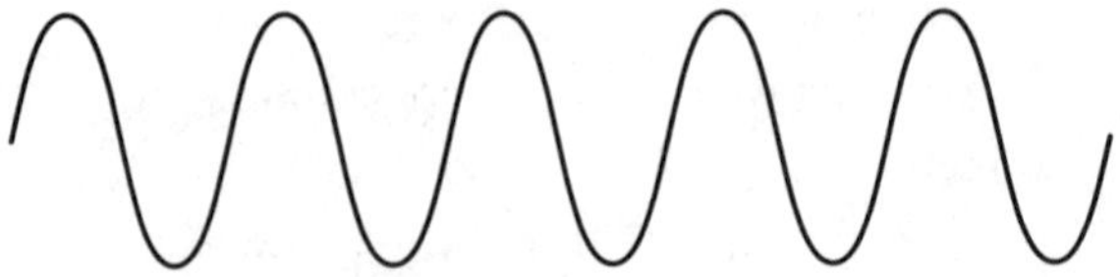

Figure 2.6
A sine wave.

Surprising as it may seem, even the messiest wave can be approximated by some number of different sine waves. Figure 2.7 shows an example of how three simple sine waves at the top add together to produce the much-more-complex form at the bottom. Although it's not obvious from this simple example, the reverse process also works—given a wildly complex periodically repeating wave, we can figure out a collection of sine waves that add up to produce the complex shape. Now, this business of adding up sine waves is

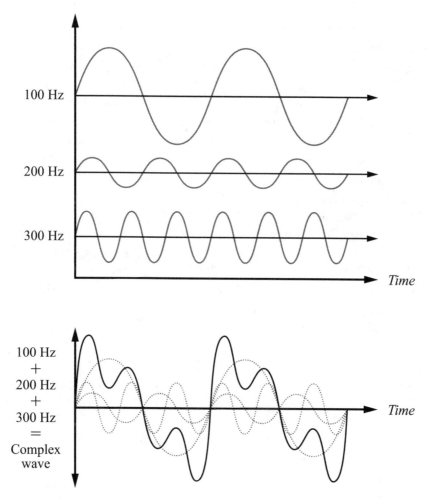

Figure 2.7
Adding together multiple sine waves for a more complex wave.

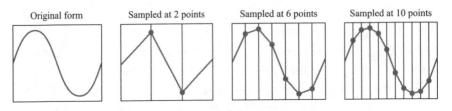

Figure 2.8
Increasing sample frequency produces a more accurate reconstruction.

not guaranteed to be perfect. Instead, as we add more and more component waves into the mix, we come closer and closer to an exact match...but may not ever reach it. But we can pick some threshold at which we say that the match is "close enough," and declare victory.

The second handy piece of knowledge is that if we have any kind of repeating wave, we can copy it perfectly if we *sample* at the right speed. Sampling here means that we are doing incomplete measurement—rather than measure continuously, we measure occasionally but regularly. Effectively, sampling is a kind of "stepped" or intermittent measurement. Figure 2.8 shows the way that samples let us reconstruct a signal. The more samples, the better the reconstruction.

The right speed to sample is at least twice the frequency of the wave. Sampling more often is okay, but if we want to make a perfect copy, we have to sample twice as fast as the rate at which anything is changing in the wave we're trying to copy. Why twice as fast? The underlying math is a little complicated, but the physical intuition is that if you're sampling at least twice as fast as anything happening in the wave, you never miss anything—you catch every meaningful change in the wave's behavior.

For example, you probably know that household electricity in a wall socket is a kind of wave. In the United States, this "electric wave" wiggles back and forth 60 times each second (or, we can say, the frequency is 60 Hz). So if our wave is one of these U.S. alternating-current waves at 60 Hz, we can sample it 120 times each second and be confident we can reassemble those readings into a perfect copy. Engineers talk about this reassembly from samples as *reconstructing* the wave.

As we mentioned, the sounds you hear are the result of waves in the air reaching your ear. Let's pick some particular musical note as an example. If you know music, then you will understand a description like "the A three octaves above middle C." If you don't know music, we're just picking some note, and it doesn't much matter which one it is. That particular note (the A three octaves above middle C) happens to have a frequency of 3520 Hz. So if we sample it at twice that frequency (that is, 7040 times each second) we can reconstruct it perfectly.

Both the alternating current wave and the pure musical tone are sine waves, but this frequency-doubling technique doesn't require sine waves—sampling at twice the wave's frequency is sufficient to reconstruct waves that don't look even a little bit like sine waves. And again, let's emphasize that this is a perfect reconstruction of the wave—as long as the wave repeats *exactly* at the stated frequency. (In the real world, lots of complex sounds actually grow, decay, or change in various ways rather than being strictly repeating in this sense.)

Let's recap the two techniques we've examined. The first, "adding-waves" technique lets us take apart even *nonrepeating* waves into collections of repeating sine waves. When the collection of sine waves is added together, the result is approximately the same as the original wave. In a complementary fashion, the second, "sampling" technique lets us perfectly reconstruct any *repeating* wave from only a sample of the points.

The great thing is that we can use these ideas together: we can take any wave apart into lots of repeating waves, which we can then represent perfectly with sampled measurements. In combination, these two techniques mean that we should be able to perfectly represent any sound by taking digital samples. We just have to be sure that we sample twice as fast as the frequency of the highest-frequency wave in the collection.

In practice, there are some problems with this approach. One problem has to do with determining what is the highest frequency that matters. If human perception is involved (as it often is), we have the challenge of whether this "perfect representation" really has to be perfect for all people, or just apparently perfect for the vast majority. Some unusual individuals can see or hear much better than almost all other people; building systems to accommodate their special talents makes everything considerably more expensive while delivering no value for that vast majority.

Accordingly, most digital audio and video systems involve trade-offs that produce visible or audible "glitches" for some but are undetectable for most people. Your friend who complains about the sound quality of some recording may really be able to hear things that you can't.

Born Digital

Do we need to worry about these sampling and reconstruction issues for everything of interest? No. Recall that some items of interest are most usefully understood as digital representations already. For example, this book was written as a series of characters inserted into a word-processor file stored on a laptop. It was "born digital." Although it's possible to identify analog elements of the writing process (the movements of the author's fingers to press keys; the specific shapes of letters and spaces between letters as visible on the laptop's screen), those are not the elements that were crucial and selected for storage. None of those analog aspects affected the version that has passed down through multiple stages of editing and production to be read by you now. All that really mattered in that first act of writing was the selection and storage of a particular sequence of characters—and a sequence of discrete characters is a fine example of something that has an obvious digital representation.

We can contrast that writing process with what would have been required if the author had written the original manuscript with a fountain pen. At some point the original handwritten text would need to be typed up, a kind of digitization process with some of the same hazards that we've identified for music.

To summarize:

• We can use digital representations for both digital and analog data.
• Digital data is easy to store and transmit correctly.

Together, these characteristics help explain why it is appealing to digitize all forms of media.

In addition, digital storage costs have dropped dramatically over time—a phenomenon that we'll examine in the next chapter. Those cost reductions provide an additional incentive for the widespread transition to digital representations.

3   Processes

In the previous chapter, we looked at the idea of stair steps as the "digitized" version of a ramp. We compared stairs to ramps as a way of getting a perspective on what it means to be digital versus analog. Now let's consider the idea of moving forward in discrete steps—not necessarily on a stairway, but just as separate and distinguishable steps. These are the kind of "digital actions" that make up the behavior of software. In the same way that we wondered in the previous chapter about a pixelated world around us, now we will consider what it would mean to have all activities (ours and others') similarly "pixelated." In the course of the chapter, we'll work our way down from abstract ideas of steps to some very concrete characteristics of computing hardware.

Our first steps of interest are like a person walking deliberately, not walking quickly or running. Each step is either yet-to-be-taken (has not yet had any effect) or has-been-taken (has had its effect). We are moving from one stable standing position to another, with the move caused by a single step. We said previously that we don't assign a distinct meaning to partly raised fingers when we're counting on our fingers; likewise, we don't see any "partial" steps, any "halfway" results, or the like.

A step is the smallest indivisible atom, and everything is built up from there. This approach contrasts with everyday intuitions about time: we tend to assume that time can be divided as finely as we want. Our best available stopwatch may be unable to measure a unit of time smaller than a hundredth of a second, but we nevertheless believe that there are smaller intervals of time that could (in principle) be perceived or measured with more elaborate instruments. In contrast, in this world of steps, there is nothing smaller than the smallest step size.

Reading as a Process

With the simple definition of process as "sequence of steps," we can see processes everywhere. For example, consider reading a book—as you are doing now! Scientists have learned that reading is a startlingly complex process when examined in terms of its physiological/neurological/psychological mechanisms. We won't try to cover all of those details. Instead, we'll focus on the experience of reading and pick out elements that help us build up more general ideas of how processes work.

We can see reading as a process with each page read being a different step, starting at the first page and ending at the last page. Or we can see reading as a process with each sentence read being a different step, or each word, or each letter.

As shown in figure 3.1, we can think of reading an excerpt from a book as reading a sequence of pages, or reading a sequence of sentences. Notice that the sentence boundaries do not coincide with the page boundaries, so a step at one level may not correspond exactly to a step at another level.

Similarly, in figure 3.2, we can think of reading a section of text as reading a sequence of sentences, or reading a sequence of words. Since it's not possible for a single word to be split across sentences, it's possible to find an exact word boundary for every sentence boundary (but not necessarily the other way around).

All of these different kinds of steps are acceptable as descriptions of some kind of process. We could even get sophisticated and combine these descriptions, so as to capture the relationships: pages contain words, which contain letters, while sentences also contain words, which contain letters; but sentences often cross page boundaries, so it wouldn't be correct to claim that a page contains only whole sentences.

There is a potential source of confusion here, because there are some circumstances in which we will be dealing with something that seems like a

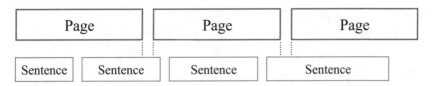

Figure 3.1
Pages and sentences.

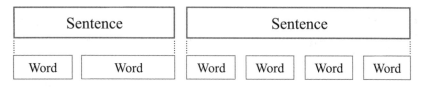

Figure 3.2
Sentences and words.

partially taken step. As in the case of letters, pages, words, and sentences, it is sometimes useful to build smaller steps into sequences of steps, and then treat such a sequence as a single larger step. Sometimes that sequence will fail to act like a single step and will be prone to partial completion, partial changes, and the like. However, that difficulty doesn't change the nature of the digital model. If we look inside a partially completed step, we'll find smaller steps being grouped together. Somewhere, down low enough, is some kind of indivisible step. The bottom layer of the system is some kind of machinery that accomplishes a single step cleanly, indivisibly, repeatedly.

For the sake of generality, we will sometimes talk about a lower layer as the "step-taking machinery." That term can certainly refer to a "computer" as it is commonly understood: readily purchasable hardware. When we look carefully at one of those computers, we see an electrical device. We have to plug it in or provide battery power for it to work. If we open it up, we see various chips and widgets that perform electronic or magnetic tricks, powered by the electricity. It's easy to think that the electricity and the exotic parts are required for computation. But actually, none of that is really essential except for its being an extremely fast step-taking machine. Even if we think of some bizarre future or alternative computer with no electricity, electronics, or magnetic components involved, our ideas here will still be relevant as long as it's a step-taking machine.

Turing Machines

There is a simple model of this generic step-taking machine. It consists of two elements: a kind of "cheat sheet" and a kind of "scratch pad," as shown in figure 3.3.

The cheat sheet is like a specialized, customized dictionary. However, the details are a little different from a dictionary: instead of looking up the

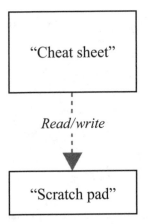

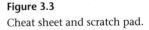

Figure 3.3
Cheat sheet and scratch pad.

definition that corresponds to a particular word, the machinery uses the cheat sheet to determine what it should do next. So the machine's actions are completely determined at each step by the combination of what's on the scratch pad and what's on the cheat sheet. For a given machine, we can set up its cheat sheet however we want, but the machine doesn't modify that cheat sheet once it starts running. In contrast, the machine does modify the scratch pad. The machine has a simple repeating cycle: it looks at what's on the scratch pad, then looks up the corresponding behavior on the cheat sheet, then writes something on the scratch pad. Surprising as it might seem, this arrangement is basically a computer.

The scratch pad is actually a little more structured and a little more limited than you might think from the preceding brief description. First, the scratch pad is divided into discrete areas arranged in a row. Conventionally, these areas are cells big enough to write a single character, but they could be small enough that you could only write 0 or 1, or (in principle) big enough to write a novel. It's crucial that there should be clear boundaries between the cells (so there's no confusing one of them with another). It's also crucial that a cell's contents should be recognizable in a single machine step—this is the reason why people don't actually make the cells big enough for a novel. Finally, there have to be enough of these cells that we don't worry about running out. To save ourselves any concerns about having enough cells, we just say that there are always more cells available—an infinite number of cells, if necessary.

The step-taking machine has one particular cell that is its current focus: the machine reads or writes only the current cell. The machine can also change the current cell, but it does so only by shifting its focus one cell left or one cell right.

This machine takes steps: one step at a time, repeatedly. From one point of view, every step is identical: it consists of reading the current cell, looking up the corresponding entry in the cheat sheet, writing the current cell, and moving left or right to a new cell. From another point of view, every step is different:

• Whatever is read in the current cell may be something that's never been read before in this computation;

• the action to be taken may be something that's never been found before on the cheat sheet in this computation; and/or

• whatever is written into the current cell may be something that's never been written before in this computation.

So even though the outline or structure of every step is identical, the detailed content of any particular step—its inputs, actions, outputs—may be unique.

A computer scientist would refer to this step-taking machine as a *Turing machine* (see figure 3.4). It is named for its inventor, mathematician Alan Turing. The computer-science name for the cheat sheet is a *finite state machine*.

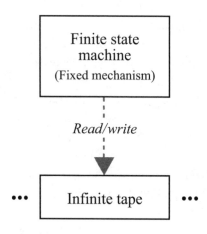

Figure 3.4
Turing machine.

In Turing's original formulation and most other descriptions, the part we have called a scratch pad is described as a kind of *tape*.

Rather surprisingly, this odd combination of cheat sheet, scratch pad, and repetitive simple steps turns out to be enough to represent any computation.

You can see the shadow of a Turing machine if you look the right way at a modern computer. A modern computer has some hardware with a fixed set of repetitive functions, like the cheat sheet/state machine of the Turing machine. A modern computer repeatedly performs a cycle of fetching the next instruction and performing its corresponding actions, in much the same way that a Turing machine repeats its simple read/lookup/write behavior. And a modern computer can read and/or write to any of a large collection of locations in memory or on disk, in much the same way that a Turing machine can read and/or write to any of the infinite number of cells on its scratch pad/tape.

A modern jet airliner has nothing specific in common with the first powered airplane flown by the Wright brothers, yet we can still recognize the common features. In much the same way, a modern computer is far more sophisticated and capable for practical computations than is a Turing machine, but we can still see the family resemblance.

Infinite Processes

Reading a book is typically a process with an identifiable beginning and end. Most often the process starts at the first page and ends at the last page. But sometimes reading is an unending process. For example, some people adopt a routine of reading a few verses of the Bible each day. When they reach the end of the book, they restart from the beginning.

In talking about these issues, it's helpful to separate specification from behavior. A specification is a higher-level description of what we want to happen, whereas the behavior is what actually happens. Once we separate specification from behavior, we see that it is possible to have a compact specification whose corresponding behavior is very noncompact—long in time, massive in space. An easy example is a process that simply prints "Hi," then pauses a second and repeats (see figure 3.5).

It's not very useful, but it does make the point: its description is short, its activity goes on without end, and the number of times it will print "Hi" is unbounded. We might refer to the description/specification here as a

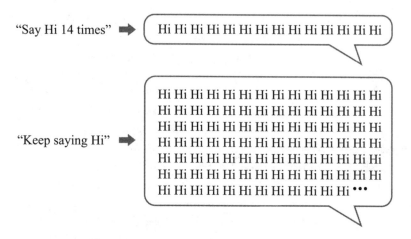

"Say Hi 14 times" ➡ Hi Hi Hi Hi Hi Hi Hi Hi Hi Hi Hi Hi Hi Hi

"Keep saying Hi" ➡ Hi Hi Hi Hi Hi Hi Hi Hi Hi Hi Hi Hi Hi Hi
Hi Hi Hi Hi Hi Hi Hi Hi Hi Hi Hi Hi Hi Hi
Hi Hi Hi Hi Hi Hi Hi Hi Hi Hi Hi Hi Hi Hi
Hi Hi Hi Hi Hi Hi Hi Hi Hi Hi Hi Hi Hi Hi
Hi Hi Hi Hi Hi Hi Hi Hi Hi Hi Hi Hi Hi Hi
Hi Hi Hi Hi Hi Hi Hi Hi Hi Hi Hi Hi Hi Hi
Hi Hi Hi Hi Hi Hi Hi Hi Hi Hi Hi Hi •••

Figure 3.5
A finite process and an infinite process.

program, although it's a very informal kind of program. As we see with this example, a small program can specify a process that continues endlessly.

Execution

What happens in a process—its actual behavior—is also referred to as the *execution* of a process. The execution of a given process (for example, one of the reading processes) depends on something taking steps, supplying the energy to proceed. In the case of our example reading process, the reader is supplying the energy to go to the next step. In the case of a computer program, ultimately it's the hardware that supplies the energy. Indeed, that's what a computer ultimately is: something that transforms energy into steps.

On one hand, the process is something real that can accomplish effects in the world; on the other hand, it is just the shadow cast by the step-taking machinery as driven by some program. To shine a different light on execution, we can ask, What is the relationship between a reel of movie film and the movie projected on the screen? Or, What is the relationship between a phonograph record and the music coming from the speakers? To a computer scientist, these are both analog versions of the relationship between program and process. The reel of film and the record are both like programs, while the projected movie and the playing music are both like processes. The movie projector and record player are both machines for this transformation, like the step-taking machinery we have described.

We can say that a program is a static description of what a process does, or we can say that a process is a dynamic realization of what a program describes. Either way, it's important to see that program and process are at one level alternative descriptions of the same thing, and at another level are completely different from each other.

Both movie film and phonograph records are like programs in that they are *mechanically interpreted*—we place an emphasis on their consistent playback, and great effort goes into ensuring accuracy of reproduction. There is a looser analogy to programs and processes when we consider the relationship of a musical score to an orchestral performance, or the relationship of a recipe to a cooked dish. Although there is the same sense that the score and performance are closely related but different kinds of entities, and that the recipe and dish have a comparable relationship, we expect that the interpretation of the "program" in these cases is not achievable by pure mechanics. Indeed, many observers would judge a "mechanical" interpretation in these domains to be of low quality. Investing effort in greater fidelity of reproduction in these domains would seem to be missing the point.

Because movies and recorded music are mechanically reproducible and place an emphasis on fidelity, they have rapidly shifted away from analog media to digital media. In a few years, perhaps, most readers won't really understand the point of our analogy to film and records, because those artifacts will be so unfamiliar, completely replaced by digital versions.

Now that we understand something about what these "action steps" are, we should consider in some more detail how to realize them in practice. That means understanding something about both what is involved in making a program and what is involved in making the step-taking machinery that can execute that program.

Effective Construction

Programs are examples of what computer scientists would call *effective constructions*: things that we can actually understand how to build.

In contrast, mathematics doesn't require effective constructions. Mathematically, there's nothing wrong with assuming conditions that we don't know how to achieve, as in the old joke about a mathematician hired to increase milk production who starts the presentation by saying, "Assume a spherical cow." Similarly, there's nothing *mathematically* wrong with the following technique for finding the weight of an average grain of sand:

1. Weigh beach to determine total weight
2. Count grains of sand to determine total number of grains
3. Divide total weight by total number to determined average weight

However, we can recognize that this is not an achievable or sensible procedure: it's not clear what it really means to "weigh a beach," or what apparatus we would use. Likewise, although it might be possible to count all the grains of sand on a beach, it seems like a poor way of spending one's resources. This "beach-weighing" approach is a handy counterexample to what programmers do. For computation, each step must be effective—we have to have some means of actually performing it, not just conceptualizing or imagining it.

Hardware vs. Software

In principle, we don't need any machinery to execute a program. Indeed, the earliest use of the term "computer" was for people who performed calculations. If we were so inclined, we could always just work through the step-by-step execution of a program by hand. But execution by hand is slow, error-prone, and excruciatingly tedious. So we're almost always more interested in using some step-taking machinery to do the work.

In the terminology of computer scientists, the step-taking machinery is usually referred to as *hardware*, while the programs being executed are *software*. A handy way of making the distinction is to think about whether the item of interest could somehow be transmitted via telephone. So the design of a physical computer (its specifications and drawings) can be seen as a form of software, but the device itself isn't.

So far, we have talked about the hardware as though it is fixed, and only the software is dynamic or changeable. But this is not an accurate summary of the situation. In fact, hardware is itself an engineered artifact, and so hardware is subject to revision, redesign, and adaptation. Just as it's possible to build better programs and processes, it's possible to build better hardware. And it's even possible to take a holistic view of software and hardware, with the idea that the hardware/software boundary is subject to movement and redesign.

Further blurring the issue is the possibility of using customizable hardware. One example is a technology called field-programmable gate arrays (FPGA). An FPGA consists of a large collection of small, simple hardware resources whose interconnections can be arranged to better match the structure of the problem to be solved. Viewed in one way, such an FPGA is hardware; viewed another way, it's software.

When we can take a holistic view, it is often useful to move functionality from software into hardware to speed it up, or to move functionality from hardware into software to increase flexibility. It's possible to think in terms of a total system design approach, in which we start with all software and "crystallize" the lowest levels into faster hardware. Alternatively, we can think of starting with all hardware and then "vaporize" the higher levels into more-flexible software. Our overall goal is to strike the right balance between speed and flexibility.

The tricky part of this trade-off is that putting too much functionality into hardware can actually *decrease* the overall speed possible. So although a naïve view is that "hardware is fast," one has to be careful not to pursue this blindly. Instead, it's more accurate to say that "simple hardware is fast."

Uniformity Gives Speed

To understand why not all hardware is equally fast, consider running a warehouse that stores cans of soup for a single product line of a single manufacturer. At one level you may be handling a tremendous variety of merchandise—perhaps there are hundreds of different kinds of soup. However, at the level of handling the goods in the warehouse, all of those different kinds of soup are basically alike: they come in the same size cans, the cans are packed in the same size cases, the barcodes are in the same places on the cans. There is a lot of uniformity, and accordingly your shelving and machinery can be optimized around that uniformity.

Suppose that your success at soup-handling gives you a reputation for running a fast and efficient warehouse, and other manufacturers start to ask you to handle their warehousing. Some of their goods are different sizes from soup cans. Even when you consider only the other soup manufacturers, they don't use the exact same cans or boxes or barcode placements as the single manufacturer you worked with before. Inevitably, the reduction in uniformity makes the operation less efficient: there's now a need for more-expensive infrastructure, and any given set of operations probably takes longer.

Similar issues arise when building a step-taking machine. The more alike the operations are, the more efficient the execution of those operations can be. The more different kinds of operations we ask the step-taking machinery to do, the more uniformity decreases and costs rise.

Moore's Law and Uniformity

There is potentially an additional level of cost from nonuniformity. We can see this additional cost most clearly if the warehousing industry as a whole is focused primarily on soup cans. If there are competitive suppliers of shelving and automation, and most are delivering soup-can handling systems, we expect that there will be steady improvements in those areas— and as consumers of those systems, we expect to reap those benefits. In contrast, consider what happens if we are building our own nonuniform systems that are very different from what the industry as a whole is building. We may benefit from having a very different market niche, but we will be unable to benefit from those soup-can-focused improvements that the industry is delivering.

Likewise when we apply this thinking to computers, we can see that it's possible to build custom hardware of various kinds to address particular computational problems. That custom hardware yields benefits in the near term, but we lose out in the longer term to the continuing process improvements driven by mainstream computing.

This observation leads us to recognize that there is a significant economic element at work here. In 1965, Gordon Moore published a paper about the trend of transistor density in the semiconductor products we've come to call "chips," but which are technically called integrated circuits. Moore observed that in the period from 1958 to 1965 this density had doubled every year, and that the trend was likely to continue for a number of years to come. The increased density means both *more* devices and *faster* devices for a constant amount of money. In line with Moore's observation—subsequently dubbed Moore's law—computing devices have had many years of dramatic improvements in their cost and performance.

Moore's law is often cited as an amazing and counterintuitive aspect of the modern development of computing, and it is indeed remarkable to see the way in which speeds and storage capacities have expanded while costs have declined. A common way of capturing the extreme nature of these improvements is to recast them into another domain, like transportation, and ask people to consider what it would be like if a modern commercial aircraft only cost $500, circled the world in 20 minutes, and used only 5 gallons of fuel to do so. Because of this dramatic history of improvement, people sometimes invoke Moore's law as though it will solve all problems of having enough computation within another few years. The reality is a little more complex. In the rest of this chapter we'll work out what Moore's law really says. A later chapter will explain why even the startling improvements from Moore's law do not overcome the costs of some computational problems.

Moore's law is a statement about the rate at which hardware improves over time. When you get into the details, there are actually multiple slightly different versions of Moore's law—so it's not as lawlike as its name would suggest. For our purposes, we'll treat Moore's law as saying that the density of transistors on chips roughly doubles every 18 months.

An important qualification to Moore's law, frequently overlooked, is that it applies to what might be described as the mainstream of computing. The computing tasks and computing machines that are of the most interest to the most people receive the most attention from engineers, and are the areas of keenest competition. So in addition to our observation that "simple hardware is fast" we also need to be aware that "common hardware is fast." This principle is a little counterintuitive, so it's worth explaining carefully.

Moore's law is a special version of a more general economic principle. In any manufacturing business, we expect that we will benefit from economies of scale—if we can sell more identical copies of the widget we produce, we will be spreading our fixed costs across more sales, lowering our overall costs. In addition, larger-scale production typically benefits from more attention by smart people concerned with lowering manufacturing costs. This can lead to a virtuous cycle in which customers are attracted to these bigger-selling widgets because they are cheaper than alternatives.

Moore's law is really about the rate of improvement in the most popular choice(s), and its underlying engine is this virtuous manufacturing cycle.

The further removed we are from the most popular family of products, the less we benefit from Moore's law. Although it's often presented as though it were related to electronics or computers in general, Moore's law is really more about the progress of the technological mainstream.

Even without the benefit of any further improvement from Moore's law, the modern world contains amazing step-taking machinery that is readily available to us. We have devices that can execute literally billions of (simple) steps each second, with the cheapest such devices costing only pennies.

4 Names

How can literature work in translation? In some ways it's surprising that an excellent book in one language can still be an excellent book in a completely different language. In fact, it is hard to find an example of a book that is genuinely untranslatable. I initially thought that Dr. Seuss's *The Cat in the Hat* or James Joyce's *Finnegans Wake* would be examples; but in fact there is a highly praised French translation of *The Cat in the Hat*, and a Chinese version of the first third of *Finnegans Wake* has been a surprise hit. In most cases there appears to be a core set of ideas, characters, and plot that can be rendered effectively into a language very different from the language in which it was originally written. Of course, there are likely to be some elements that work poorly in the new language, but there may occasionally be elements that work better in the new language due to happy accidents or the skill of the translator. For example, in the Asterix books, the (translated) English name Dogmatix is funnier than the French original Idefix. Both have the connotation of single-mindedness...but since this is the name of Asterix's dog, the English version is appropriate in a way that the French version can't match.*

There is a similar sense in which computation can happen in different models—in translation, if you like—while nevertheless retaining some of the same essential qualities. Those shared qualities can be the same effects or lack of effects, the same limits, and so forth, along with some untranslatable bits and/or happy accidents of improvement. In this chapter we redevelop our ideas about steps, but in a new way. The basic step of this new approach is to substitute a value in place of a name.

* One reviewer of this book was unclear about why Dogmatix is a better name than Idefix, so I will spell it out: *Dog*matix is a *dog*. *Ide*fix is a *chien*. There is humor in the first coincidence but not in the second noncoincidence. I hope this explanation is helpful.

This chapter has more notation than any other. If you're a person who is comfortable with mathematical notation or you like to play word substitution games, there's probably nothing in here that will worry you. But if you're not all that comfortable with the notation or the way the chapter goes, feel free to skip ahead at any point to the next chapter. You'll be missing some of the "local flavor" of computing in this new approach, but you won't miss anything fundamental.

What's in a Name?

In everyday life, we usually don't have too much trouble distinguishing a map from the terrain that the map describes. Usually the map is a different material: it's printed on paper, or it's a display on a mobile phone. Meanwhile, the actual terrain is land, roads, buildings. Usually the map is also a different scale: we might fit whole neighborhoods or cities into just a few inches, whereas the terrain of interest might well take up miles.

Just as we are usually not confused between the map and the terrain the map represents, we usually don't get confused between names and what's named. Our typical uses of names and quotation in speech or writing are usually not very complicated.

Computer science involves issues of names and naming to an extent that may be surprising. The naming systems turn out to be more elaborate than those used in ordinary language; in addition, the "material" or "stuff" of which names are made is often very similar to the "material" or "stuff" of what's being named. In contrast to our everyday experience, in this domain there is a chronic risk of confusing map with terrain, or confusing the name with what's named.

Let's start with a simple case. Barack Obama is the name of a man. We can use the name as a kind of substitute for the man (see figure 4.1).

If we didn't know his name, or didn't want to use his name, but he was in the vicinity, we might point at him or use a roundabout construction like "that man standing over there" (see figure 4.2).

In a written document like this one, we can use a picture as another kind of "naming" to indicate a particular person we're talking about. In a sense, our picture is a name for Barack Obama, since we can't actually include the real person in this book.

Barack Obama

Figure 4.1
A name and the named person.

Figure 4.2
Gesturing instead of using a name.

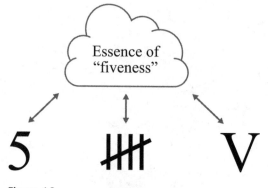

Figure 4.3
Three different names for five.

Here's another example: the Arabic numeral 5, the Roman numeral V, and the hashmark consisting of four vertical marks crossed by a diagonal mark all represent the same number (see figure 4.3).

But they are all *names* for the number, rather than *being* the number. The number itself is some kind of abstract concept of "fiveness," not the particular marking on the page with this shape: 5.

Even if Barack Obama is standing right next to us as we speak, we can't express a statement like "Barack Obama was the first U.S. president who was raised in Hawaii" without using some kind of name. Instead of saying "Barack Obama" we could gesture at the man standing next to us, but that's just a different kind of name. We can't pick up the person physically and slot him into the opening phrase of the sentence: a physical human being is the wrong kind of entity to be in a sentence, just as the name "Barack Obama" is the wrong kind of entity to be tucked into bed with his wife at night.

Quoting

Let's push the naming ideas one more level to distinguish between Barack Obama and "Barack Obama" (the quotes here are crucial). Consider these two correct sentences:

Barack Obama was the first U.S. president raised in Hawaii.

"Barack Obama" is twelve characters long.

and contrast them with these two structurally similar but incorrect sentences:

"Barack Obama" was the first U.S. president raised in Hawaii.

Barack Obama is twelve characters long.

Some people notice this kind of error and find it irritating. Structurally, the sentences are still acceptable: they are both still simple predicate sentences, we have just swapped the subjects. But the incorrect versions have mismatched meanings. The quotation vs. usage structure is wrong, and strictly speaking the sentences make no sense. The first one claims that a string of characters could serve as president, while the second claims that a person can be measured in terms of text.

Remember that we aren't discussing these issues for grammatical purity: we're going to further develop names vs. what-is-named to illuminate some important ideas of computer science. It's tempting to push past this topic while waving our hands and saying, "everyone understands names." But most people don't *really* understand names—or at least they don't understand names once the naming system is more complicated than everyday usage.

Our example sentences show the use and misuse of quoting. In principle, we can keep applying the quoting mechanism as long as we want. In practice, it's only workable for a couple of levels when people are using languages like English to communicate with each other.

Computer scientists would call English and other similar languages *natural languages*. Although we're starting with examples of quotation in English, we'll soon shift to dealing with artificial languages. The artificial languages are simpler and more regular in their structure because they are deliberately constructed that way. The issues of naming and substitution may still seem a little tricky, but it's important to be aware that natural languages have some additional complexity that we won't try to tackle.

The following example already feels confusing and contrived to many readers:

'"Barack Obama"' is a way of quoting the name of Barack Obama by adding a double quote on each side: "Barack Obama."

In this sentence, there are three occurrences of the same president's name text, each a little different:

• The first occurrence of the president's name is a nested quote: we are talking about *how* we can quote a name. This usage is unusual because we don't

often see quotes inside quotes, although it does sometimes occur for reasons other than contrived examples in books.
• The second occurrence is unquoted because it is a reference to the person
(although it is embedded in a phrase, "the name of Barack Obama" ...which
effectively quotes it!).
• The third occurrence is another example of quoting the name.

Interestingly, this rather elaborate construction doesn't actually depend
in any way on whose name is being used. We could equally well have said
something like

'"George Bush"' is a way of quoting the name of George Bush by adding a
double quote on each side: "George Bush."

The resulting sentence is equally true as long as we somehow substituted
the exact same person's name throughout.

An ordinary person's thought process might simply move on from here
to some other topic, but a mathematician or a computer scientist is likely to
think that it might be handy to have a way of talking about these patterns.
As a bonus, figuring out a way to express these common patterns and perform the substitution leads us into computation.

Leads us into computation? Where did that come from? Weren't we just
wandering down this path so we could be ultra-hyper-careful about what is
a name vs. what is the stuff that's being named?

Well, yes, but one view of computation is that it's fundamentally about
repeated renaming. We learned in previous chapters about "step-taking
machinery" and a kind of mechanistic perspective on computation. In that
approach, there's some kind of a machine that just repeatedly takes a step.
Computation is what happens when the machinery is operated according to
a plan—what we called the program—and the operation of the machinery
according to the program is the process.

But just as 5 and V are different but equally valid ways of referring to an
underlying "fiveness," there's another, equally valid, view of computation
that starts with a kind of renaming game. There are still steps to the computation, but now those steps are the simple renamings or substitutions that
occur. The program is the text that we start with, and the process consists
of the transformations of the text that happen while following the rules of
the substitution game.

Sentence Patterns

Let's take this complicated sentence that we previously mentioned:

'"George Bush"' is a way of quoting the name of George Bush by adding a double quote on each side: "George Bush."

and start playing the substitution game on it. Our reward for going down this path is that we will invent our way into computation along the way.

The substitution game is like a kind of algebra with text. Recall that in high-school algebra a variable like x might occur several times in an equation. Perhaps x was the key answer we were trying to find, or perhaps it was just some intermediate answer that helped us on the way to the final answer. In our current context, looking at naming and named objects, we can think of a variable like x as a *name* for its value. For our complicated sentence, we'll use x as a replacement for the name of a president and get the generalized pattern:

'"x"' is a way of quoting the name of x by adding a double quote on each side: "x."

This sentence might be true in some sort of technical/philosophical way— but it doesn't feel very useful, or make a lot of sense. That's OK, because we were just trying to capture a pattern. This sentence isn't really intended to be a meaningful sentence itself, it's more like a sentence-generator: something we could use to produce the Barack-Obama-version and the George-Bush-version (and many others beside).

An alternative way of thinking about this new sentence is that it's been freeze-dried like instant coffee. It needs to be reconstituted with the removed ingredient (the real text), just as instant coffee needs to be reconstituted with hot water. (If this analogy doesn't work for you, just ignore it.)

It would be helpful to have some kind of a marker to warn the reader that this sentence needs to be reconstituted. Because of how we developed the sentence just now, we know the version with x's isn't really supposed to be understandable. But if we just ran across it somewhere in a book, we might not recognize it as a sentence-generating pattern. We might instead think that it was trying to express some deep philosophical insight about x, and waste time trying to understand it in those terms.

Lambda

Rather than invent a new kind of marker, we'll use the same notation that computer scientists sometimes use in a similar situation, using the Greek letter lambda (λ). If we write "$\lambda x.$" (pronounced "lambda ex dot") in front of our pattern, it effectively means "in the following text, x is just a place-holder for something that will be supplied later."

To get a handle on this new notation, let's use it in really simple cases first. Let's suppose that we want to capture a sentence pattern that just "doubles" a piece of text: so if we put in "blah" we get out "blahblah" and if we put in "Barack Obama" we get out "Barack ObamaBarack Obama."

Here's a doubling pattern, which delivers a new text containing two copies of the text we give it:

$\lambda x.xx$

Let's first say this out loud so it doesn't seem alarming: "lambda ex dot ex ex." Then let's consider what it means. The dot divides this line into the *body* to the right of the dot, and the *formal parameter* to the left of the dot. The formal parameter (or just *formal*) tells us the placeholder name that gets substituted—in this case, x. The body tells us the text in which the substitution occurs—in this case, xx. The whole thing taken together—lambda, parameter, dot, body—is called an *expression*.

Figure 4.4 shows those parts labeled on the same expression.

So we know that the x's that occur in the body will be replaced by something else. What is substituted for x? Whatever is supplied to the expression. The expression doesn't care exactly what the substitution is, it works pretty much the same way regardless of what's supplied.

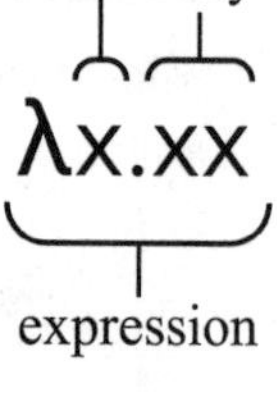

Figure 4.4
The parts of an expression.

What does it mean to "supply" something? Well, you just write whatever you are supplying to the expression right after it. Here's an example where we are supplying the letter a to our doubling expression:

λx.xx a

The stuff to the left of the space is just the exact same lambda-expression we wrote before. The stuff to the right of the space is just the letter *a*.

We're usually more interested in the *result* of this kind of combination, rather than just writing the expression. We can draw a rough analogy by observing that it's correct but unhelpful to say that $(237 + 384)$ has the value $(237 + 384)$. Most people are more interested in knowing that its (final, simplified) value is 621. We'll introduce a right arrow "→" to indicate that the stuff on the left side of the arrow can be simplified or reduced to the stuff on the right side of the arrow.

λx.xx a → aa

Here's another example:

λx.xx abc → abcabc

These first examples used only textual joining (sometimes called *concatenation*), where we put two pieces of text next to each other and treat them as a single piece of text afterward. This notation is also powerful enough to express arithmetic—although we won't be concerned with exactly how to do that. Instead, we'll just take advantage of our knowledge that it can be done to write some examples using simple arithmetic operations. For example, we can write a simple add-one expression (what computer scientists would call an *incrementing function*). It just adds one to whatever number it is given:

λx.(x + 1)

And then consider what the results are for a couple of uses of the function:

λx.(x + 1) 3 → 4

λx.(x + 1) 17 → 18

Finally, here's an even simpler example, what computer scientists call an *identity function*: whatever you supply to it is also what comes out:

λx.x

Here's an example of using the identity function:

λx.x 2 → 2

With this notation we can also say things like

λx.x "Barack Obama" $\rightarrow$ "Barack Obama"

We can see from these examples that this identity function doesn't care whether it's applied to numbers or pieces of text.

The amazing thing to keep in mind when learning about names is that the world of computation that's reached via names is identical to the world of computation that we've already reached via steps. Whether you think of computation as programs running on machines or names being replaced by other names, it's all the same "computingness" underneath.

Simple name substitution is generally pretty easy to understand. The next level of complexity in using names is often a little harder to grasp, so we'll approach it from the angle of slightly silly humor.

5 Recursion

In the previous chapter, we considered name substitution as a form of computation. As you likely already know, an *acronym* is a specific kind of name substitution: for example, the two-letter acronym "US" can be expanded to "United States," and the four-letter acronym "NASA" can be expanded to "National Aeronautics and Space Administration." Three-letter acronyms like IBM, FAA, and NSA are so common that sometimes people will refer (usually with tongue in cheek) to a TLA—that is, a Three-Letter Acronym. The humor arises, at least in part, from self-reference: TLA is itself a TLA.

We can push self-reference to another level with an example like XINU, an acronym that expands to "XINU Is Not Unix." At one level this expansion "works," in the sense that it provides additional information about the meaning of the letters—but in another sense the expansion "fails," because it still contains the unexpanded acronym XINU. Repeating the process doesn't improve the situation; we just get

XINU Is Not Unix Is Not Unix

which doesn't even make sense, and it still contains the unexpanded acronym.

A human reader can find humor in this self-referential and somewhat paradoxical expansion; however, a purely mechanical substitution fails as the initial XINU is repeatedly expanded.

This definition of a name in terms of itself is called *recursion*. Although recursion is used only for humorous purposes in these acronym examples, it's one of the more important (and slightly mind-bending) concepts in computer science.

Why is recursion important? As we've seen already from the XINU example, recursion lets us express something that is infinite, or potentially infinite, in a finite form. In the XINU example, that infinite expansion is not useful—except in prompting an amused reaction. However, we will see that better-behaved recursion can have practical value. In particular, we'll see in chapter 15 that some of the naming infrastructure of the web is best understood in terms of recursion.

As with other aspects of computation, we can reasonably ask whether something is interesting only because it's "something programmers do" or whether it has larger significance. In this case we might well ask, Is "recursive thinking" something real and useful? If so, what is its utility? We'll return to that question after we understand a little better what recursion is and how it works.

Factorial

Let's consider two examples of recursive definitions that are more serious than the recursive acronyms. The first example is mathematical; the next one is linguistic. (If you think of yourself as a person who "doesn't like math," you may prefer to skip this example and go directly to the following one.)

Our mathematical example is the definition of factorial. The factorial of some positive integer n is the result of multiplying together all the numbers from 1 through n. The factorial of n is written "$n!$" and so one way to define it would be

$$n! = 1 \times 2 \ldots \times (n-1) \times n$$

This definition takes advantage of our understanding of how a series works and what is meant by the ellipsis "..." to leave out the "middle" terms of the series. We can make this construction a little clearer by distinguishing two different cases:

For $n = 1$: $n! = 1$

For $n > 1$: $n! = 1 \times \ldots \times (n-1) \times n$

That is, we've split the definition into two cases: the first for the case where n has the value one, and the other for all cases where n is more than one. Let's consider an alternative formulation using recursion, but retaining the case-analysis framing:

For $n = 1$: $n! = 1$

For $n > 1$: $n! = n \times (n-1)!$

In contrast to all our previous definitions of factorial, this version uses the factorial sign "$!$" on the *right-hand* side of an equals sign. In fact, the second line looks circular: the factorial of *n* is being defined in terms of another factorial. We can immediately see the risk of infinite expansion here (revisiting the problem we saw with expanding XINU earlier). What are we gaining that makes this useful?

The first line provides one alternative (what computer scientists would call a *base case*): it ensures that for some simple version of the problem we can provide a compact answer. The second line is another alternative (what computer scientists would call a *reduction step*): it ensures that we can repeatedly move toward the base case as we compute a partial result. So the recursive definition effectively provides us a means of computing *n!*: we can repeatedly invoke the definition, as in this example of computing *4!*:

$$4! = 4 \times 3!$$
$$4! = 4 \times (3 \times 2!)$$
$$4! = 4 \times (3 \times (2 \times 1!))$$
$$4! = 4 \times (3 \times (2 \times 1))$$
$$4! = 4 \times (3 \times 2)$$
$$4! = 4 \times 6$$
$$4! = 24$$

All we've done here is repeatedly substitute the definition of factorial until we reach the base case, then simplify.

The House That Jack Built

Now let's look at a linguistic version of recursion. There's a Mother Goose tale that is relevant here because it effectively teaches the repeated use of a modifying clause:

This is the house that Jack built.

This is the malt that lay in the house that Jack built.

This is the rat that ate the malt that lay in the house that Jack built.

The story goes on in the same vein, eventually building a sentence involving 11 different noun phrases:

This is the farmer sowing his corn,

That kept the cock that crowed in the morn,

That waked the priest all shaven and shorn,

That married the man all tattered and torn,

That kissed the maiden all forlorn,

That milked the cow with the crumpled horn,

That tossed the dog,

That worried the cat,

That killed the rat,

That ate the malt

That lay in the house that Jack built.

It seems likely that all reasonably intelligent children exposed to this story eventually notice that the same mechanism is used repeatedly and that the ending point is flexible—the tale could plausibly be extended yet again.

If we analyze this story, we can break it down into just a few rules. First there is a kind of frame for the extension:

This is [ ] the house that Jack built

Here we're marking with brackets a place where "other stuff" gets inserted while the surrounding frame stays the same. If we look at the things that go in there, we see a pattern:

[ ]

[the malt that lay in]

[the rat that ate [the malt that lay in]]

[the cat that killed [the rat that ate [the malt that lay in]]]

That might be where we stop if we were thinking conventionally, but if we're thinking like computer scientists, we would like to design rules that would generate these kinds of phrases.

We can start by saying that one rule is about picking nouns. In the examples just preceding we have only three nouns, so let's stick with those. Wherever we use a noun, we'll use "malt" or "rat" or "cat." We can write that rule like this:

noun = malt | rat | cat

The vertical bar "|" represents a choice or alternative, roughly analogous to the two cases we had in defining the factorial function in the previous example. It's usually read aloud as "or"—so in this case, the noun could be "malt" or "rat" or "cat."

Similarly, in our examples above we had only three verbs, so we'll stick with those. Wherever we use a verb, we'll use "killed" or "ate" or "lay in."

verb = killed | ate | lay in

We can then see that nouns and verbs are combined in a particular way that we can call a "that-phrase." Our examples are "the malt that lay in," "the rat that ate," and "the cat that killed" so what we notice is that it's always "the," then a noun, then "that," then a verb:

that-phrase = the noun that verb

To capture the lengthening phrases, we use a recursive definition that lets us nest that-phrases the right way. We can keep adding more that-phrases "bracketing" what we've built up, and the overall phrase will still make sense. For example, we already saw

[the cat that killed [the rat that ate [the malt that lay in]]]

and it's still grammatical (if conceptually strange) if we wrap that in another phrase like this:

[the malt that ate [the cat that killed [the rat that ate [the malt that lay in]]]]

So the scheme here can be summarized by the following rule:

compound-phrase = compound-phrase that-phrase | that-phrase

Notice that *compound-phrase* is both the thing being defined (on the left-hand side of the equals sign) and part of the definition (on the right-hand side of the equals sign). Why isn't this a meaningless or silly kind of circularity? We're OK because there is a nonrecursive alternative. We can stop "choosing" the recursive part and instead pick the part where the compound-phrase is only a that-phrase. We already know that a that-phrase has a nice compact (and nonrecursive) definition.

We saw a similar structure in the factorial definition—there the base case was the situation where $n = 1$, because in that situation the answer is just 1, not some computation that depends recursively on the definition of factorial. For the phrase generator, the base case is when there's only a that-phrase and no additional compound-phrase.

If we apply these rules, making random selections each time there is a choice, we can generate some plausible if uninspiring new verses for the Mother Goose tale, like

This is the malt that killed the rat that lay in the cat that lay in the cat that ate the rat that lay in the malt that killed the house that Jack built.

That's not great literature, but neither is it ungrammatical. Contrast it with a nonsentence like

This is malt rat killed cat cat the house that Jack built

The second one is worse than the first one; while the first one may be silly or meaningless, it's not incoherent or garbled in the way of the second one. As computer scientists we can demonstrate that lack of coherence by comparing it to the rules we derived. Alternatively, as speakers of English we can notice it intuitively. The simple mechanical rules seem to have something in common with what's happening in our brains when we are dealing with language, which in turn suggests (but doesn't prove) that our brains may use some kind of similar rules.

Finite and Infinite

Now let's return to the question of whether, and how, recursive thinking matters for a nonprogrammer. Recursion arguably underpins the capacity of language to be *infinitely generative* but *finitely comprehensible*. That is, we each have only a finite amount of capacity for producing or understanding language. Our brains may be big and complex compared to most other mammals, but they are still definitely finite...and actually quite small when compared to an infinite amount of anything! However, the finite brain doesn't imply a finite bound on language. Even if we could somehow catalog all of the utterances produced by all humans across all time, we would not have exhausted the possibilities of language because we could add an additional clause in the middle or at the end of one of those cataloged expressions. There seems to be no clear limit to our ability to generate new sentences and embed sentences as clauses in other sentences. The set of words and sentences used by an individual at any instant is finite, but there is nothing that prevents that person from understanding new words and sentences—there is no point at which either the brain "runs out" or the language itself "hits a wall."

While human language contains many additional features and complexities not captured in such a simple arrangement, it's nevertheless compelling as a "proof of concept" that a finite apparatus can produce and consume infinitely varied languages. Even if natural languages do not use exactly the same recursion that computer scientists and mathematicians know, the computer-science recursion seems like a handy metaphor.

Recursive thinking is also a problem-solving technique. For example, we can approach a problem with the mindset of looking for a small number of simple base cases and then looking for recursion steps that allow us to decompose bigger problems to the simple cases. Viewed in this light, recursion is a special case of the general principle that one can divide and conquer. In a problem-solving context, the infinite extensibility of recursion means that the sheer size of a problem need not be a limitation. In the same way that we don't worry about "running out of" language, a recursive formulation means we don't "run out of" ability to slice up a big problem into smaller, more-manageable pieces.

6 Limits: Imperfect Programs

Up until now, we've considered only small ideal programs and processes. Starting in this chapter, we take the first step toward a more realistic view by understanding some of the limits the universe imposes on the construction and running of processes. In this chapter we take up various ways in which processes are flawed, while in the next chapter we consider the limits even when processes are perfect. However, both chapters assume only a single process running on correctly functioning step-taking machinery. In later chapters we'll encounter still another set of problems caused by multiple processes (chapter 8) or by failures (chapter 16).

All Software Is Flawed

Professional programmers tend not to criticize each other solely for the presence of flaws in programs. It would be strange for company A to criticize company B's software product simply because company B had published a list of known problems with its product—because the reality is that company A's software product almost certainly has a roughly similar list of known problems. Can we ever expect to have software that is free of flaws? Today, that is not a realistic expectation. What we can hope—but cannot guarantee—is that the flaws are not serious. Even that condition is sometimes hard to achieve, and it's worth understanding why.

There are program design techniques to help us make programs that are easier to understand, and there are tools that can help us to identify likely sources of error; but the normal state of software is that it contains some errors (sometimes called "bugs") and accordingly can fail to meet the expectations of its users.

This acceptance of bugs often comes as a surprise to people who are not programmers. Some of the problems are caused by bad practices in the software industry, but most of them are related to the fundamental nature of software—and so they're not likely to go away any time soon.

In this chapter we take up four key problems that lead to software flaws:

1. Use of discrete states
2. Massive scale of state changes
3. Malleability
4. Difficulty of accurately capturing requirements and building corresponding implementations

The next chapter considers some additional problems that arise even when software is *not* flawed. But for the rest of this chapter, we take up each of these flaw-producing issues in turn. These problems are limits imposed by reality; we might consider them to be the hazards imposed by our inability to have perfect computation.

Discrete States

Let's first consider that the use of discrete states can itself be a source of error. We've previously looked at the digital nature of both data and action in the world of software and processes (chapters 2 and 3). A digital view of the world sees it as composed of discrete levels of value; in contrast, an analog view of the world sees it as composed of continuous, smoothly varying curves of value. We need to revisit the digital view of the world to understand that it can be a source of error—particularly if we make the mistake of thinking only in analog terms.

Analog elements are typically not only analog (smoothly varying) but also *linear*: each small change in input produces a corresponding small change in output. For example, when we turn a volume knob up one notch, we expect that the relatively small change in the position of the knob corresponds to a relatively small change in the perceived loudness of the sound.

In contrast, digital elements are typically not only digital but also *nonlinear*: that is, knowing the size of the input change doesn't give much ability to predict the size of the output change. Turning a system on is a kind of digital change. When we turn a power knob from "off" to "on," the knob may only move as much as we moved the adjacent volume knob to make an almost-imperceptible change in the volume. But with the power knob, the relatively small change in the position of the knob gives no information whatsoever about how large the resulting change in loudness will be. Depending on how the volume was set and/or how the system is constructed, it might start up very quietly or very loudly.

Testing

For a linear analog system, it's not hard to come up with a simple and sensible set of tests. There is some range of acceptable input: think of a volume knob, for example. We would want to check performance at the lowest acceptable input (knob turned all the way down); at the highest acceptable input (knob turned all the way up); and probably also at some middle input in the range between the two extremes. If the system performs acceptably on these three tests, and if the system is subsequently used for inputs only between the expected lowest setting and the expected highest setting, then the testers can have a high degree of confidence that the system will perform acceptably.

If the designers want to be conservative and cautious, they can build in a "safety factor" or "margin of error" by ensuring that their system performs acceptably for a range of input values much wider than the input values that are really expected to occur. This approach is essentially how modern society is able to build tall buildings or long bridges. We can rely on them because they are overbuilt for what we expect will happen to them.

Successful as that approach is in many important domains, it doesn't work at all for programs, or in general for any system with many discrete states (such as computer hardware). To see why, consider this slightly ridiculous example of an infinite program that responds to numbers chosen by a user:

1. Print "Pick a number"
2. If the chosen number is exactly 27,873 then detonate a large pile of dynamite
3. Otherwise print "OK" and go back to step 1

If you encounter a computer running this program and you don't have a way of seeing these steps that make up the program, then it's not obvious how you would learn about the particular value that detonates the dynamite. You could type a few different numbers at the program, but it would most likely look like a program that simply replies "OK" in response to any number at all. Even if you happened to try the immediately adjacent numbers 27,782 and 27,784, you'd get no indication that the number between them could have such an enormously different effect. This is nonlinearity with a vengeance!

It would be bad enough if these discrete nonlinear behaviors were the only source of trouble. They aren't.

Massive Scale

Let's assume that we have found a way to construct a process with smooth and linear behavior or that we have a tool that verifies the linear behavior of our process. Are we now in a position where it's easy to write correct and predictable processes? Unfortunately, no. Now we have to be concerned about our second key problem: massive scale of state changes as a source of error.

What do we mean by massive scale? It's not that any single change is itself a problem. It's unusual for a problem with a computer program to be something conceptually deep and intellectually challenging, so that only a few brilliant people can understand the issue. (The problem of deep intellectual challenge is partly true for coordinating multiple processes, to which we will return later, but not for most kinds of programming.)

Instead, the typical problems with computer programs are roughly analogous to the problems of an architect designing a building. There are lots of small decisions to make and lots of rules as to how those decisions should be made for the best result. Any single problem in isolation is typically not very hard to solve. The challenge arises because there are a lot of decisions to be made, and sometimes they interact in unanticipated or unpleasant ways. "The breakfast nook should be about this big for comfortable seating...the mud room should be about this big...the back door should be here...oops, we're close to the lot line now so let's move the back door, oops, now the door swings into the breakfast table...."

So our problem in programming is not only the digital, nonlinear nature of the states we manipulate, as we previously mentioned. Those problems are even worse than they initially appeared, because of the sheer number of states that could be involved.

Modern computers are really fast—almost incomprehensibly so. When a computer's specifications include a number with its "clock speed," usually specified as some number of gigahertz (GHz), you can think of that as representing approximately how many additions the computer can accomplish every second: 1 GHz is a billion sums performed every second. That high speed is good because it means that computers can do really long sequences of steps to solve really hard or interesting problems, in ways that seem magical to a plodding human. But all that speed has a matching bad aspect: as we'll see shortly, even relatively simple programs can have such large complex branching structures that they can't be tested exhaustively. Of course, it's not the speed itself that makes large untestable structures. Rather, increasing speed makes it feasible to build longer and more complex sequences as elements of our solutions. It is tempting to think that increasing speed of computation should be matched by increasing speed of testing, so that this issue wouldn't really matter in the end; unfortunately, that casual optimistic analysis turns out to be incorrect.

Doubling

To give some context for the problem, a relevant story is about doubling on each square of a chessboard. In one version of the story, a fabulously wealthy emperor of old offered a reward to a cunning inventor (in some versions, the inventor of chess itself). The inventor asked "only" for one grain of gold on the first square, two grains on the second square, four grains on the third square, and continuing the doubling until the sixty-four squares of the chessboard were covered. The emperor felt very wealthy, wanted to reward the inventor, and was unfamiliar with how fast doubling grows. So he thought that the arrangement sounded OK, and agreed. As a result, he ended up handing over all his gold (and all his other possessions!) well before the board was covered.

To understand what happened in more detail, we can represent the number of grains of gold on each square using exponent notation. (You can just skip to the conclusion if you don't like or don't understand exponents.) The first square has 1 grain, which is 2^0, and the second square 2 grains, which is 2^1, the third square has 4 grains, which is 2^2, and so the nth square has 2^{n-1} grains of gold on it. As it happens, people who think about these things have estimated that all the gold ever mined in the world is less than 3 trillion grains. That's a lot of gold, but 3 trillion converted into this exponent notation is less than 2^{42}. Accordingly, we can see that well before even the

43rd square of the 64-square chessboard, the unwise emperor would have run out of gold.

Branching

In the case of a program, the doubling to be concerned about is not the doubling of grains of gold but the doubling of test cases. If we have a simple program like this one:

If something is true **then** do thing 1; **otherwise** do thing 2

then we can see that we need at least two test cases: one where we "do thing 1" and the other where we "do thing 2." Figure 6.1 represents this two-way choice.

With the chessboard doubling, things got worse with each additional square to be covered. Our version of marching along to the next square of the chessboard comes if the program gets just a little bit more complicated. Let's assume that "do thing 1" has more choices inside, like this:

If something-else is true **then** do thing 3; **otherwise** do thing 4

and "do thing 2" is similarly more complicated inside:

If yet-another-thing is true **then** do thing 5; **otherwise** do thing 6

Figure 6.2 captures this new branching.

We've been deliberately vague in this description. We're just trying to capture the idea that each time we introduce another two-way choice we're potentially doubling the number of test cases involved. The chessboard had only 64 squares, and that level of doubling was already enough to overwhelm the treasure of an empire. Now consider that the clock speed of a computer

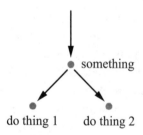

Figure 6.1
A two-way choice.

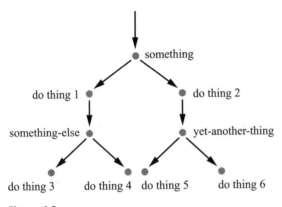

Figure 6.2
Multiple levels of choice.

is also roughly the speed with which it can choose between possibilities—clearly when clock speed is measured in units of GHz (one billion actions per second) it doesn't take long to build up an incomprehensibly large set of alternative paths.

Of course, no real program actually makes a new two-way choice at every single opportunity—it does some kind of "real work," along with deciding which things to do. So a billion opportunities to make choices doesn't necessarily mean a billion different choices. Even so, it's easy to have a ridiculous number of alternatives.

What does the increase in possibilities mean in practical terms? It means that we have to abandon any idea of "complete coverage" or "exhaustive testing" for any but the very smallest and simplest programs. There are just too many possibilities. So if our programs contain errors, we have little confidence in our ability to find all of them.

But if we could find those errors, would we be in good shape? No. Surprisingly, the flexibility of software undercuts our efforts to build it well…as we'll see next.

Malleability

In some ways, software seems like an ideal material. We don't have to worry about its weight or its strength, and it doesn't take heavy tools or enormous factories to produce it. If we can think clearly about a solution and write it down accurately, we don't have a difficult fabrication process ahead of us—instead, we have basically produced the end product. Software offers very little resistance of its own and is easily shaped. Paradoxically, this very *malleability* of software is our third key source of trouble. Software exposes the weaknesses of our design skills and thinking.

Because it's "easy" to write a line of program, it's also "easy" to correct a line of program. That ease means that it becomes (apparently) less important to write any given line of software correctly. In fact, software professionals often want to make a program available to users as early as possible—typically, at the first point where it can be expected to be a net benefit for that user. At that early stage (which sometimes goes by a Greek letter like "alpha" or "beta") the program likely still contains a huge number of known but unfixed errors. The expectation is that those errors will be found and fixed later.

This early-release behavior is economically rational in many cases, although it is unpleasant for an unsuspecting consumer. Often there is a premium on being first to market with the first viable implementation of some new product or feature; while you are the only available choice, you can rack up sales without competition from others. As long as your version is first to market and not too awful in its flaws, you will probably come out ahead of a competitor who is more careful but comes to market well after you.

Downloading fixes or new features has become widespread, even for products that were once sold as simple unchanging appliances. Embedded software in consumer electronics (such as a TV) used to be constructed with the expectation that it could not be updated once it left the factory. The software was built primarily around the expectation that it should work reliably without ever being updated, and accordingly it was not very sophisticated. However, modern consumer electronics are increasingly built with an expectation of internet connectivity and sophisticated software capabilities, with the corresponding increase of "software update" approaches to fixing or extending functionality.

Many people object to the practice of releasing poor software and fixing it later. There have been various attempts to solve this problem by essentially moralizing about it, shaming programmers in various ways, and/or pretending that the software is less malleable than it really is. But in almost all serious programming efforts, there comes some point at which a difficult choice must be made. At those times, the reality of software malleability almost always wins out over mere good intentions. In some unusual settings (like old-school consumer electronics, or NASA programming the space shuttle) there are real physical constraints on when and how software can be updated, and the malleability problem is accordingly less of a concern; instead, the concern is with ensuring that this essentially unfixable software is carefully built so that it doesn't fail. But anywhere that the software is actually malleable, it is somewhere between rare and impossible for that malleability to be constrained and for people to focus on delivering programs that work the first time. Instead, customers are increasingly taught to be familiar with support websites, from which they can download "updates" that are improved versions of programs they already have. Or they use "cloud" services across networks, where the services available may be updated invisibly at any time. (We will look more at networks and clouds in chapters 13, 14, 18, and 19.)

Making Things Worse

Even worse is that the work done to fix detected errors sometimes introduces new errors. The underlying causes of flaws (human cognitive limits, misunderstandings, poor choices under pressure) don't typically change between the first implementation and the correction or reimplementation. In some cases these problems actually get worse: "maintenance" work is low-prestige and so is often handed to less-capable programmers, even though the task of understanding and correcting someone else's program is typically harder than writing a new program.

It's glamorous to do something new, with the possibility that the result will be great. By comparison, it's pretty unpleasant to deal with some old pile of junk and patch it yet again. Since programmers often aren't very motivated to work on older programs, it's common to see situations in which an attempt to fix a problem inadvertently creates a new problem, which might even be worse than the original problem. This phenomenon is a key reason why computing professionals are often distrustful of new versions of critical programs. Those same professionals often make elaborate arrangements that allow them to "roll back" to previous versions even after they install a new (and allegedly improved) version.

Some computer scientists have measured error rates in certain kinds of large programs. Those studies support the idea that there is actually a point at which it's better to leave the program unfixed, because on average each "improvement" makes things worse. However, just as it's hard to have the discipline to get programs right in the beginning, it's very unusual to have the discipline to forgo "fixing" old programs. As with our other problems created by the apparently attractive malleability of software, it just seems so simple to go and fix the problem.

A closely related concern is the common misunderstanding of how expensive it really is to add a feature to a software product. Often it seems as though the work required to implement some small change is trivial—and the change, considered in isolation, might well be only a tiny effort. Unfortunately, it is very common for any such tiny change to have huge costs. The source of those costs may be only weakly related to the actual change required, but those costs are nevertheless unavoidable. One such cost is the integration of the new feature with the existing program—for example, a modified user interface to control the new feature's behavior. Another such cost is the testing of the new feature, ensuring that it doesn't break any of the program's other features. There is no way to take short cuts on these costs. After all, if the feature isn't made available to users, it isn't actually useful. And because software is digital and nonlinear, involving enormous numbers of states, there really are no "small changes" that can bypass testing. Every programmer with extensive real-world experience has stories of how an apparently harmless change had severe unexpected effects.

Requirements

From earlier sections we know that the number of possible paths through a program can grow very rapidly as the program gets longer and has more decision or branching points. If there are any errors in our implementation, they may be hard to find. But if we put aside that concern with some kind of magical testing tool, are we OK? Unfortunately, no. We then run into the difficulty of accurately capturing requirements: our fourth and last key problem of this chapter.

Sometimes it's hard to even decide what a system should do. For example, if the system is to be used by another person, we have to make some judgments about what that person will like or not like, what they will find helpful or annoying. Often we have trouble knowing our own minds, especially when dealing with complex trade-offs—but the problem is much harder when trying to establish someone else's preferences.

Consider a program to sort numbers. At one level, it doesn't seem very hard to say that the program should accept some numbers that might be out of order, and then provide the same numbers in sorted order. We might not have any idea how to do the sorting well, but surely it's easy to explain what it means to sort numbers. But when we actually start trying to do the explaining carefully enough to build a program, we see there are challenges.

For example, how will the numbers be provided? (Typed in from a keyboard? Read from a file? Scanned from a document?)

Then we might ask, How will the result be delivered? (Displayed on a screen? Written into a file? Printed?)

Generally, when a program like this is written, it's not running alone on the "bare metal" of the step-taking machinery. So there may be various kinds of services available to help tackle some of these questions for us, almost like magical spells we can invoke. Let's assume that we can hand off many of these details so the program "only" needs to deal with the stream of input numbers and the stream of output numbers. Even so, there are still some design choices to be made where it's partly a matter of judgment, rather than mathematically provable correctness.

Even when we have those supporting services to help us, there are questions that those services probably don't know enough to solve. Are negative numbers OK, or are they a symptom of a misunderstanding? Are numbers with a fractional component or in scientific notation OK? Are words OK, and how should they be sorted in comparison to numbers if they are OK? Some of these comparisons can get quite bizarre, especially in terms of how they look on a page: for example, the zero-length (null) string "" compared to a single blank " " compared to two blanks " "—these are all different items, although we don't usually find ourselves comparing them. It is possible to sort these, but is that really what we wanted?

Further, it's not just user-to-program interactions that can be hard to design. There are challenges in taking a program that we've already constructed, and figuring out how to best have it interact with a new program that we're building. For example, our number-sorting program may need to take numbers that are generated by some other measurement or analysis program. What is the format of the numbers generated by that program? How often does it generate them? How many numbers does it generate? How does the sorting program know that all of the numbers to be sorted have been received?

We've been getting a flavor of the challenges involved in fleshing out a vague problem statement into the requirements for a real working program. It's even harder to take two programs written by *other people*, where these various trade-offs and detailed design choices may well be unknown, and figure out how to best combine them so they will work well together. And yet that is the kind of task that faces real-world system builders all the time.

Expressing Requirements

Separately from the serious problem of how to figure out what the requirements are, there is a serious problem of how to express the requirements so that they can be understood. Even if you believe you know something about how a complex system will work, that's not the same as expressing it so that another person will have the same understanding.

For example, you might have a high degree of confidence that you, personally, would be able to separate numbers from non-numbers and sort the numbers—but that doesn't necessarily mean that you have the same degree of confidence that you could write down all the tests and cases for someone else to behave in the exact same way. As we solve problems, it is easy for us to rely on tacit knowledge: knowledge that we may use without being aware of it and without necessarily knowing how to articulate it.

If you are an adult reader of this book, there's a fairly good chance that you know how to ride a bicycle. But your ability to ride a bicycle doesn't mean that you can write a book that would allow someone with no previous experience to ride a bicycle well.

A further, closely related question is whether you can express some procedure so that a computer or mechanical implementation (rather than a person) can match your understanding. To return to riding a bicycle, we can see again that being able to ride a bicycle does not imply an ability to write a program so that a robot could ride a bike.

Specifications

Even if we have some good way of expressing requirements so that we can distinguish between success and failure in solving the problem, we may still struggle with expressing specifications. The specifications express some preferred set of solutions that meet the requirements. Compared to the requirements, they are closer to the ultimate implementation technology while still preserving some implementation flexibility.

Most statements of requirements and specifications are written informally in human (natural) languages. Those descriptions have the advantage that they are comfortable for the reader, but they are hard to write precisely—natural languages seem to all come with a considerable degree of ambiguity and fuzziness in their typical usage. As a result, it's hard to write natural-language text that is sure to be understood exactly the same way by different readers. For an informal confirmation of this problem in a different domain, we can look at court cases. Although some legal disputes turn on different versions of facts and the evidence supporting those contested versions, there are also a surprising number of cases where the facts are not in dispute but the correct application of the law is in doubt. Even when regulatory agencies attempt to produce very detailed rules, there are often disputes about what terms mean or how they apply in particular situations.

In contrast, formal (artificial) languages can be much more precise and can be used to produce specifications that represent the same functionality when analyzed by different readers. By developing exact grammars and rules, and using formal semantics, we can be very precise about the meaning of a statement like

$$P \rightarrow A \mid B \mid C \bullet D$$

(This equation doesn't necessarily mean anything interesting. It's just an example of how these kinds of statements look in various formal languages.)

However, any such formal language requires specialized knowledge, making it unlikely that "real users" will be able to genuinely understand and review the description for accuracy.

There seems to be an awkward but unavoidable trade-off. On one hand, there are languages that are imprecise but can be reviewed for accuracy. On the other hand, there are languages that are precise but cannot be reviewed for accuracy. To date, the best compromise between precision and accuracy probably occurs when formal specifications are produced and then converted into natural language by people who are competent in both the formal language and good (natural language) writing. However, such a process is expensive and inevitably introduces additional opportunities for error, since there are additional translation steps required.

Mock-ups

Building a mock-up (a limited implementation) is another common approach to capturing requirements and specifications. Building a "quick and dirty" version of a sorting program, for example, would force us to identify issues about the boundaries of the acceptable inputs—so we would then be better prepared to ask the right questions of the users. In addition, having the users try out our sorting program might well prompt them to notice things we hadn't done right (or to confirm the things we had done right).

Such an approach is often particularly useful for certain domains where a language-based description is hard to understand: for example, when trying to design how a website looks and how users will interact with it. However, the approach is not a universal solution. Mock-ups by their nature leave out details. Ideally, those details don't matter. But it is sometimes hard to be sure what matters and what doesn't.

One response to these problems has been to build programming practices around repeated iterations of small changes to the product or service. This approach sidesteps some of the problems of requirements and specifications in favor of a belief that repeated tinkering eventually leads to recognizable improvements. The lurking hazard is that there may never be a point at which anyone is thinking about the whole system in any kind of architectural or strategic way. If we start with a small car for a job that really needs a semi-trailer truck, it won't matter how many after-market accessories we add or how many times we repaint the exterior—the car will still be inadequate for the job. Sometimes there is a similar challenge when people think entirely in terms of small increments of functionality, even though the approach is appealing for limiting the scope and risk of any given change.

Implementation

Now we know that there are problems with capturing and specifying what systems should do. Let's put those problems aside for a moment. Repeating a common pattern in this chapter, there are still problems lurking: even if we assume a perfect specification, there is still the problem of ensuring that the implementation matches the specification.

A specification is the "higher level" description of what we want to happen. Correspondingly, an implementation is the "lower level" realization of how we want it to happen. A correct implementation is one that exactly meets its specification. Given a complete, precise, accurate specification, building a correct implementation is much easier; many programming errors arise from problems of specification incompleteness or inaccuracy, not from programmers being unable to write correct programs. Nevertheless, it is also true that having a good specification is not always sufficient to write a flawless program; errors can also arise from misunderstandings or the incompetence of programmers.

It's very unusual for a programmer to build something that doesn't work at all, in at least some important cases. But it's very common, bordering on universal, for a programmer to neglect at least some minor, obscure, or unusual cases—or to get a boundary condition "off by one."

This clustering of problems along boundaries is one reason that testing a program can be useful, in spite of the explosion of possible paths we mentioned previously. Although the program's execution may proceed along many different paths, programmer errors will tend to cluster along only a few of those paths. We may recall our example (earlier in this chapter) of the program that exploded on a particular single input value. Although it is possible in principle for a program to have such a completely arbitrary behavior, in practice that situation is unusual. Instead, human problems of poor communication and/or cognitive limits tend to produce particular kinds of implementation errors, which can often be prevented, or found and removed.

From the use of discrete states to the challenges of implementation, we've now identified some of the most important ways in which programs are usually flawed. We'll next take up some of the ways programs are limited even when they are flawless.

7 Limits: Perfect Programs

The previous chapter described various ways in which programs are imperfect and thus fall short of what we might want them to do. In contrast, in this chapter we take up the ways in which programs can be flawless but nevertheless unable to do what we want them to do. It may be surprising, but even perfect programs still have limits.

Environment

The first problem is that the program may well be correct at a particular instant of time, but we also have to consider the *environment* of the program—everything in the universe that isn't the program but with which it interacts. The evolving environment of a program leads to additional challenges beyond the ones we've already considered.

Most changes in the environment are irrelevant. For example, consider a program that I might write to print "Hello world" when I choose to activate it. Such a program's operation or utility would be unaffected by a change in the price of coffee, the love affairs of movie stars, or the phase of the planet Jupiter. However, that program does depend on assumptions about the computer on which it's running, the operating system services available on that computer, and the display device on that computer. A naïve programmer might think that his or her simple "Hello world" program would be totally immune to changes in its environment, and over short timescales that view would be correct. But if we consider a "Hello world" program that might have been written on a Bell Labs or MIT computer in the 1970s, there is no way to take that exact program, unchanged, and run it on a readily available modern computer, unchanged.

There are two ways to get the program running on a modern machine. The first, a process called *porting*, requires that we modify the program to adjust to its new environment. The second, a process called *emulation*, requires that we create a layer of additional program that recreates the 1970s-era environment as expected by the old program. We can adjust the program to the new environment, or adjust the environment to the old program, or some combination—but we can't just count on today's correct program remaining tomorrow's correct program indefinitely into the future.

This phenomenon of program/environment mismatches developing over time has a colloquial name of "bit rot" among programmers. It's a term that implies decay over time for software, which is certainly what it seems like experientially—even though the programs are actually made of a wonderful nonphysical "material" that never has any kind of wear or deterioration.

Big Problems

We will be concerned later in the book with how to scale up systems to tackle big problems. So another important limit on even a perfectly constructed program is that the problem to be solved might be too big for the available resources. What do we mean by saying that a problem might be too big? Suppose that we have *some* measure of how big a problem is. For example:

• If we are looking for one instance of a word in a particular (single) book, then looking in a different, longer book is probably harder.
• If we are considering a particular single word in a particular single book, then looking for all the occurrences of the word is probably harder than just looking for any one occurrence.

Just knowing that one problem is vaguely harder than another is not much help, though. We would like to identify what the limiting elements are. We are familiar with this issue in other contexts. Suppose that we have a car capable of speeds up to 100 miles per hour, and we need to drive 10 miles through the city. Can we simply divide 10 miles by our 100 mph speed and conclude that the driving time will be 0.1 hour (6 minutes)? Probably not. In a typical city, there will be speed limits well below 100 mph for the entire route, and traffic lights at some number of intersections are likely to stop us for some of the time as well.

Suppose that we tried such a drive and found that it actually took us 24 minutes instead of 6 minutes to go 10 miles; and further suppose that we found that speed unsatisfactory. Would it be sensible to buy a much more expensive car that could go twice as fast, 200 mph? No, because the car's top speed isn't the limiting factor. The limiting factor is something else, and we would need to identify and correct it to get any significant improvement in performance.

In general, it's not easy to identify what the limiting element is in a program. If there is no other information available, finding the limiting element involves a careful analysis of the program's activities, particularly as the inputs are increased in size and/or number. The measurement of program performance is called *benchmarking*, and improving the performance of programs is called *tuning*. The concepts involved in benchmarking and tuning are not very different from what people do when racing cars—indeed, the terminology is largely borrowed from there.

Computational Complexity

However, computer scientists also have an approach to understanding and improving performance that is quite different from the steps taken to improve performance in race cars. That approach is called *computational complexity*. Professional programmers design programs with an eye on how they scale up to large problems, making design choices with an awareness of the computational complexity of various potential solutions. A good education in computer science provides an awareness of these issues and the consequent ability to make sensible choices about key implementation concerns. However, simply knowing "how to program" doesn't necessarily imply a good understanding of these topics.

Computational complexity hinges on two tricks:

1. We think about a program's performance only in terms of the elements that will be dominant as the problem gets bigger—the real bottlenecks or limits at large scale.

2. We characterize that performance by a kind of mathematical analogy. Rather than developing a detailed analysis of the program's performance, we understand whether it is similar to one of a small number of common mathematical functions.

Just as we can sort socks into piles of black, white, and colored socks without worrying too much about exact colors or patterns, we can sort programs into piles based on how quickly they run out of resources as the problem of interest gets bigger. As with the sock-sorting, there may be some tricky edge cases, but we can still use the approach to get a better sense of what we have—and we know we'll at least distinguish black socks from white socks.

Instead of sorting socks into piles based on color, we'll sort programs into groups based on their complexity. The "color" of a program is the mathematical approximation that is closest to the program's behavior, and that "color" is what is meant by the complexity of the program. Here the word "complexity" is not just an informal term for something complicated; instead, it has a precise meaning for how hard a problem is.

Ignoring Constants

Let's return to the first "trick" of computational complexity to understand it better. When we're looking at performance, we want to focus on a limiting factor—we don't want to be distracted by something that's not the "big issue." As we noted with the example of the fast car going across town, it doesn't make any difference to speed up something that's not the limiting factor.

We're going to turn that reasoning around and assume for our discussion of computational complexity that we are focused on cases where the size of the input drives the overall cost. We're assuming that lots of good detective work has already removed quirky or unrepresentative performance, so that we're now dealing with a cleaned-up situation where the performance of the program is basically determined in some way by the size of its input.

If we consider a program to sort numbers, the size of the input would be how many numbers we want to have sorted. We call that input size n. In this example, it's the number of items to be sorted, but in other cases it could be something else. We drop any aspect of the cost that doesn't include n. That is, if there's some fixed overhead that we always have to pay that doesn't change with the problem size, we ignore it. The technical term for this perspective is that we *ignore constants*—we are interested in how the cost grows as n grows, and any constant overhead simply drops out of that comparison because it doesn't grow at all.

Perhaps more surprisingly, we also ignore constants when they are "only" multiplying the cost. For the purpose of this analysis, $2n$ is the same as n, which is the same as $n/2$—they're all just "variants" of n. The technical term for this perspective is that we also *ignore constant factors*.

Ignoring constants and constant factors might seem strange. Is it justifiable? Yes and no. As a way of getting to core scaling issues, it's absolutely reasonable. Recall that what we're heading toward (our second "trick") is grouping the behavior of different programs into "piles" that share an underlying growth characteristic. As we will see, the differences *between* those families completely dominate the differences *within* each family. We might think of the underlying complexity as a vehicle and the constant factors as the effort of the vehicle's driver or rider. If we're comparing a sports car to a bicycle, the crucial comparison is between the vehicles, not how hard the rider or driver is pushing the pedals. And it's important not to be misled by a hard-pedaling cyclist vs. a light-footed driver into thinking that the car is slower.

However, once we are past this core analysis—understanding which "vehicle family" corresponds to the program's behavior—constant factors and overhead come roaring back to our attention. A theorist specializing in computational complexity might dismiss a given approach as "only changing a constant factor," and thus irrelevant; but making something run twice as fast (or perhaps even just a few percent faster) can make a huge difference to real-world applications of computing.

For example, in the annual ranking of the world's supercomputers, the difference between being the fastest in the world vs. being at the bottom of the list is meaningless from the perspective of a theorist. In a discussion among theorists, the distinction between these is merely some constant factor, which in a theoretical analysis is dropped as insignificant. However, if you have a specific problem you want to be solved and it can be solved on either computer, you will be much happier getting to solve it a thousand times faster on the fast machine...and you will cheerfully ignore the theorists' comments that this difference "doesn't matter."

Categories of Complexity

Let's assume that we are given the complexity of a program rather than having to somehow figure it out. It's useful to compare the growth rates of some plausible complexity functions to get an intuition for how they behave. Table 7.1 shows some values of complexity functions that a program might have.

The column labeled n represents the size of the input, like how many numbers need to be sorted. The values in the other columns give an idea

Table 7.1

Some examples of how problem sizes grow with n

n	n^2	n^3	2^n	10^n	$n!$
1	1	1	2	10	1
2	4	8	4	100	2
3	9	27	8	1,000	6
...	...	...	...	...	...
10	100	1,000	1,024	10,000,000,000	3,628,800
11	121	1,331	2,048	100,000,000,000	39,916,800
12	144	1,728	4,096	1,000,000,000,000	479,001,600
...	...	...	...	...	...

of how many steps are required if the program falls into that category for its complexity. (If mathematical functions are not your friends, just think of these as slightly weird names we're giving to some useful growth trends: they could have names like "Carol" or "Ted" instead, if you prefer.) The crucial part for our exploration is just to see how big or small some of the numbers in the table get, not to spend a lot of time with the underlying math. In particular, we notice that the columns to the right have crazily large numbers in them.

If you are acquainted with spreadsheets, it's not hard to build a chart like this yourself. Making your own chart means you can explore these numbers and functions yourself or test out some other functions for comparison.

Our simple, no-real-math-involved observation is that it makes a big difference which column of this table most closely resembles our program's behavior. Some of these trends grow very much faster than others.

In chapter 3 we mentioned Moore's law and the surprising way that computing performance has improved over time. Despite its startling effects, Moore's law does not promise growth as fast as some of the possible complexity categories we've just seen. We might find ourselves taking the tone of a spoiled child and complaining that Moore's law "only" promises repeated doublings (that is, the 2^n column). Although it is a remarkable benefit to receive, we could want more: any of the really fast-growing problems will stay out of our reach even with the help of Moore's law.

We haven't said much about how to establish a connection between a particular process and the closest growth trend representing its computational complexity—and we won't, because that's a hard topic that doesn't yield much value to nonspecialists. There are three important insights to summarize:

1. Problems typically grow harder as they get bigger.
2. Not all problems grow harder in the same way or at the same rate.
3. Some problems can grow faster than our ability to supply resources to solve those problems.

Uncomputability

One of the great mind-benders beloved of amateur philosophers is the notion of limits on omnipotent beings. One way of raising this issue is to assume an omnipotent God. Then ask, can God create an object that's so large that even God can't lift it?

The problem with answering is that no matter how we answer, we seem to have put limits on the defined-to-be-omnipotent being. If we say "yes," then that means we are saying God can't lift the object … so God is limited, and thus not omnipotent. If we say "no," then that means we are saying God can't create the object … so God is limited, and thus not omnipotent. The problem seems to be in our casual assumption that "omnipotent" is a coherent concept. Instead, it seems like the designation of God as "omnipotent" is the start of the problem. As we'll see, there are some vaguely similar logical problems in considering the power of computation.

To recap, to get to this point we have considered a variety of limits on programs and imagined our way past each. So now we are considering a perfectly specified, perfectly implemented program with an unchanging environment that has also been checked to ensure that it has sufficient resources. One final limitation relates to what is impossible to express as a computation, or *uncomputability*. This limitation can seem esoteric and bizarre when first described. However, uncomputability turns out to have some important practical implications.

A common first reaction to the idea of uncomputability is to reject it. What can it possibly mean to say that there are programs that can't be computed? We can readily grasp the idea that it might be hard to capture requirements, hard to write correct programs, hard to ensure there are sufficient resources to execute the program. But the idea that there are well-specified programs that are nevertheless impossible to compute seems to violate what we've implied previously. As we first considered the digital world (chapter 2) we saw that we could use bits to represent analog data; no matter how complex the wave form, if we were willing to use enough bits we could produce as good a copy as we wanted. Similarly, when we examined programs and processes (chapter 3) we saw that we could build up very elaborate processes from many tiny steps. So after all of that rah-rah positive attitude about computing, it seems like a real step backward—a contradiction, even—to say that there are things we just can't do.

Formal Logic

Indeed, if we were to assert that everything is computable, we would be in distinguished company. Famed mathematician David Hilbert made a comparable incorrect assumption in 1928 when he posed his "decision problem" (which sounds much more impressive in the original German, where it is "*Entscheidungsproblem*").

Part of the intellectual ferment at the time was an effort to build all of mathematics from a foundation of logic. Logic is the study of valid reasoning, and its relevance for this discussion is in the idea of *formal* logic. Formal logic starts from distinguishing the form of an argument from its particular content. The form is the structure or skeleton of the argument; in contrast, the content is what the argument is about.

For example, we can make a variety of claims about a subject like elephants, some of which will be valid and some of which will be invalid. Similarly, we can make a variety of claims about a subject like strawberries, with some being valid while others are invalid. The key insight of formal logic is that the validity of a statement may be determined by its form, not its content. What does that mean? There are circumstances in which a claim about strawberries is related to our knowledge about strawberries: for example, "Ripe strawberries are red." That particular piece of knowledge is relevant only to strawberries and their color; it doesn't let us determine much about anything else.

In contrast, consider the two statements: "No strawberry is an elephant" and "No elephant is a strawberry." Taken together, these two statements and the rules of formal logic allow us to conclude that "nothing is both an elephant and a strawberry." Better yet, that same structure is applicable to something other than elephants and strawberries. For example, we can also reason about the unrelatedness of giraffes and grapes, or indeed even move away from animals and fruits to (say) cars and vegetables.

Seen from the perspective of everyday experience, it can seem quite peculiar and excessively philosophical to make this separation between form and content. However, with the benefit of hindsight we can appreciate that it's exactly this bizarre-seeming emphasis on abstraction and rules that led to today's computer age. Computers are very much embodiments of formal logic, applicable to many different kinds of content.

No Solution to Hilbert's Problem

To return to Hilbert's ambition: the thinking at the time was roughly that a mathematical system could start with a few simple assumptions (what mathematicians would call *axioms*) and some combining rules. The rules would allow those axioms to produce additional logical statements that were also true (proven) as a consequence of the axioms. With the right axioms and rules in place, all of mathematics could follow as consequences.

In that context, Hilbert posed the task of constructing a decision process that could be given a statement in a particular kind of logic and answer "yes" or "no" depending on whether the statement was or wasn't reachable by applying the rules to the axioms. Computer science arguably dates its birth to this problem. Two foundational figures of computer science—Alan Turing and Alonzo Church—independently used their own computational models to explore this problem. We have already encountered Turing's computational model in the form of the Turing machine when we first looked at processes (chapter 3). Then we saw Church's computational model in the form of lambda calculus, when we looked at names (chapter 4). As we saw there, lambda calculus is not at all machinelike. Instead, it "operates" on the basis of substituting values for names.

Remarkably, despite the surface differences in their approaches, Church and Turing reached the same conclusion: Hilbert's problem is not solvable. Church and Turing in turn were building on a startling discovery that yet another logician (Kurt Gödel) had made a few years earlier about the intrinsic limits of mathematics and logic.

In all of these cases, the limits arise from applying the system to itself— that is, the limits of a universal system arise from the ability of a universal system to turn a mirror on itself. The next few sections develop the slightly convoluted thinking required to demonstrate this limit in the universe. If you like logic puzzles, this is great stuff; if you're not all that keen on logic, you may want to skip forward a few sections to "The Halting Problem," where we talk about what this means for real-world systems.

Russell's Paradox

To work our way up to this sort of self-mirroring and the problems that arise, let's consider an even earlier logic problem called Russell's paradox. Russell's paradox arises from the work of Bertrand Russell, yet another famous logician and philosopher who was a contemporary of Hilbert, Gödel, Church, and Turing.

One way of talking about Russell's paradox is to talk about clean-shaven men in a small town with a single male clean-shaven barber. The barber shaves everyone in town who does not shave himself.

The paradox arises from trying to classify the barber within the stated rules:

• If he shaves himself, he is not shaved by the barber, which means he *doesn't* shave himself. Or…

• If he is shaved by the barber, he is shaved by himself, which means he *isn't* shaved by the barber.

With either decision, we arrive at a contradiction. How annoying!

We can acknowledge that this is a paradox, but it seems a bit pointless and pedantic. We might well wonder about its significance to the problem of computability that we are trying to approach. Part of the answer is that the elements in play here will also matter for computability. In particular, to have this paradox we need to have three elements together:

1. Universality (a rule that applies to *all* the clean-shaven men);
2. Negation (those who shave themselves are *not* shaved by the barber);
3. Self-reference (men who shave *themselves*).

If we eliminate any one of these elements, the paradox disappears:

• If we eliminate universality, the barber can simply be an exception to the rule.

• If we eliminate negation, the barber can be both shaved by himself and shaved by the barber.

• Finally, if we eliminate self-reference, then we would simply be discussing the set of men who are or aren't shaved by the barber, which can certainly include the barber.

Halting vs. Diverging

Russell's paradox is a fine logic puzzle, but why does it have any relevance to computability? We are going to take those same ideas of universality, negation, and self-reference and apply them to the "answerability" of computational questions.

We start with the idea that each process either gives an answer or it doesn't. If a process gives an answer, we say that it *halts*—it doesn't take any more steps after it comes up with the answer. If a process never gives an answer, we say it *diverges*—that is, it just fiddles around taking meaningless steps endlessly.

Then we create a process about processes, with a special kind of "clairvoyant" quality. This clairvoyant process can be given a program as its input, and will determine (somehow) whether that program's corresponding process halts or diverges.

Let's pause here and consider what we've done. It doesn't feel like we've done anything wrong—yet. We've just said that we are going to build a program that looks at other programs. Examining a program to determine whether it halts or not seems like something useful that a program can do, much the same way that cutting hair is something useful that a person can do. Indeed, there are real-world examples of programs that examine other programs to determine if the examined programs contain errors. We can view this clairvoyant program as a very simple abstract example of the larger class of programs that examine programs.

Determining whether a program halts is less familiar than cutting hair, but otherwise nothing here seems alarming. Just as it might take a lot of training to cut hair well, it might take a lot of sophistication to build this clairvoyant program. But in the best traditions of mathematics, we'll just assume we can solve the problem rather than worrying about how!

Building a Paradox

For the next step in our pursuit of paradox, we build a *negated* version of that clairvoyant process. The negated clairvoyant process halts if the input process diverges and diverges if the input process halts. In contrast to the unknown complexity of building a clairvoyant process, the negation step seems easy and obviously implementable. Whatever you were going to do, just do the opposite.

The final step in assembling this paradox is to ask what happens when the negated clairvoyant process is given *itself* as input. After all, the negated clairvoyant process is just a process, and its corresponding program can be examined just like any other program to determine whether it halts or diverges.

But the situation is dire when we do apply the negated clairvoyant process to itself. If the negated clairvoyant process halts when given itself, then it diverges; but if it diverges when given itself, it halts. Ugh! There is a contradiction, which we can trace back to our assumption that we could build the clairvoyant process.

Once again we used the combination of universality, negation, and self-reference to achieve a contradictory result.

The Halting Problem

What does this contradiction mean? Our seemingly harmless assumption that we could determine the halting behavior of a program now looks like it was the first step on a road to ruin. We've now exposed what computer scientists call the *halting problem*.

Its real-world implication is that we have to be a little concerned about whether our computational system is powerful enough to let us play this trick. If this trick is possible, then in general we can't tell whether a program will work correctly. We know for sure that any universal model of computation will definitely have this problem. After all, if a system is sufficiently powerful to write any program, then it's also powerful enough that we can write the program(s) required to play this trick on any supposedly clairvoyant program.

If we really want to be able to guarantee whether programs will work, we can weaken the model of computation so that it's not universal, and then perhaps we can't build the contradictory example. But people who have tried that path have found that it is frustrating to write programs in such a mode—the elements that give a language expressive power are the same as the elements that are problematic in terms of predicting execution.

Indeed, a part of what Gödel proved in the larger realm of mathematics is that there is essentially a trade-off between completeness and consistency. If a mathematical system is large and powerful enough to prove *all* true statements about arithmetic, some of the statements in that system are inconsistent with each other. But if a mathematical system is careful enough to prove *only* consistent statements about arithmetic, it also omits some true statements.

The halting problem itself is narrower than Gödel's much broader concerns about mathematical systems, but it still feels very philosophical. At this point it seems unlikely to be of any practical concern. However, we will see that it is quite important in chapter 22 when we start to consider defending against attackers.

II Interacting Processes

8   Coordination

In the previously described "reading world" (chapter 3) there was a reader process interacting with a book. There are two different ways to add in a second activity: we can add a second reader, and/or we can add a second book. We can diagram it as a 2×2 grid of possibilities (table 8.1):

- one reader, one book (which we described in a previous chapter);
- two readers, one book;
- one reader, two books; or
- two readers, two books.

We'll fill in this table to cover the different cases. Initially we just put a question mark for each of the new combinations.

The one-reader, two-books case is a reader who is trying to make progress in two books at once. This implies that the reader spends some time reading one book, then switches to the other and spends some time reading that book. The reader then switches back to reading the first book, and the alternation between the books continues. A computer scientist would refer to this as "timesharing" or "multitasking." This alternating approach turns out to be very important to how computer systems operate. It's also challenging to get it right, as we'll see in chapter 10.

One thing we know for sure is that we don't want the reader to start from the beginning of the book each time there's a change of books. For the

Table 8.1

	1 Book	2 Books
1 Reader	No multiprocess issues	?
2 Readers	?	?

reader to make progress within this arrangement, there must be some kind of marker or reminder of where to restart: possibly a bookmark or a pencil mark on a page, or a memory retained in the reader's brain to identify a starting point. Without such a marker, each switch to a different book restarts reading at the beginning; in such an arrangement, the reader may stay very busy but doesn't make much progress.

As soon as we are concerned with multiple processes, there is some additional data that's not really related to the problem being solved—it's just related to the work of coordinating the processes. This particular kind of data is what computer scientists usually call *context*. In general, the context of a process lets the process be bundled up and put away, then later resumed from the same place.

Sharing a Book

The next case to consider is two readers, one book. Two readers are each separately trying to make progress in the single shared book. Because the book is a single shared thing, there must be some kind of *controlled access* to it, or else the two readers will interfere with each other's reading. For example, our first reader (named Alice) may be ready to turn from page 5 to page 6, but turning the page will prevent our second reader (named Bob) from finishing his reading of page 5. In a possible annoying scenario, the two readers could each briefly grab the book, flip the page to where they want it, read something there, and then let go of the book—only to have the other reader immediately flip the page back again to where it was previously. It's possible to make progress under these circumstances, but it's frustrating.

In an even worse scenario, the two readers might grab hold of the same page at the same time and pull it in opposite directions, tearing it. Such a disaster is like the kinds of damage or corruption that can happen if two or more processes have uncontrolled access to some shared data in a computer. Fortunately, there are tools that we can use to avoid those problems; we'll learn more about some of those tools in chapter 10.

Multiple Books and Multiple Readers

We've now covered both the one-reader-two-books scenario and the two-readers-one-book scenario. You might well think that the two-readers-two-books case is the most complex of all, and in a sense that is correct.

Table 8.2

	1 Book	2 Books
1 Reader	No multiprocess issues	Timesharing
2 Readers	Controlled access	No sharing: No multiprocess issues
		Sharing: Controlled access

However, that case really adds only a little new difficulty to the issues that we've already discussed. In one arrangement, the two readers are each reading a distinct book, so there's nothing shared between them. That means we effectively have a single-reader, single-book arrangement that just happens to be next to another single-reader, single-book arrangement. If there's no interaction between those two setups, it doesn't really matter if they're next to each other or on different planets—they'll still both have the same experiences as any other single-reader, single-book arrangement.

In the other "two readers, two books" case, the two readers are *both* reading from *both* books. Because there is sharing, this situation requires the same kind of controlled access that we needed when two readers were reading from one book. It almost doesn't matter how many different shared books there are, or how many readers. As soon as there's the possibility of a book being shared, there needs to be some kind of controlled access to it. Table 8.2 summarizes all of the cases we've considered.

Deadlock

There is one new wrinkle in the two-book, two-reader case compared to what we saw previously. That new wrinkle is that there's now a simple way to get "stuck" if the two readers both want to gain exclusive access to both books at once.

What do we mean by getting "stuck?" To see how the problem arises, let's return to our two readers who we have named Alice and Bob. We'll call the books Dickens and Shakespeare. Let's further assume that *both* Alice and Bob want to grab *both* Dickens and Shakespeare before either one does something with them...perhaps comparing them page-for-page, looking at differences. Alice plans to grab Dickens, then grab Shakespeare. Meanwhile, Bob is planning to grab Shakespeare, then Dickens. They will get "stuck" if Alice successfully grabs Dickens while Bob successfully grabs Shakespeare.

They will each be politely waiting for the other one to give up what has been grabbed. If they are obtuse and stubborn, they will each cling to what they have and wait for the other to give up—which might not ever happen.

Getting "stuck" in this way is called *deadlock*. Deadlock is easy to see in a two-process case like this, but the problem can also occur with larger groups of processes. Any arrangement with multiple shared resources and multiple processes poses some risk of deadlock until we figure out how to avoid it. Any time that a process has grabbed some of the shared resources it needs, but still needs other resources that are currently grabbed by other processes, there is a risk of deadlock.

Gridlock

It may seem implausible to imagine deadlock among readers sharing books, but there's a real-life example that's probably not hard to imagine…and which you may even have experienced, if you drive in a crowded city like Boston. A traffic gridlock is a form of deadlock. Every intersection is shared among the various cars on the road. Cars are like processes, and their forward motion is analogous to steps (although of course cars are not digital in their movements!).

In a simple case with a badly designed intersection, two cars facing each other and both trying to turn left can block each other. Each car is occupying part of the intersection that the other one needs in order to leave the intersection.

In a simple gridlock like this one, it is easy for both drivers to see that there is indeed a "stuck" situation. It's also simple to resolve the situation by one or both drivers giving up their attempt to turn left. What makes a large-scale gridlock more hazardous is that the collection of drivers and intersections may be spread across a number of blocks, so that there is no single intersection where it's obvious that ordinary traffic behavior has broken down.

Bad driving habits can spread the gridlock. In Boston, it's common for a driver to enter an intersection without having a clear path to exit the intersection. These naughty drivers usually get away with this behavior even if they are stranded in the intersection for a cycle or two of the traffic lights, because traffic eventually moves forward and gives them some space outside the intersection. There are some intersections where this kind of ugly intersection-blocking behavior happens as a matter of course for both the roads that are crossing. But if something happens further down the road to create a genuine blockage, the intersection can't clear as it usually does—it stays blocked. The newly blocked intersection in turn blocks traffic in all directions, which in turn creates problems for traffic leading to that intersection—especially if that traffic is in turn coming through intersections blocked by misbehaving motorists.

Detecting Deadlock

If we know what processes have grabbed and what processes are waiting for, then we can understand exactly when deadlock has occurred by drawing a diagram of waiting processes. We draw an arrow from process A to process B whenever process A is waiting for a shared resource that process B has grabbed. We previously mentioned that Alice is waiting for Bob, since Bob is currently holding Shakespeare and Alice needs Shakespeare before she can proceed further. Figure 8.1 captures that A-waits-for-B relationship.

If we draw in all the arrows wherever one process is waiting for another, we can look at the diagram to see if there are any loops. Figure 8.2 is our diagram for when Alice has Dickens and Bob has Shakespeare, but each of them is also waiting for the book the other has.

If there's a circle of processes waiting for each other, with the arrows leading back to our process of interest, then there's a deadlock among all the processes in that loop. Part of the challenge is that there might be a lot of processes in the loop. Figure 8.3 shows six processes in a deadlock. Looking at any one pair of processes doesn't reveal the deadlock—only the whole group of six has a loop.

Figure 8.1
A waits for B.

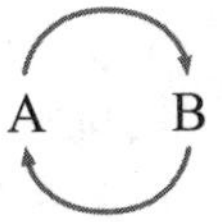

Figure 8.2
A cycle of waiting, A and B are deadlocked.

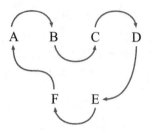

Figure 8.3
Six processes in a deadlock.

Breaking Deadlock

We've seen that we can detect deadlocks in the diagram of who is "waiting-for" whom, by looking for loops. That diagram is also useful for fixing the problem. Any process that notices such a loop can choose to leave it, and thereby break the deadlock. The leaving process stops waiting for whatever it currently needs, and/or releases whatever it has that others are waiting for. The remaining processes are no longer deadlocked and can make progress.

An alternative to this "noble volunteer" approach uses a kind of overseer process that tracks the behavior of some collection of other processes. When the overseer sees a deadlock, it can choose at least one "victim" from among the deadlocked processes. The victim will have to lose its grabbed resources so that others can proceed. With the involuntary, pick-a-victim approach to breaking a deadlock, the victim process may not be prepared for its demise. Simply taking resources away from a process doesn't necessarily give a good result: the process might have already changed some of the items that it grabbed. If we simply wipe out a process in the middle of its activities, and then hand its resources to some other process, we might create a mess. After all, if you have to stop some cooks in the middle of making a meal and send them home, you also want to clean up whatever they've left behind in the kitchen, not just parachute in a new cook to start cooking more stuff in addition to what's currently on the stove.

Fortunately, there are elegant mechanisms available to "undo" whatever has been done by the victim process, if we know that we may have to break deadlocks. We're not going to get into those details; instead, we will just wave our hands and declare that we can reliably reverse all the steps taken by a process that has become trapped in a deadlock situation.

Livelock

A subtle trap is that it's possible to replace a deadlock with a *livelock*—that is, a situation in which no process is "stuck," but there is also no forward progress. For example, assume that there's a group of processes that have somehow reached deadlock in a ring configuration, like the group in figure 8.3.

Each process (labeled A through F) is waiting for something. Although the processes may be unrelated to each other and unaware of each other, we can see that they have a kind of relationship through these shared items. If each of the processes handles a "stuck" situation in the exact same way, then each may choose to release and then regrab items at the same time. Bizarrely, the collection of processes will repeatedly create a brief deadlock that is then "resolved." Although there is ongoing activity in such a system, it's not doing any real work in any of the processes—each of the processes is just repeatedly grabbing a resource and then releasing it.

A real-world experience that's like a different kind of livelock can happen in a large bureaucracy like a university or a state government. A difficult issue may fall into a gray area where it's not clear who should solve the problem, and so department A will redirect an inquiry to department B, which may in turn redirect to department C. No one actually provides an answer, only a pointer to someone else who might be able to provide an answer. If this sequence of redirections leads back to a previously encountered department, we are in a redirection loop and can't ever expect to get an answer no matter how many more times we're redirected.

Now, when a person actually follows such a sequence of redirections, they usually notice if they find themselves back at a place they've visited previously. But that only means that this particular kind of livelock is easy to detect. In general, detecting livelock is hard. Although deadlock is readily detected by constructing the "waits-for" graph, there is no comparably easy way to detect livelock. In the scenario where each of the processes is repeatedly in a deadlock and then out of a deadlock, it's not obvious how any particular process can tell the difference between livelock and a run of bad luck. In the worst case, detecting livelock requires predicting the behavior of programs. Such prediction is equivalent to solving the halting problem—and as we learned in chapter 7, the halting problem is unsolvable.

Thrashing

Thrashing is a situation where multiple processes are spending all of their time in coordination overhead rather than in doing real work. Thrashing is similar to livelock in some ways but is distinct from it. The usual cause of thrashing is overload—as a step-taking system divides its resources among more and more processes, each process's share of steps gets smaller. Eventually, that share is no more than the steps required for housekeeping and bookkeeping associated with each distinct process.

We also see a similar class of problem in everyday life: as people try to increase their intensity of multitasking, they eventually reach a point where they are ineffective because they are spending too little time "on task" vs. too much time being interrupted or reminding themselves of what they should be doing next.

The difference between livelock and thrashing might seem academic—after all, the real point in either case is that there's a lot of activity but not much real progress. But it's useful to distinguish them and understand what the differences mean. Livelock is not something that typically develops or goes away based on how much work needs to be done. Instead, livelock usually reflects some underlying design error that affects the correctness of the system. Something in the sequencing or arrangement of the processes means that it's impossible for them to make progress, because they get in each other's way.

In contrast, thrashing both appears and disappears based on how much work needs to be done. Thrashing is essentially about implementation costs. In thrashing, there is no structural or design problem with the processes that keeps them from working; instead, the process-related coordination overhead has become so high relative to their real work that little or no useful work is being done.

9   State, Change, and Equality

Although we have considered both the "stepped" nature of digital data and the steps taken by an executing process, we haven't yet looked very closely at how those ideas interact. We have already seen that a data item can change its value: the "scratch pad" or "tape" of the Turing machine has cells that can be read or written (chapter 3). As we start to consider multiple processes, it's useful to understand this changeability and its implications more carefully.

As with our examination of names in chapters 4 and 5, some of this examination of changes may seem overdone. But in a similar way, we'll find that we benefit in later discussions of computer systems and infrastructure. It will be helpful later if we're careful now about distinctions that may initially seem unimportant.

To start with an everyday example, consider an ordinary coffee cup. Part of what makes a typical coffee cup useful is that it undergoes changes that we can view as different states. A coffee cup typically starts out empty, then it's filled with coffee, and then it's partially or wholly emptied by someone drinking the coffee. It may or may not be cleaned before it is refilled with coffee—or if it's disposable, it will be discarded rather than being cleaned. It usually makes sense to think of it as the *same* coffee cup throughout the activity: we do not usually think of its identity changing, even though its role in our life may change as it is filled, drained, cleaned. Indeed, there may even be completely different people involved in the filling, emptying, and cleaning (or discarding) stages.

There are many ways we could represent the state of the coffee cup. For example, we may distinguish a few levels like full, partial, or empty. Or we may think of the cup's state as being clean (ready to be filled) or dirty (ready to be washed). Or we may think of the cup's state as numbers describing the quantity of coffee contained and the temperature of the coffee there.

To pick another household example, we can consider the slots of a silverware drawer. When all the silverware is out on the table, all of the slots in the drawer are empty. When all of the silverware is freshly washed and put away, the knife slot is full of knives, the fork slot is full of forks, and the spoon slot is full of spoons. In fact, we could even use the silverware slots as a kind of computation mechanism to let us know how many items remain to be put away. Suppose there are eight sets of silverware: eight knives, eight forks, eight spoons. And further suppose that we look in the drawer and see the slots have two knives, five forks, and eight spoons. We can easily figure out that the table or the dishwasher or the sink must have the remaining six knives and three forks. Putting silverware away or taking it out is an analog process (a hand moving continuously through space, with no identifiable discrete "steps" to those hand motions) but we can comfortably view the silverware-in-slots state as being digital: a spoon is either present or absent, and it's not really interesting or useful to focus on the in-between instants right when the spoon is being taken out or put away.

Stateless vs. Stateful

State complicates behavior. That claim might seem surprising since it wasn't hard to understand the previous household examples of state. So let's consider how state adds complexity.

Some circuits or machines have a very simple relationship between inputs and outputs, and identical inputs always produce identical outputs. For example, consider a gadget that's an adder (not the snake kind), taking two numbers in and producing a single number as a result. An adder that's given "2" and "3" will always produce the output "5." There's no need for any state or history, and no value to adding state. Engineers refer to these as *combinational* or *stateless* systems. All you need to know is the combination of inputs to predict the output, because there's no hidden state to affect that output.

Other circuits or machines depend on some element of previous history to determine outputs. If we see such a machine at an isolated instant of time and without knowledge of the previous history, it's unwise to try predicting the output. For example, consider the following gadget: each time it's given two numbers, it adds them both to its previous total. This gadget is not an adder, it's what a computer scientist would call an *accumulator*. Like the adder described earlier, this accumulator could also be given "2" and "3" as inputs. But unless we have reason to know its previous total was "0," there's no reason to believe the result will be "5."

Whereas the adder had a simple rule that was applicable for all time, the accumulator has a complex rule that's contingent on information that we might not know. Engineers refer to systems like the accumulator as *sequential* or *stateful* systems. You have to know the sequence or history or the state to predict the output, because the inputs alone are insufficient.

Assignment

When we do simple mathematics, we assume that elements behave in the combinational or stateless way that we described for the adder. If we have a simple algebra problem to solve, we might determine at one step that $x = 3$. For example, we might have a pair of equations like

$2x = 6$

$y = 3x$

Once we've learned that first piece of information about x having the value 3 from the first equation, we don't have to worry that at some later time x might have changed its value to 42. We just go ahead and use the knowledge that $x = 3$ to determine from the second equation that $y = 9$.

Indeed, if we are working through a proof and find that there's some kind of collision of values for a variable (say, we find by one path that $x = 3$ and by some other path that $x = 42$) then we'll declare that there's a contradiction— and use that contradiction as a basis to reverse some assumption that we made earlier in the proof. For example, if we're confronted with the following two equations

$2x = 6$

$x = 42$

then there's no solution possible. We would either say that this problem is unsolvable, or we would backtrack to some earlier step of solving the problem to understand whether an earlier error gave rise to the contradiction.

In contrast, a programmer would not be at all surprised to deal with a process in which x has the value 3 at one point and the value 42 at some later point and would see no contradiction or failure. The programmer would simply say that the variable x is *mutable*; we wouldn't ordinarily use that word for the changeability of the coffee cup or the silverware drawer, but it's describing the same characteristic. The mathematical view of variables is correspondingly *immutable*. In math we might not (yet) know the value for a variable x, but x can have only one value, or else there's something wrong. In programming, we might see that the same variable x has different values at different times, and that's OK.

This difference is the root of why state makes it hard to think about processes and their behavior: the same name can have different values at different times in a process's execution. State means that a particular pairing of a name with a value is not necessarily stable over time. When state is described as an instability of naming, or an instability of values, it becomes a little easier to see why it might not always be a good thing.

Referential Transparency

The very idea of equality has some tricky issues lurking once we introduce mutability into the picture. As we've noted, mutability implies that a single name can mean different things at different times. That changeability wrecks a fundamental trick of substituting names for values or vice versa, and means that all kinds of simple statements about the process have to be hedged to the point that they're essentially useless. Instead of being able to say "x has the value 3" we wind up saying something like "x has the value 3 unless something else changed it, in which case it could be pretty much any value at all"—which in turn seems like a fancy way of saying "we know almost nothing for sure about the value of x."

It's handy when a name always has the same value, as in simple mathematics. There is a technical term for this attractive property, and that term is *referential transparency*—that is, it's always clear (transparent) what a name refers to. So another way of expressing our concern here is to say that state destroys referential transparency. We can also say that what makes substitution work in our math/algebra examples is that there's referential transparency. In general, if there is referential transparency, we can say something simple and clear about relationships between names and values; if we don't have referential transparency, then reasoning about names and values tends to be complex and contingent, often to the point of adding little benefit.

Is State Necessary?

As we start to see the drawbacks of state and how it undercuts referential transparency, we might reasonably ask, Why bother having state? Shouldn't we get rid of it?

There are two good reasons to have state at least some of the time: *expressiveness* and *physical necessity*.

Let's first consider expressiveness. There are many kinds of activities in the world that are most readily understood or modeled using some kind of mutable state. Our opening example of the coffee cup is one such case. It would be possible to think of the "empty cup" as a completely distinct entity from the "full cup," and that we somehow switch over from using one to using the other—but it wouldn't feel very natural as a representation of our everyday experience. If we make a movie of the coffee cup, every frame of the movie has a separate picture of the cup; in a similar fashion, we can break our "stateful" experience of change into a "stateless" form, where change is replaced by multiple instances. But just as it's more natural to watch a movie than to examine its individual frames, it's often more natural to deal with state directly, rather than to try to express a stateful behavior in a stateless vocabulary.

In a wide variety of cases, it's possible to find ways to describe such activities without using mutable state, but those descriptions often seem unnatural and unhelpful to the users who have to judge them. In general, it's not yet clear whether the advantages of referential transparency are enough to overcome such objections when they are raised. Overall, the rough consensus seems to be that it is a good idea to avoid mutable state when possible but that it's unwise to outlaw state entirely. It's nice to have a programming language that *allows* a state-free style, but not so nice to have a programming language that *requires* a state-free style.

Now let's consider physical necessity, and start by returning to a simple program we mentioned when we first started looking at processes (chapter 3). That program prints out "Hi" then pauses a second before doing the exact same thing again, endlessly. When we first mentioned this program, our goal was to point out a simple example of a finite program that corresponds to an infinite process. This program's endless execution doesn't require any mutable state: after all, the only activity is printing out the exact same text every time, so the program really doesn't need to change anything.

But now consider what happens if we modify the program slightly, so that instead of just printing "Hi" repeatedly the program prints "Hi 1" followed by "Hi 2" and then "Hi 3" and so on. There's nothing about this simple change that requires us to use mutable storage in our program. Although it might seem awkward, we can certainly write the program so that there is a new piece of text created after each previous text has been printed. We can even write the program so that the incrementing counter is simply the next element of an infinite sequence of numbers 1, 2, 3, ... No mutable state is logically necessary in the expression of what this program does.

However, if we run the program and it really has no mutable state used anywhere, it will eventually run out of space. How can we be so sure it will run out of space? Because at each iteration it creates an entirely new text to print—in principle, an infinite number of texts!—and any real step-taking machine has only a finite amount of storage. There's also something particularly foolish about the way this program runs out of space: it's full of old numbers and old (already printed) texts. All that leftover data is actually of no value whatsoever for what the program needs to do next.

Of course, there is also a more sensible alternative implementation. We could keep a mutable counter that increments repeatedly through values 1, 2, 3, etc. and then converts that value temporarily into a text for printing, then reuses that space for the next text on the next iteration. It's not hard to think in terms of a reusable chunk of storage that has "Hi " at the beginning and then space at the end for a variety of different text representations of numbers like "1" or "2" or "437892" or indeed any other number. But that space-saving approach only works if the counter and text space are mutable, if they can have different values at different points in time.

If we are particularly cunning, we may notice that we could support the *appearance* of an infinite supply of storage if we were allowed to recycle the old and irrelevant values previously used. Instead of changing the program to use mutable storage, we could change the underlying machine so it looks like it has infinite storage. From the perspective of the program, that's not mutability—it never sees any value changed. But something is definitely being mutated, because as we watch the machine we can see that a particular storage location holds different values at different times.

Does this issue arise only for infinite programs? No, it's just easiest to see the problem there. Very similar issues arise whenever a program's usage of storage might exceed the amount of storage available. Being able to reuse space makes many more computations possible.

Two Kinds of Equal

Whenever there is mutable state, we have to distinguish between (at least) two kinds of "equal." One kind of equality is an unchanging relationship: two entities that are related by it are *always* related by it. The other kind of equality is a changeable relationship: two entities that are related by it now might not be related by it later. We'll call the first relationship "equal-now-and-forever" and the second one "equal-now-but-might-change."

If we have established that two entities are equal-now-and-forever, then we have referential transparency and we can play substitution games freely. If we have only established that the entities are equal-now-but-might-change, then we don't have referential transparency. We have to be mindful that we don't know a lot about how long the two entities will have the same value, unless we know something about how other processes may or may not change them.

If we're being very careful, we would say that only eternally unchanging entities can ever be "the same as" each other—everything else necessarily changes over time. After all, at a cellular level, you are not exactly the same person you were yesterday. Considered in terms of the interacting atoms and electrons in constant motion, your laptop is not "the same" laptop that it was even a nanosecond ago.

If we do adopt this strict and rather unhelpful perspective, does anything remain equal-now-and-forever? Numeric values don't change. The value 3 remains equal to every other 3, for example. (We certainly don't expect the number 3 to suddenly have the value 17.) Similarly, the text "hello" is the same as every other instance of the text "hello." There's no risk of it suddenly changing to the string "good-bye."

Same Object vs. Different Object

The unchanging nature of a value like 3 or "hello" is completely separate from the question of whether some name in the program (like x) has an unchanging value. If we know that a particular name always has the same value, we call it a *constant*. If we know that a name might not have a value (yet) but can only ever refer to a single value, we can call it a *single-assignment variable*. In contrast to a constant, a single-assignment variable might not have a value at some point in time; but once it gains a value, that is its value forever, just as if it were a constant with that value. When we looked at simple algebra problems, the mathematical notation behaved like single-assignment variables. If our programming notation only allows names to be constants or single-assignment variables, then that notation will ensure that we always have referential transparency. Such a notation can be called a *single-assignment language* or a *functional language*.

But if we don't have those restrictions, a name might be able to have different values at different times. Whenever that's true, it doesn't make much sense to compare using equal-now-and-forever—because anything mutable can't be equal-now-and-forever to something else, not even itself! The strongest possible form of equality for something mutable is equal-now-but-might-change.

However, saying that we compare mutable state in terms of equal-now-but-might-change isn't the whole story. In addition, we can (and should!) distinguish between *same-object-equal* and *same-value-equal* (see figure 9.1).

To understand the difference, let's consider two names *x* and *y*. And let's say that at the moment both *x* and *y* have the value 3. So that means they are same-value-equal (right now!). Finding out that they both have the value 3 doesn't really give us any information about whether they are same-object-equal.

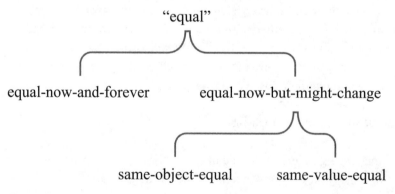

Figure 9.1
Different kinds of equality.

Figure 9.2
x and y are equal now and forever with the value 3.

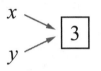

Figure 9.3
x and y name the same mutable cell containing 3.

Figure 9.4
x and y name the same mutable cell, now containing 17.

For example, it could be that x and y are both bound eternally to the value 3, as in figure 9.2.

That means that x and y are equal-now-and-forever to each other as well as to the value 3. Effectively, x and y are just synonyms for 3.

A seemingly similar situation with very different implications is that x and y are two different names for the exact same mutable cell (which happens to have the value 3 at the moment), as in figure 9.3.

The box around the value 3 captures the idea that this is a mutable cell: we can see some later state of the exact same system in which that cell's value has been changed, as in figure 9.4, where it now has the value 17.

But yet another configuration that would initially look the same is that x and y could be two completely different things, which just happen to have the exact same value of 3—as in figure 9.5.

In this diagram we have a privileged view in which we can tell whether the names x and y are actually aliases for the same object. We have a means of distinguishing same-object-equal (the two names are actually for the same

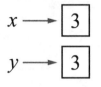

Figure 9.5
x and *y* name different mutable cells, both containing 3.

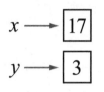

Figure 9.6
x and *y* name different mutable cells with different values.

object) from same-value-equal (the two names happen to have the same value). It's an important general principle that sharing the same object is quite different from having a separate copy with the same value, and we will pursue that issue further in the next chapter.

If we don't have a direct means of determining whether two names refer to the same object, is there any way to tell? Yes, it's possible to do a kind of experiment: for example, assigning the value 17 to *x* and then examining the value of *y*. We will likely conclude that they are not same-object-equal if *y* still has the value 3, as in figure 9.6.

What if *y* now also has the value 17? A likely conclusion is that *x* and *y* are same-object-equal. However, both of these possible conclusions are actually not as solid or straightforward as you might think: they partly depend on what else might be happening between the actions involved in changing one name's value and examining the other name's value. In chapter 11 we will look in more detail at the possibility that other activities are happening in between the steps that we take.

Although at one level state is a familiar everyday concept, we can see that there are a surprising number of subtleties once we examine it closely. On one hand, we seem to live in a stateful universe. It's easy to find examples where content changes while the identity of the container stays the same—like the coffee cup at the beginning of the chapter. On the other hand, as soon as identity and content can be separated, we have to be very careful about what we mean when we say that two things are "the same" or "equal." Simple reasoning seems to depend on avoiding state, while realistic implementation seems to depend on using state. We might paraphrase a famous saying of Erasmus: State, can't live with it, can't live without it.

10 Controlled Access

Now that we understand a little more about the general challenges associated with state, we're ready to look at the problem of controlled access to shared state. We mentioned in chapter 8 that there are risks if we have uncontrolled access to shared resources. One kind of risk was that we might somehow corrupt the data, and another kind of risk was that we might get "stuck" in some kind of deadlock or livelock. If we want to have well-behaved access to shared resources, how would we go about doing that? To explore this topic, we don't want to start with thinking about human readers and books, because humans are very sophisticated. Instead we want to think about really simple mechanisms. The simpler we can make the mechanisms, the more readily we can use them.

So instead of trying to share a book, we'll look in more detail at sharing a cell. We first encountered cells on the infinite tape of a Turing machine (chapter 3), and then we used them again as small pieces of mutable state that could have more than one name (chapter 9). A cell is just a slot where we can put a single small item of information—a single character like "w" or a single number like 1257.

We're going to be a little vague about exactly how big a cell is, because it partly depends on how much ingenuity we use in implementing it. But by the scale of things that matter for everyday life, the contents of a cell are always pretty small: not really huge numbers, no more than a single character of text.

Lost Update

We'll consider two very simple processes sharing a particular single cell. We'll use the cell to hold a number, and each of the processes will update the number in that cell to be the value one larger than it was previously. That is, each process will take the following steps in sequence:

1. Read the value in the cell.
2. Figure out the new value by adding 1 to that existing value.
3. Write the new value into the cell.

So if we start with the value 0 in the cell, and we have two processes that each increment that value by 1, we'd expect to wind up with the value $0+1+1=2$ in the cell. When people build and run little systems like this, it's disturbingly easy to end with the value 1 in the cell, as though one of the processes had completely failed to do its job. This is a *lost update* problem, and it's worth looking at the situation in a little more detail to understand how it can happen.

First, though, let's consider why solving this problem is important. If we are only talking about these numbers unconnected to any particular meaning, we might not much care whether the answer is 1 or 2. But now let's assume that the cell represents a bank balance, and that the discrepancy corresponds to a missing dollar that belongs to us. Now it starts to seem like more of an issue. Or if we assume that the number represents a geographic coordinate on a GPS system issuing us driving directions, or is the target of some oil-drilling crew, again the single-digit error starts to seem important in terms of causing large problems—taking a wrong road, drilling in the wrong field, all kinds of ugly situations we'd prefer to avoid. And in all of these cases it's not likely to be much consolation if someone tries to reassure us that these problems don't happen very often—indeed, it's actually *more* of a problem that these lost updates happen unpredictably.

After all, if a failure occurs consistently, we can adapt to it. If we *always* get 1 instead of 2, we can just add one to the result consistently. Or if we always get 1 on Tuesdays, or when the moon is full, we can just add one to the result on those occasions. But if the failure occurs only occasionally, inconsistently, and unpredictably, then we don't have any way to fix it. So instead we need to prevent it. To prevent it, we need to understand how it arises.

Two Processes, in Detail

Let's think in terms of Alice and Bob acting out the steps of the two processes sharing the single cell. Although the two processes have the exact same steps, it's helpful to be able to name every step of each process separately.

So we'll write A1 to mean "step 1 of Alice's process." We'll also write "A1 →
A2" (and say that as "A1 before A2") to mean that step A1 *always happens
before* A2.

Alice's process can be summarized as

A1 → A2 → A3

which just means that A1 always happens before A2, and A2 in turn always
happens before A3...which is what we implicitly specified with the numbered list of steps that we used before. If we want to be clearer about what's
actually happening, we can replace these names like A1 with the action
that's happening:

Read cell to get x → compute $x+1$ → write $x+1$ into cell

Or we could summarize it like this:

Read → Compute → Write

Those are all alternative summaries of the single process that Alice is
executing.

Here's a summary of Bob's process:

B1 → B2 → B3

So now we have Alice's process and Bob's process, three steps each, that
we can write alongside each other:

A1 → A2 → A3

B1 → B2 → B3

Now we have all of the machinery in place, and we have a lost-update
problem to solve.

Interleaving

To understand why lost updates can occur, we have to understand the interleaving of steps of the two processes: that is, what orderings are possible
for the steps. This discussion of interleaving may be easier to follow if you
actually make up a set of six index cards, one for each of the three steps in
each of the two processes. Then you'll be in a better position to arrange and
rearrange them to see what's possible and what's not possible.

Before we go further, let's ask a question in terms of these names: what is
the *always-happens-before* relationship between A1 and B2?

It seems pretty easy to say that one possible relationship, B2 → A1 is not true. That is, we don't have any trouble seeing that A1 *can* happen before B2. After all, Alice's process is listed first on the page; step A1 is further to the left; step A1 is the first step of Alice's process, while B2 is after the first step of Bob's process. So there are lots of cues in this simple example suggesting that A1 can happen before B2, which in turn must mean that B2 *always* happening before A1 is not correct.

The trickier part is thinking through whether A1 → B2 is true. (Spoiler alert! It's not.) In this case, all those same cues from the text are suggesting that *of course* A1 happens before B2. But we need to be careful to understand what it means to "take a step" in this kind of process.

How does step-taking really work? If we think of Alice and Bob as independent step-takers, then each of them simply takes steps at their own speed. They don't need to be "fair" or "consistent" or "sensible" or anything like that. So we have to be careful not to assume that they have those kinds of constraints. Alice might take steps very quickly while Bob takes them very slowly, or vice versa, or they might go at roughly the same speed. When we consider the range of speeds each might have—instead of assuming that they are roughly the same—it becomes clearer that we can't guarantee that A1 happens before B2.

Multiprocessing and Multiprogramming

When Alice and Bob each have the ability to take steps that are completely independent, computer scientists would call it *multiprocessing*. A different situation that's also important to consider is where Alice and Bob are actually sharing a single underlying step-taking machine. A given step may be Alice's, or it may be Bob's, but each single step only advances one of them. If Alice is taking a step, Bob is not (and vice versa). We encountered this approach previously in chapter 8, where we called it timesharing or multitasking. Sometimes computer scientists use the term *multiprogramming* when comparing this approach to multiprocessing.

In the multiprogramming example, the actual "step-taker" is a third person, Chuck. We'll modify the Alice-and-Bob example a little to make it clear how they can share a single step-taking machine. Chuck doesn't do anything very interesting himself; he just picks who gets to take a step next. When Alice or Bob is ready to take a step, they raise their hand; Chuck picks the next one to take a step from among whoever happens to have a hand up. When the chosen one finishes their single step, Chuck picks again. Chuck never picks someone who doesn't have his or her hand raised, but otherwise his choices are not predictable. Again, he doesn't have to be "fair" or "consistent" or "sensible." He won't pick a process that's not ready, but otherwise he can be as fair or unfair as he likes.

Since we can't predict Chuck's actions in general, we have to consider the possibility that he'll choose Bob twice before he chooses Alice. If that happens, then B2 happens before A1, which in turn means that A1 $\rightarrow$ B2 isn't true.

Some Example Interleavings

To summarize, we can say that there are some "inside-the-process" combinations that are always-happens-before relationships, but so far we haven't found any such relationships across different processes. In general, the steps of the two processes may be interleaved in any way that preserves their inside-the-process ordering constraints. It's a little like shuffling together two ordered decks of cards. A "good" shuffle is fair and the cards from the two sides alternate; but even if the shuffle is pretty bad and the interleaving isn't very even, it's still a shuffle and we still use the result. The combined deck will have unpredictable sequences of left-hand cards vs. right-hand cards—but the riffling together doesn't change the order of any of the cards within the left-hand deck, or the order of the cards within the right-hand deck.

Returning to our simple example, there are several equally possible orderings, like "all Alice first" or "all Bob first" or "alternating steps" (and several others as well). Here's what some of those orderings look like:

- *All Alice first:* A1, A2, A3, B1, B2, B3
- *All Bob first:* B1, B2, B3, A1, A2, A3
- *Alternating:* A1, B1, A2, B2, A3, B3

Now recall that we started down this path of looking at interleavings so that we could understand the lost-update problem. To get there, let's focus on contrasting two of these, the "all Alice first" interleaving and the "alternating" interleaving.

To do that comparison, we're going to switch around the way we write out the process steps. The processes will still be the same, but different notation helps make different aspects clear—just like 0.25 and 1/4 are different ways of writing the same fraction, and we could use whichever one makes a problem easier to solve. With our previous "A1, B2" notation we've been emphasizing that there are two processes A and B while being a little fuzzy about what is happening in each of those different steps. To be clear about the cause of the lost write, we effectively have to turn our notation inside out. Instead of emphasizing the processes and downplaying the specifics of each step, we'll now emphasize each step's meaning, with just enough information about each process so we can tell them apart. So now instead of calling a particular step "A1" we'll call that exact same step "Read$_A$."

Where does that notation come from? We summarized these processes previously as the three steps Read, Compute, Write. Recall that Read reads the value from cell x, Compute figures out a value for $x+1$, and Write writes that value back into the cell x. Both processes A and B have identical steps, so we use a subscript to keep track of which process is doing each step: "Read$_A$" is Alice's process doing a Read, while "Read$_B$" is the comparable Read step...but in Bob's process.

Using this new notation, figure 10.1 shows what's happening in those two different interleavings.

Let's focus on the two Read steps, Read$_A$ and Read$_B$. In the upper (Alice-first) interleaving, Read$_A$ and Read$_B$ read *different* values for x. Read$_B$ reads x after it has been updated with a new value (increased by one) that was computed by Alice's process. That arrangement gives the correct final result, in which x has been incremented by 2.

But in the lower (alternating) interleaving, Read$_A$ and Read$_B$ both read the exact *same* value for x. Read$_B$ reads x the very next step after Read$_A$ has read x—so Alice's process hasn't yet had a chance to update x. That arrangement causes a lost update, in which x only gets incremented by 1.

All Alice first:

Read$_A$	Compute$_A$	Write$_A$	Read$_B$	Compute$_B$	Write$_B$

Alternating:

Read$_A$	Read$_B$	Compute$_A$	Compute$_B$	Write$_A$	Write$_B$

Figure 10.1
Two different interleavings of the same steps.

Each process did all the right steps so that each one would increment the value. But because of the way those steps were interleaved, we've unfortunately lost the effect of one of the incrementings.

Is This a Real Problem?

If we think about Alice and Bob as people carrying this out with pencil and paper, this lost-update problem seems pretty unlikely. Alice and Bob would be aware of each other's presence, and the piece of paper itself would serve as a kind of coordinating mechanism. They're not really going to blindly compute the same value and then have the second person's result overwrite the first person's result. So this all may look a little contrived.

It may help to think about an "idiot" version in which neither person has an ounce of common sense and is just exactly following a list of instructions, without any higher-level thinking about what's to be accomplished. It's easy to think that this is such an easily avoided problem, so how can it be a real concern? But our computers are indeed just dogged step-takers, performing their given instructions without any common sense or higher-level reasoning. So we have to be concerned about how to give them the exact right instructions to avoid this sort of error.

Is it possible to prevent the problem of lost updates? As we've described the arrangement so far, any interleaving can happen. Instead, we'd like to arrange the system so that only certain interleavings can happen—specifically, only those that give the correct answer.

In our small example, we know we could get the correct answer by arranging to only run one process at a time—and indeed, that's always a worst-case solution that is available to us. In principle, we can always avoid the problems that can arise from multiple processes with shared data. One possibility is that we simply execute only one process, to completion, at a time. Another possibility is that we eliminate sharing by giving each process its own copy of all data. But those solutions seem kind of drastic, and probably not workable in general. For example, if Google search were a service that could only perform one search at a time for one user at a time, it's hard to see how it could have become a valuable resource for millions of users on the web. Eliminating multi-process behavior or eliminating sharing would be running away from the lost-update problem, not solving it.

Mutual Exclusion

Our problem here is *concurrent* access—access by multiple executing processes. We need to build something to briefly limit concurrent access to the cell x, long enough to stay out of trouble. And more broadly, we need to have such a mechanism not only for cell x but also for shared state in general. This specific problem is what computer scientists call *mutual exclusion*: "exclusion" meaning that a process can somehow keep other processes away from shared data, and "mutual" in that any single process can use similar mechanisms to exclude other processes.

Let's imagine a simple mutual exclusion mechanism that would eliminate our lost-update problem. We'll call the mechanism a *lock*. Somehow—we won't worry about the details—the mechanism ensures that only one process at a time is *holding* the lock. There are two things a process can do with a lock: "Acquire" and "Release." After a successful Acquire operation, the executing process is holding the lock. After a successful Release operation, the executing process is no longer holding the lock.

Despite the name, this lock is not very much like a household lock on a front door or a gym locker. It's not really trying to keep out burglars and thieves, nor does it have a special key or combination that lets only certain people open it. Later in the book we'll see some computational mechanisms that do have keys and are about enforcing security of various kinds, but that's not what these locks accomplish. These locks are just about limiting the ways that concurrent processes share state.

Fans of espionage may be happier with an analogy to a "dead drop." That's a way for a spy to pass information to the spy's handler (or vice versa) while never having the two parties in the same place at the same time. The sending party leaves the information at a designated place and the receiving party picks up the information at that designated place, with some signaling or timing constraint to ensure they are not both there at the same time. Either the spy has possession of the information, or the handler has possession of the information, but the spy never hands the information directly to the handler or vice versa. With the dead drop, spy and handler have effectively implemented a form of mutual exclusion on the shared data.

Using a Lock

We can tweak the Alice and Bob processes to use Acquire and Release. The only changes we'll make are to introduce locks that work as described and to use those locks to avoid lost updates. Our goal is to ensure that every possible interleaving of their steps will end with x incremented by 2 (which is the correct result). Just as the previous version using uncontrolled processes, both the Alice and Bob processes will contain identical steps—but now those identical steps include a couple of operations on locks:

1. Acquire Lock$_x$
2. Read x
3. Compute $x + 1$
4. Write x
5. Release Lock$_x$

The heart of the process is still the exact same Read-Compute-Write steps we had before. But we have effectively wrapped those steps inside an Acquire-Release pair. Acquire and Release are a little like left and right parentheses: they have to match, or else there's some kind of a problem.

What progress have we actually made? The crucial new capability here is that we can have confidence in the result when we allow the two processes to run concurrently. The lock lets concurrency be dynamically restricted, only in the places where it matters. We didn't have to pick in advance whether process A or B would run on its own, nor did we have to decide in advance which one would run ahead of the other. If the processes didn't have any shared resources, they can run to completion in parallel with no sequencing at all between them. Locks are a simple mechanism to control concurrent access dynamically. Once we have this simple mutual exclusion problem under control, it becomes possible to build much larger, more complex systems with concurrency and shared state.

11   Interrupts

We have referred to the step-taking machinery as though it proceeded simply, smoothly, consistently forward. Most programs are written as though they run that way, but if we look at the activity of the underlying machinery we see something different. Instead of a steady flow of simple steps, a physical machine performs a combination of both smooth forward motion and abrupt unpredictable transitions called *interrupts*.

Figure 11.1 shows four abstract steps labeled with letters. This simple diagram reflects the way that an ordinary program is written and the way that a programmer would usually think about its execution.

Figure 11.2 takes the same four steps with the same labels and shows a possible view of the steps actually taken by the machine. Instead of simply proceeding directly from one step to the next in the original program, there are two deviations from the simple flow: one with the two steps $x1$ and $x2$, the other with the step y. Our task in this chapter is to understand why this more complex behavior is useful.

Being interrupted is a familiar everyday experience. We can distinguish between what we were doing before being interrupted—some activity that we expected to continue further—and the event that prompts us to shift our attention and actions away from that former activity. Indeed, we could say that the dashes in the previous sentence effectively interrupt the flow

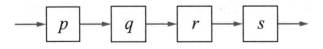

Figure 11.1
Four steps as the programmer sees them.

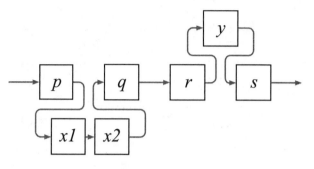

Figure 11.2
The same four steps, a possible execution.

of the sentence to insert a modifying subordinate clause, then return the reader to the original sentence. Likewise in computation, an interrupt changes the ordinary flow for a short period of time. (The more grammatical noun might well be "interruption," but "interrupt" is well-established as the technical term—so that's what we'll use.)

The Unpredictable Environment

Why are interrupts necessary? They let the step-taking machinery achieve two hard-to-reconcile goals. With interrupts, the machinery can both deal with unpredictable outside events and support a fairly simple approach to programming for most processes. Let's first look at why we might have to deal with unpredictable outside events, then see how that problem is awkward unless we bring in interrupts.

One source of unpredictable events is any interaction with the world outside the computer. In particular, there is an *input/output* (I/O) system that allows the step-taking machinery to read in or write out data that is somewhere outside the machine itself. The step-taking machinery can set and follow its own rules about how quickly steps happen, or what happens during each step. But the outside world doesn't respect those rules. There is no necessary relationship between the timing of program steps and the timing of an I/O-related event such as the following:

- a user presses a key,
- a message arrives from across a network,
- a spinning disk reaches the right position to write information,

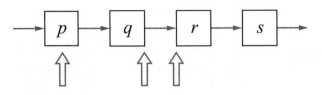

Figure 11.3
The same four steps with some possible interrupt times.

• a display is ready to be updated with new items, or
• a network is ready to accept a new message to be sent.

Any of these changes can happen at essentially any time.

In Figure 11.3, we have taken the same four-step program we considered previously and indicated with vertical arrows some of the places where an outside event could occur. It might happen:

• in the middle of a step (left vertical arrow),
• as the machinery is moving from one step to another (middle vertical arrow), or
• at the very beginning of a step (right vertical arrow).

Although the machinery has a very regular, consistent, repetitive behavior, the outside world has no obligation to match its events to the machinery's pace.

Check, Check, Check …

Let's consider just the simple case of dealing with characters being typed on a keyboard. To the user, a keyboard is a collection of different keys that can be pressed one at a time or in certain combinations. But to a computer, a keyboard is just a mutable cell like the ones we considered previously (chapter 9). The physical keys of the keyboard are just the way that a user controls the value of that cell, and they don't otherwise matter to the computer.

Some of the time the cell contains a single character, representing the key that's currently being pressed. Each character value is actually represented as a short sequence of bits, but we'll ignore that detail here. Some of the time the cell contains a special "nothing" value corresponding to "no key pressed." Let's assume for a moment that we could watch that cell, and that we had the ability to "see" the bit patterns there. It would look a little like figure 11.4. (Unfortunately, the cell doesn't really display the character in a way that we could just look at it with our eyes and see a letter.)

If someone types a piece of text like a speech from Shakespeare, we would see the cell successively changing values as different characters were pressed. So typing the phrase, "To be or not to be" would first show up as the character "T" (see figure 11.5).

Likewise, we could see something similar for "o" and " " (that is, a space) and "b" and "e," and so on.

Depending on how fast the user was typing, the special "no key" value might be appearing between some or all of those letters and punctuation.

keyboard

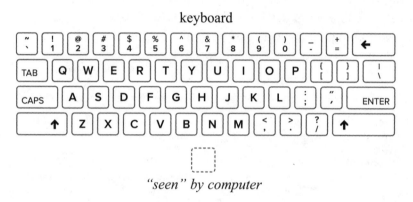

"seen" by computer

Figure 11.4
A keyboard and its associated cell.

keyboard

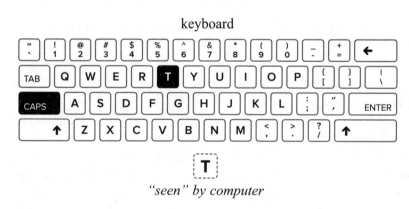

"seen" by computer

Figure 11.5
Typing the letter "T"

If we wanted a program to just watch the keyboard, that program would be pretty simple to write. The program just repeatedly looks at the incoming values in the cell, much like the program we saw earlier that prints out "Hi" endlessly in figure 3.5.

From the computer's perspective, a keyboard is basically a means for a cell to take on a sequence of values. But as a user of a computer, our view is a little different. When we type that Shakespearean phrase at the keyboard, we want the whole sequence of characters to be recorded. How would that work? Let's first figure out how something even simpler works without interrupts.

We'll start by assuming that we have a step-taking machine running some program. It doesn't much matter what that particular program is doing, but we know roughly what's happening for any program: the machinery is repeatedly fetching instructions and data, and performing the instructions on the data. The program doesn't initially interact with the keyboard at all.

Now assume that we actually want an improved version of that program to read input—perhaps it is drawing patterns on the screen, and pressing different keys changes the color of the current pattern. We have to modify the program so that it periodically checks to see if a key has been pressed (computer scientists refer to such an event as a *keystroke*). If a program has to repeatedly check the keyboard's cell to collect each keystroke, the timing constraint may be fairly tight: to notice the keystroke correctly, the program has to "look at" the keyboard often enough so that it "looks" during the time that the key is down and providing a signal. So whatever the program used to do before, now it has to repeatedly check the keyboard. Previously, the program looked like this:

Do tiny step 1

Do tiny step 2

Do tiny step 3

Now the program has to look like this:

Do tiny step 1

CHECK KEYBOARD

Do tiny step 2

CHECK KEYBOARD

Do tiny step 3

CHECK KEYBOARD

So even this tiny simple sketch of a program got twice as long and annoyingly repetitive. The changes are actually even worse if the program is longer or more complex. Why is it necessary to do this repeated checking?

Let's suppose that we check less often. If the program doesn't check the keyboard often enough, it might miss some keystroke, and the experience of typing something into the computer would become frustrating—some keystrokes would be missed if we were typing quickly, which might prompt us to slow down and press the keys for longer times, or we might get frustrated and find some other way of entering the information.

The problem of "looking" often enough to catch transient events like keystrokes becomes more difficult as both the number and complexity of devices increase. And even if we set aside this risk of missing characters, consider the task facing programmers who want to use the keyboard to communicate with their program. They don't want to have to write their program mostly about the keyboard.

If each program has to check on various devices for possible changes, it's hard to tell what the program is really doing. The problem of interacting with those devices dominates the problem of whatever real work we wanted the program to accomplish. Effectively, "the tail is wagging the dog" and even the simplest program ends up being affected by the need to check for inputs. In addition, every change to the computer's collection of devices potentially requires every program to adapt. This approach seems unattractive and unworkable.

Interrupts and Handlers

Interrupts allow a different approach to this problem. With interrupts, an "ordinary" program—one that's trying to accomplish some task unrelated to the devices and machinery—no longer has to check each of the various devices itself. Instead, a change of state on any one of those devices causes an interrupt. Effectively, the checking on each step becomes part of how the step-taking machine works. When the interrupt occurs, the execution of the ordinary program is halted temporarily—that is, steps are no longer allocated to executing that program, so it pauses. Instead, the machinery's steps are allocated to a different, specialized program designed exactly for this purpose: an *interrupt handler*. After the interrupt handler has done whatever work is required, control returns to the interrupted program and it resumes execution as though nothing had happened.

The interrupt handler typically takes the new input (such as which key was pressed) and puts it into a safe place for subsequent processing. The intermediate storage—the safe place—is usually called a *buffer*.

The interrupt handler for a keystroke interrupt can be a very simple program: it knows the location of a buffer to be used for keyboard characters, and it puts the current keyboard character into the next available cell of that buffer. Later, when the program is ready to look at one or more characters from the keyboard, it actually reads them from the buffer. For example, our pattern-drawing program might be either in the middle of actually interacting with the screen (so that it's impossible to change the color that was just used) or in the middle of some calculation unrelated to color (so that there's no need to deal with color yet). So when do we want to check? The place we want to check for keyboard input that might affect the color displayed is just before the program next starts to interact with the screen.

Shared Services

Without interrupts, we had a difficult trade-off between responsiveness and simple programming. If we wanted a program to be responsive to transient conditions, we had to make that program a mess of frequent checks; or if we wanted the program to be simple, we had to accept that it would miss some transient events. An interrupt mechanism lets us have both responsiveness to transient conditions *and* a simpler programming model most of the time.

However, if our only concern is programming simplicity then interrupts are not the right solution. The mechanisms for handling interrupts and buffers are admittedly more complex than simply exposing the keyboard directly to a program. It was kind of stupid to repeatedly check the keyboard for a possible character, but it had the merit of being straightforward, as compared to this convoluted business of transferring to a different program, storing a character away, then resuming the original program. Interrupts are appealing when we want to balance responsiveness and simple programming.

The good news here is that the extra complexity of interrupts is not really a problem in practice. Once we've built those interrupt handlers and buffer managers, we can reuse them for lots of different programs that want to interact with a keyboard. Even more important, we no longer need for all those different programs to be written in terms of a particular keyboard arrangement. Instead, we've achieved a separation of concerns: the program can deal with its main purpose, while the interrupt handlers and buffer managers can deal with the details of the hardware. The program doesn't really need to know much about how the keyboard works; likewise, the interrupt handlers and buffer managers don't really need to know much about how any other programs work.

The interrupt handling and buffer management are examples of shared services for ordinary programs, making the step-taking machinery easier to use. Another name for a collection of those shared services is an *operating system*. We've previously mentioned some examples of popular operating systems, but this is the first time that we've considered a possible definition for the term. Another helpful way of thinking about an operating system is that it's a program for running other programs. There's no contradiction between these two definitions—they just emphasize different aspects of what an operating system does.

Ordinary (non-operating system) programs are typically called *application programs*, or *applications*. An application usually runs "on top of" some operating system. The operating system uses buffers to isolate smooth-running processes from the unpredictable peculiarities of the outside world, allowing each program to deal with keyboard input and other unpredictable events in a sensible way. With support from the operating system, applications don't need to obsessively check the keyboard for fear of possibly missing a keystroke.

An aside: we can see an interesting perspective embedded in computer science terminology if we notice that input and output devices are collectively referred to as *peripherals*, as though they were somehow unimportant to the more central task of computation.

In reality, a computational device without I/O is completely irrelevant. Indeed, an old computer-science joke says that ordinary rocks have extremely fast computers inside—but the I/O system is really bad.

Frequent Check, Rare Problem

The same arrangement of using an interrupt and an interrupt-handler is also useful for handling problematic situations that could occur frequently, but only actually occur rarely.

For example, there is a potential problem with *overflow* of numbers. Many physical step-taking machines have instructions to perform arithmetic on integers, and every one of those machines has some limit on how big a number it can use. One possible (and relatively easy to understand) limit is related to 32 bits, and is either a little bigger than 4 billion (roughly what you can represent with 32 bits) or a little bigger than 2 billion (roughly what you can represent with 31 bits). Every single addition operation on that machine has at least the theoretical possibility of producing a result that exceeds that maximum size—an overflow. However, in most programs the vast majority of additions don't cause an overflow. Even if we write a program that deliberately triggers an overflow by starting at zero and repeatedly adding 1, it will perform literally billions of additions before triggering the overflow.

Just as it was foolish to write program steps to check the keyboard in between every "real" action, so it would be foolish to wrap every single addition operation in a tiny program that checks to see if an overflow occurred. It makes more sense to leave all of those overflow checkers out of the program's text, and instead write an overflow handler that is called only when an overflow does occur. The common pattern that we are starting to see here is that we can separate out something that is logically checked very frequently, when there is a strong skew to the expected results of the check— we expect the common case to be that nothing is wrong and nothing needs to be done, but occasionally we have to do some kind of fix-up. We also notice that because this checking is done very often, it makes sense to build it into the step-taking machinery rather than asking the programmer to do it over and over again.

In fact, one way of thinking about I/O is to view it as a source of frequently checked but rarely triggered conditions. Because computers are so fast, even I/O that seems fast to a person is incredibly slow for a computer— there are typically many steps taken between any two I/O activities. To return to our keyboard example, you would be a very fast typist if you could type at 180 words per minute (wpm)—the fastest typists in the world are up around 212 wpm. A speed of 180 wpm is 15 keystrokes per second, which in terms of human speeds is amazingly fast. However, even relatively modest devices like mobile phones and tablets can have processors running at 1 GHz or more, which means they are taking a billion steps or more every second. So that amazingly fast typist is only affecting the next step taken by a computer roughly 0.00000015 percent of the time, or approximately never. An I/O event is something that could happen on any step but almost never does; if we think about the situation from the perspective of a smooth-running application, an I/O event is almost like an error.

Input/output and commonly possible but rarely occurring errors share the characteristic that they *could* all be handled explicitly by the program— but taking such an approach would lose the real meaning of the program under a mass of redundant detail. In all of these "check-often, fail-rarely" cases we have an argument for building the checking work into the step-taking machinery, and then using an interrupt to invoke a handler when the unusual case arises.

Protecting Memory

We've noticed that every integer addition potentially causes an overflow. In a similar fashion, every time a program reads or writes a memory location, that access potentially causes a different kind of error: a kind of trespassing within the computer's storage.

We know that the operating system is a program. Like any other program, it uses some of the available space of the machine for its instructions and data. Those particular instructions and data should be reserved for the exclusive use of the operating system; no application program should be looking at or changing any of those locations. An application program using the wrong part of memory may violate limits that are set up to protect the operating system.

Protecting the operating system from the applications is a situation like overflow: it makes sense to check a condition frequently, but we expect the check to only fail occasionally. We expect that in the vast majority of cases, each access by an application is no hazard to the operating system. What should we do in the rare case where an application may be doing something it shouldn't? That's a situation where it's important to stop the offending behavior as quickly as possible.

To protect the operating system from application programs, we need to designate some locations that are available *only* to the operating system. The operating system is allowed to read and write to those locations without limitations; but when an ordinary application attempts to read or write any of those locations, an interrupt occurs. Much as a check for overflow happens in hardware on every arithmetic operation, this boundary check happens in hardware on every read or write of memory. If there is an illegal use of memory, the interrupt occurs and transfers control to an interrupt handler, which in turn will stop or redirect the offending program.

In contrast to our previous examples (keystroke, arithmetic overflow), we simply can't solve this protection problem without some kind of interrupt. Even as a thought experiment, there is no sensible way we can leave this problem to explicit checks by the application program. Why? Because the problem we need to solve is precisely an error or failure of the application. Whether the inappropriate access is accidental or intentional, we have to ensure that an application can't interfere with the operating system—or else the operating system will be unable to reliably provide services to its users. If there is no protection mechanism and we're simply trusting all of the applications to "play well together," we are effectively running a kind of race to see which application can most quickly seize control of the operating system, and thus the machine.

System Calls

We've already seen that a real-world computing system needs to have interrupts, and the operating system needs to be involved in handling those interrupts. We could turn that observation inside out and note that the interrupt-handling system has to be able to handle all of the details required to transfer control from any application process to the operating system, and also transfer control back.

That's a useful insight when we consider that there are also situations where an application program simply needs to ask the operating system to do something useful. These requests are collectively referred to as *system calls*. A system call is simply a request, and logically doesn't require an interrupt—there's nothing "unexpected" or "unusual" about it. However, in most cases system calls are implemented by reusing the interrupt mechanism. This leads to the slightly strange situation where a program requests an operating system activity by interrupting itself.

Is this kind of interrupt-based transfer the only way for one program to access another program? No. It's far more common for one program to *call* another program, so that the second (called) program performs some activity and then *returns* to the original program. It's the same kind of going-away (to the called program) and then coming-back (to the calling program), but there's no interrupting happening—just ordinary steps, one after another.

So why can't an ordinary program just call the operating system? In principle, it can; and in some systems, it does. Regardless, there is a collection of housekeeping that has to happen whenever there's a transition from an ordinary program to the operating system, or vice versa. In particular, at the start of a system call the machine has to be tweaked so the operating system can use its (otherwise off-limits) resources; and at the end of a system call, the machine has to be tweaked back so that the operating system resources are put off-limits again.

The transition between application and operating system (in both directions) is crucial to handle correctly and efficiently on every interrupt. As a result, there is usually special hardware support for interrupt handling. Designers often find that it is both faster and more reliable to reuse the interrupt mechanism for system calls rather than develop a separate system-call mechanism, even though that approach does sometimes seem a little bit convoluted.

12 Virtualization

In the previous chapter, we recognized the need to sometimes interrupt a computation to perform some short urgent task. That approach is also useful in other settings, where the connection to interrupts might not be obvious. Interrupts are vital to sustaining certain kinds of useful illusions.

We can make a historic reference here to "Potemkin villages." The phrase and associated story are familiar to many, although historians dispute whether any of it actually happened. In the late eighteenth century, Catherine the Great was the ruler of Russia. According to the story, she was traveling with her court and foreign ambassadors through Ukraine and Crimea, shortly after those areas had been conquered. Grigory Potemkin was the recently appointed governor of the territory, which had been devastated by the military campaigns. The queen's party was traveling by barge down the Dnieper River. To create a better impression for the Russian monarch and the ambassadors, Potemkin arranged for a small number of mobile fake villages to be placed on the banks of the river, populated by Potemkin's men pretending to be peasants. As the royal party passed, the village would be dismantled and moved downstream to look like another village. The effect was to create an illusion of population and wealth where both were severely lacking.

In a roughly similar fashion, certain specialized kinds of software can create the illusion of an unshared, enormous computer when the actual computer available is small and shared. Such software takes advantage of interrupts that happen whenever an event occurs that threatens to break the illusion. By handling each interrupt appropriately, the software quickly fixes each threat.

We have previously observed that our step-taking machinery usually emphasizes speedy simple steps rather than slower, more sophisticated steps.

Instead of building ever more elaborate hardware machinery, we use software to extend the capabilities of this underlying machinery. Broadly speaking, *virtualization* is about building better versions of the step-taking machinery by adding one or more layers of software. The general pattern is to start with some underlying "real" thing and then make a new, more-flexible "virtual" version of that thing.

Thus we can have a "real machine" built of hardware or a "virtual machine" that is built of software wrapped around the real machine. We can likewise have a "real memory" that is built of hardware or a "virtual memory" that is built of software wrapped around the real memory. We can have a "real network" that is built of hardware or a "virtual network" that is built of software wrapped around the real network. In each of these cases, the virtual version is typically more flexible but slower than the real version. But since computer systems typically have plenty of "spare steps" or "unused speed," building something slower but more flexible is often a good trade.

The real physical step-taking machinery is still focused on supplying fast, simple steps. So those capabilities are still available for programs that primarily need lots of raw speed. Virtualization is a way to have sophisticated facilities even though the underlying machinery is simple—a kind of way to have our cake and eat it too.

Managing Storage

We have described virtualization generally; we will next consider virtual memory specifically. When we have a computational problem to solve, it's handy to be able to work on it without worrying too much about space limitations. That's the problem that virtual memory solves.

Let's start by assuming that you have the problem of dealing with luggage at a family reunion. Lots of people are coming from all over the world with lots of luggage, and you have to find places to put it. Because they're your family, you probably know something about their quirks (such as who will need their luggage when). If you're familiar with the venue, you know something about the spaces available and how to best use them. But even with all of that familiarity, it's still a lot of work and you still make mistakes—you can't predict all of your family's behaviors in advance. Worse is that even after you survive one family reunion, that doesn't necessarily give you any advantage for the next family reunion, because that will take place

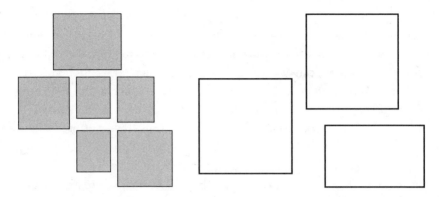

Figure 12.1
The boxes need to be stored in the available spaces.

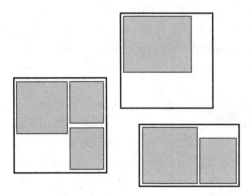

Figure 12.2
One solution to the box storage problem.

at a different venue with different storage spaces and with different family members in attendance.

In figure 12.1, there are some boxes on the left to fit into the spaces on the right.

Figure 12.2 shows a solution that packs the boxes into the spaces. Of course, this particular solution doesn't necessarily help us much if we are presented with a different collection of boxes and/or a different set of spaces.

It's a similar experience when dealing with limited space for programming: the space-related arrangement that works in one setting may not be relevant for another. If we work out how to fit our data structures into (say)

16 megabytes of space, that set of arrangements isn't likely to be useful if we then try running the exact same problem on a computer with half as much space. We'd have to redo the work of figuring out how to fit the data into the space available. We can also have the reverse problem: if we find ourselves using a computer that has twice as much space, we won't be able to use the extra space if we stick with our detailed 16-megabyte layout. So we'd likely have to redo the work of figuring out how to best use the available space in that case too.

An alternative to working out a data layout for each size of memory could be to put even more work into an adaptive scheme that would expand and contract our use of space to match what was physically available. In the luggage-storage world, this approach would correspond to developing better skills at learning where storage space was and how to use it.

But as we develop such an adaptive scheme, we are likely to realize that many different programs share the goal of adapting to the space available. We don't really want to be managing the data layout ourselves. We want there to be a service to take care of it for us.

In the luggage-storage example, we're just working to support a family reunion. We don't actually want to spend time and effort to get better at storing luggage. Instead, we would really prefer a bellhop or similar service that will take care of the details for us. That service might be less efficient than what we could do if we were willing to work hard and use our knowledge of our relatives' particular quirks. But broadly speaking we'd rather hand the job to someone who specializes in it, and devote our energies to something else.

Virtual Memory

To avoid at least some of these space-related problems, operating systems often implement an analog to the luggage-space-managing service that we imagined. The operating system version of that service is *virtual memory*. With virtual memory, each executing program has a simple view of the space available: each program appears to have as much memory available as the machine is capable of holding. So every program apparently has sole possession of a computer full of memory. Meanwhile, the physical reality is that the computer may have far less than the maximum possible amount of memory. In addition, not all of the physical memory is necessarily available; the operating system and/or other programs may occupy a substantial fraction of it.

So how is it possible to create this illusion of a full, and fully available, memory? Our good fortune in the modern era is that our step-taking machinery typically has unused speed; our machines spend much of their time idle. This available speed is a part of what lets virtual memory work.

Our examples so far have only needed to deal with a small number of locations at a time, but that's somewhat misleading. A modern computer actually has a vast number of memory locations, each with its own unique numeric address. We can talk about the whole range of such numeric addresses as the *address space,* and in principle the computer can examine any element of the address space at any time. However, a conventional computer has no way to survey the entire field of possible memory locations in a single step. Although it can request any address at any time, the program examines only one or two addresses at any one step. The address space is not a huge field laid out in bright sunshine so that the program can take it all in with a single sweeping glance.

Instead, it's like a huge dark closet full of individual slots. The executing program has one or two flashlights, each with a beam that's just wide enough to illuminate one slot at a time. As the program ranges its flashlights over the slots, each slot contains whatever the program has put there and expects to see there.

So what, you might ask? We can divide up the available storage among the multiple processes. The trick is to use a small amount of the physical memory for each process, rearranging that physical memory as needed to support the process's actions in its much-larger virtual memory space. We let every process "pretend" that it has the whole address space, and fill in bits of physical memory as needed to sustain the illusion. We are taking advantage of the computer's extreme speed, finding ways to switch back-and-forth fast enough that we can create illusions of whole systems from parts of systems.

Virtual Addresses and Real Addresses

To build virtual memory, we separate the process's memory space into parts that are present vs. parts that are missing.

In figure 12.3, processes P1 and P2 both have large virtual address spaces—they have the illusion of being able to use all of the address space indicated. However, only a section of each virtual address space is present in

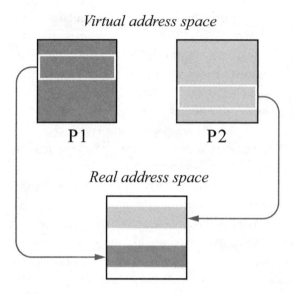

Virtual address space

P1   P2

Real address space

Figure 12.3
Two virtual address spaces sharing one real address space.

the physical machine's real address space. Notice that the location of a chunk of virtual address space within the real address space may not have any relationship to where that chunk is within the virtual address space. In order to effectively share the real machine, most application programs are *relocatable*—an address translation step allows them to operate in much the same way regardless of which real addresses they are using. The bookkeeping required to get the right addresses is simultaneously very important, very confusing, and very tedious. So we will skip it, apart from noting that this is the kind of area in which operating system programmers really earn their pay.

For an ordinary application, the step-taking machinery checks each read or write of memory to determine whether it's related to an address that's missing. If the relevant piece of memory is missing, an interrupt happens. The interrupt handler does the fixup required to bring in the relevant memory and make it present. Because space is limited, the machine might not have enough space available for what needs to be brought in. Finding enough space might require evicting something else and marking it as missing.

Marvelously, this test for absent memory can use the exact same arrangement as the one that we already saw for protection. From chapter 11, we already know how to keep an executing application away from the operating system's memory: the machine checks each memory access and causes an interrupt whenever an ordinary application is trying to use part of the operating system's space. To solve this new virtual-memory problem, we can treat all of the missing memory locations as belonging to the operating system. When an interrupt occurs because the process is apparently messing with operating-system memory, the interrupt handler can distinguish between a reference to absent memory and a genuine reference to operating system space. If the interrupt is caused by a reference to missing memory, the interrupt handler can make the necessary fixes so the memory is present; then the process can resume. If the triggering access really is a reference to the operating system's memory, the interrupt handler doesn't try to "fix" it. Instead, the process has somehow gone wrong, and the handler takes whatever actions are required to stop it.

Virtual Machines

A different kind of virtualization provides a bigger illusion. Whereas virtual memory supports the illusion of a whole memory dedicated to a single process, a *virtual machine* supports the illusion of an entire physical machine. That may not seem very impressive; after all, we already know that an operating system can present a shared machine to multiple application programs, each with the illusion of exclusive control. So we have to explain a little more about why a virtual machine is special.

Let's first consider an operating system in a little more detail. In figure 12.4, two processes (process 1 and process 2) are both using services of a single operating system that is in turn running on a single machine.

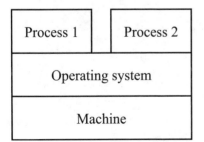

Figure 12.4
Two processes sharing a single machine via an operating system.

The operating system provides an illusion of exclusive access to both processes, while actually mediating their shared use of the single underlying machine. It also provides a variety of shared services that make it more convenient for each process.

For example, an operating system often has a file system that makes permanent storage more convenient. Magnetic disks are useful permanent storage devices, but they are awkward to use. They come in many different sizes, and each one allows the reading or writing of only a fairly large fixed-size block of storage at a time. Even worse, each of those blocks is named only in terms of a numeric disk address. A file system hides all of these annoying details and makes it possible to think instead about variable-length files with user-friendly naming.

Now consider what would be involved in providing an illusion of exclusive access to the machine—but providing that illusion to operating systems, not ordinary applications. The program that achieves this kind of illusion is a *hypervisor*. One way to think of a hypervisor is that it's an "operating system for operating systems." As we'll see shortly, that can be a misleading summary.

In figure 12.5, two different operating systems OS1 and OS2 are interacting with a single hypervisor, on a single machine. For completeness, we should show some processes in those operating systems to clarify the similarities and differences with how an operating system works.

In figure 12.6, processes P1 and P2 each have an illusion of exclusive access, provided by operating system OS1, which also provides them with a variety of other convenience features. Processes P8 and P9 likewise each have an illusion of exclusive access, plus whatever features are provided by operating system OS2. Both OS1 and OS2 are designed to be in total control

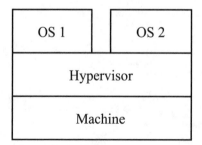

Figure 12.5
Two operating systems sharing a single machine via a hypervisor.

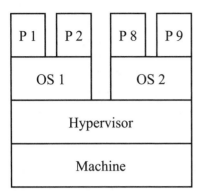

Figure 12.6
Different processes in different operating systems on one machine.

of the physical machine. But in this configuration, they are instead being fooled by the hypervisor.

Although both operating systems and hypervisors are software infrastructure layers that provide useful illusions to their users, they are otherwise aiming at completely opposite goals:

• An operating system is providing services beyond the hardware, so as to make the hardware more convenient and easier to use; it is typically providing an extended or enhanced environment for programs. An operating system both provides facilities that are missing from the hardware, and hides or smooths over inconvenient realities of the hardware.

• In contrast, a hypervisor is intended to present the illusion of the exact, complete machine to a program that expects to have full control of that machine.

There is a seeming paradox here: in building a hypervisor, we are building a complex, expensive piece of software to produce an illusion of exactly what we already have (a physical machine). What is the point, and why is it a good idea?

Sharing Servers

Once we have a functioning hypervisor, we have virtual machines. Once we have virtual machines, there are all sorts of interesting possibilities. One important motivation is purely economic. Let's first assume that we have some collection of what computer scientists call *servers*. A server can be any collection of functionality that is valuable enough and difficult enough to occupy an entire machine. The most common example of a server for most people is a *web server*—we will look at the mechanics of web services in chapters 15 and 20. However, there are many other kinds of servers like mail servers, file servers, and servers that don't have any special name because they're just a part of some complex application. The word "server" is also used to refer to the kind of machine used for a server—people will talk about "buying a new server," for example.

In the most common arrangement, a software server runs on a single hardware server. However, with virtual machines, it's possible to take two or more entire (software) servers and run them simultaneously on a single shared machine. This consolidation is possible even though each server potentially includes a distinct operating system and multiple applications. Virtual machines offer a good arrangement for the many servers that don't demand a very large fraction of the hardware's available resources.

Although we were concerned in chapter 7 about the way in which some problems can grow without bound, not all problems grow that way. For many important problems, their computational requirements remain approximately steady over time; meanwhile, Moore's law keeps ratcheting hardware performance higher, with the inevitable result that what might once have been a demanding application becomes a relatively undemanding application.

In the abstract, we might think that Moore's law means that machines of a roughly fixed capability get ever cheaper over time—and that does happen to some extent. But the more conspicuous, better-established pattern is the inverse: machines at a roughly fixed price get better over time. That means that the smallest machine we can economically buy tends to be better each time we go to purchase. So you don't really ever get to buy a whole computer for a nickel, no matter what Moore's law says. Instead, the computer you buy for a few tens or hundreds of dollars becomes increasingly impressive. This phenomenon isn't surprising if we reflect that many of the components of a computer are not items that improve with Moore's law. Even if the step-taking piece gets much better, the display, power supply, and similar "boring" components probably still cost roughly what they did before.

In the absence of virtual machines, we would need to deploy each of these relatively undemanding software servers on its own separate machine. Each of those machines would be underutilized. With virtual machines, we can consolidate servers onto fewer physical machines, saving money while not affecting performance. Virtual machines also enable cloud computing, which we will consider in chapter 20.

Building a Hypervisor

A hypervisor is conceptually simple, but it is hard to make one that's efficient. If we want the fastest virtual machine possible, every step of the real machine should also be a step of the virtual machine. However, we know the virtual machine can't always run at exactly the same speed as the underlying physical machine. At least some of the time, the hypervisor will need to behave differently from the hardware.

For example, an operating system running on a hypervisor can't really interact directly with a keyboard, even though the operating system ordinarily handles keyboard interactions (as we saw in chapter 11). Instead, the hypervisor interacts with shared resources like a keyboard so that multiple different "guest" operating systems can each have their own virtual keyboard. At the point where a guest operating system is attempting to use the keyboard directly, the hypervisor has to take control and make the right things happen so that the operating system sees the right effects, even though the operating system doesn't really have control of that keyboard.

That situation sounds a lot like what we already encountered with virtual memory. And a situation where "most of the time" we want to do the ordinary thing but "occasionally" we need to splice in a different behavior is a lot like what we already encountered with I/O and error conditions.

Indeed, modern efficient hypervisors depend on some of the same tricks of interrupts that we've already seen. The same interrupt-fixup-return idiom turns out to support not only unexpected timing of interactions with the outside world, but also a variety of useful illusions like virtual memory and virtual machines.

13 Separation

We have been looking at some challenging aspects of computation while assuming that everything of interest is nearby. We haven't needed to consider distance, because we've implicitly assumed it didn't matter. But as systems get larger and computation speeds get faster, we increasingly have to pay attention to issues of distance.

For most of human history, the speed of communication across long distances has been identical to the speed at which people could travel those distances. The local representative of a remote organization (government, trading company, financial partnership, or the like) necessarily had to operate in a semi-independent fashion much of the time. For example, in colonial times Massachusetts had a royal governor appointed to administer the colony. Although some ministry in London would have been nominally "in charge" of affairs in Massachusetts, London was a sea voyage of many weeks away; so it would have been impractical for the governor to consult the relevant ministry officials for their opinion on each question that needed to be resolved. Instead, the governor would have to exercise his judgment locally, within a relatively broad set of policy guidelines.

In contrast, for that exact same colonial governor who wasn't consulting London about every single question, it is completely plausible that he might have chosen to consult with a trusted member of his *local* staff on every single question that needed to be resolved. Turning to a local expert would be particularly likely if the person serving as governor were primarily a ceremonial or "figurehead" governor. Such a person operating on his own would be neither well acquainted with local conditions nor likely to make sound decisions.

A computer scientist would refer to the governor's relationship with the remote ministry as *loosely coupled*. In a similar vein, we could refer to the governor's relationship with the local advisor as *tightly coupled*. Although the governor could choose to have a loosely coupled relationship with the local advisor—simply consulting that person less often, or not at all—it is impossible for the governor to choose to have a tightly coupled relationship with the ministry in Britain. Distance precludes that possibility.

Distributed Systems

In our modern age of telecommunication, it is easy to imagine that distance-related concerns are only of historic interest. Sometimes it seems as though everyone can be our local contact by simply dialing a telephone. But in the world of computers and data communication, these issues still have a vivid relevance.

We start with the difference between a *distributed system* and a *concurrent system*. We have already done a fair bit of thinking about concurrency in chapter 10, as we considered the challenges of coordinating multiple processes. So what's new here? The governor was interacting with other people whether the other person was local or remote; so in either case there were "people-related" communication issues to resolve. But the remote communications had additional limits. In general, distributed systems are concurrent (involving multiple processes), but a concurrent system is not necessarily distributed. What makes the difference? Autonomy and distance.

Autonomy

Autonomy means that a distributed system is made up of independently operating elements that can fail separately, so that the system has to be prepared to handle a situation in which some elements have failed.

Consider the internet as a whole. It consists of billions of different elements. Those elements include devices like phones, tablets, and laptops that people are using to request information. Those devices are collectively called *clients*. There are also computers that store information and make it available; as we have mentioned previously, those computers are collectively called *servers*. Finally, there are many kinds of specialized gadgets that make up the "plumbing" of connections and paths to connect clients with servers.

With so many distinct parts, there is never any point at which *all* of these elements are functioning at the same time. Something, somewhere, is *always* broken. But each element functions (or fails) on its own. The marvelous thing is that the internet as a whole still functions anyway. To a first approxima-tion, it simply doesn't matter that something, somewhere is always broken.

In one sense this is nothing new. For example, we can see something similar in the collection of different ways to travel—the transportation network. The global transportation network always has something broken somewhere, but in general people can still get from point A to point B.

Autonomy also means that different elements are owned and adminis-tered separately. If you own a device, you can decide for yourself when it is working and when it is not; you don't (typically) give up that control sim-ply because you connect the device to the internet. Even when devices are connected to the internet, you can still choose to turn them off or change the services they provide.

Distance

Distance means that the elements of the distributed system are sufficiently far apart that they can't receive information simultaneously. As we have already noted, we cannot run a tightly coupled system when distance gets large enough. In contrast, in a local (nondistributed) system we may also have various communication mechanisms among processes, but we don't need to pay attention to either their delays or their failures. Instead, inter-process communication works like just another kind of computational step.

As with the royal governor, distance implies autonomy, but autonomy does not necessarily imply distance. Very distant systems have to run inde-pendently of each other; as we have seen, there is no opportunity for the governor to consult with London on every question. But it is equally pos-sible that another official who is working in London operates in essentially the same autonomous way as the colonial governor. Simply being nearby doesn't *require* the sacrifice of autonomy.

Standards

Autonomy doesn't imply anarchy. For two computers to be able to com-municate, the two sides must have some amount of agreement about how information is represented:

• Are the bits represented by electrical impulses on a wire, by variations in radio waves, by flashes of light in a glass fiber, or by some other means?

- How is a "1" different from a "0"?
- How rapidly can either side provide bits to the other side?
- Can both sides "speak" at the same time or must they follow some kind of turn-taking?

We know that a person who speaks only English can't communicate verbally on the phone with a person who speaks only Chinese. In a similar fashion, we can't expect computers to communicate without some common basis for that communication.

Thus, connecting to a network requires adhering to some technical standards. In addition, there are (usually) legal and behavioral standards we are supposed to meet in order to get connected to someone else. But those standards are relatively loose and afford us a considerable degree of freedom. In our language metaphor, we may have to speak English, but then we are free to discuss what we like.

Distance Revisited

Now let's consider the problem of distance in more detail. The Mars rovers *Spirit* and *Curiosity* offer a particularly vivid example of the challenges of distance in a distributed system. Initially, it might seem like it would be fun for someone on Earth to drive the rover around the Martian surface by remote control, like some kind of video game. Unfortunately, the physics make it impossible except in super-slow-motion. The distance between the Earth and Mars varies, but one reported time for a radio signal to reach *Curiosity* and return to Earth was 13 minutes and 48 seconds.

Figure 13.1 depicts an interplanetary version of the game "Marco Polo" where one blindfolded player calls out "Marco" and the other players immediately call out "Polo." The player on Mars is very speedy, instantaneously answering—however they don't get a chance to respond until almost seven minutes after the blindfolded player on Earth first yells out. What does this mean for driving the rover? Any view available "now" on Earth is actually the view of almost seven minutes ago on Mars, while a control movement made "now" on Earth can't affect the vehicle on Mars until almost seven minutes from "now."

Of course, most of us don't deal with the problem of remote control for Martian rovers. What is the significance of distance for more earthbound domains of interest? There are two issues. One is that light takes time to

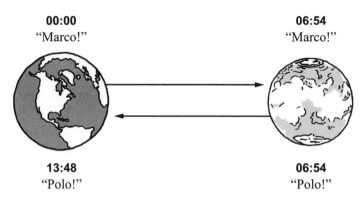

00:00
"Marco!"

06:54
"Marco!"

13:48
"Polo!"

06:54
"Polo!"

Figure 13.1
An interplanetary game of Marco Polo.

travel, and so ordinary notions of simultaneity break down. The other issue is that in the absence of communication, there is no information available about the remote party. We'll take up each issue in turn.

Light Is Slow

The fastest response you can get from the "other side" of a communication is bounded by the speed of light, and when the distance is substantial that can be a problem. As humans we are used to light being so fast that it is essentially instantaneous. We just can't perceive the time that light requires to travel human-size distances. But there is an interesting consequence of our success at building ever-faster computing: our machines are now fast enough that they can really "notice" issues related to the speed of light.

A nanosecond is a billionth of a second, which by human standards is a ridiculously short span of time. One handy rule of thumb is that in a nanosecond of elapsed time, light only travels about a foot. Now consider that various laptop computer specifications list their speeds in GHz, and that 1 GHz (1 billion cycles/second) is a frequency where something happens once each nanosecond. Modern computers generally have speeds well *above* 1 GHz, so that they have multiple things happening each nanosecond—and suddenly light doesn't seem fast at all. Every time your laptop is taking a step in some process, it's doing it so quickly that light couldn't even make it from one side of your keyboard to the other.

Naturally, this problem of "light being slow" is even worse when the distances involved are larger than the distance across a laptop, and those issues get still worse if the communication involves a lot of back-and-forth "chat-tiness" between the communicating parties. (Surprising as it may seem, computer scientists actually do refer to these back-and-forth interactions as being "chatty.") In particular, it's easy to make poor design choices when communication is local, because even many back-and-forth exchanges will still add up to only a small amount of time, perhaps imperceptible in human terms. For example, 50 exchanges that each take only 1/1000 second (that is, 1 millisecond or ms) will collectively add up to 50 ms. That's only 1/20 of a second, and not a humanly noticeable delay in most circumstances. Succes-sive movie frames appear at roughly that rate, exactly because that's too fast for them to be seen as separate. But if that exact same communication pat-tern then happens over much longer distances, it's easy for the accumulated time to become very noticeable for users.

For example, let's assume that the communication is happening between Boston and New York. A plausible network round-trip time for a single exchange might well be not 1 ms but 20 ms. At that speed, the same 50 exchanges would now take a whole second, which can be a distressingly long time ("one-one-thousand" said out loud) compared to what previously seemed instantaneous.

Now let's assume that the communication is happening between Boston and San Francisco. A plausible network round-trip time for a single exchange might well be 200 ms. Those exact same 50 exchanges at 200 ms each would take ten seconds, which would start to prompt thoughts of taking a coffee break rather than breathlessly awaiting the response.

This problem of worse performance with increased distance is not a contrived example. Indeed, I spent a decade working in the marketplace of products that helped people overcome these kinds of inefficiencies. Organizations collec-tively spent hundreds of millions of dollars each year on solutions to reduce the number of message exchanges required. Slowdown problems caused by distance are often both important and hard to fix.

Is Anyone There?

We just considered the problem that "light is too slow," which is one of the problems caused by distance. The second issue caused by distance is that we cannot tell the difference between a communicating party that is slow and one that has failed. We send a message and wait for a reply. But what does it mean when we haven't received a response? We can choose an arbitrary cutoff time to declare that the other party has failed, at least from our perspective. But there's nothing to guarantee that we're making that decision correctly. It's entirely possible that the reply we've been awaiting arrives just a split-second after we've decided that the other party has failed. Then what should we do?

This second problem can be as difficult to grasp as the speed-of-light problem, and for similar reasons. In our everyday experience, we don't usually have problems with simultaneity. We can pretty easily establish a real-time two-way communication in most cases—for example, in a face-to-face conversation or a telephone call. The difficulty with network traffic is most readily understood if we imagine a world in which the *only* communication mechanism is email (without acknowledgment). When sending an email, you know when you receive a reply that the other party received your initial message. But until you receive something back, you really don't know what the situation is. Has the other party received your message, or is the message still in transit? Has your message been lost so that they don't even know you sent something to them? If they did receive your message, are they doing anything about it? Even if they did receive your message, and they would like to do something about it, has something gone wrong? (Did they die? Are they too sick to reply? Are they too busy to reply?) Even if they did reply, perhaps something has gone wrong in the reply path. Although the reply may have been sent successfully, perhaps it is taking a long time to be delivered, or perhaps it has been lost, or perhaps in the time since you sent your message your receiving device is turned off, or not in a service area, or otherwise not able to receive the message.

We will have more to say about reliable communication in Chapter 18. For now, we can get by with just the three following observations:

1. In the general case, communication over distance is unreliable: messages can be lost or can get out of order.

2. There are ingenious techniques available that can hide the messiness of partial delivery and out-of-order delivery, if at least some messages are being successfully received.

3. Those techniques are not able to hide or fix the problem of being entirely unable to communicate with the other party. As we will see, some of those kinds of problems lead to unfixable uncertainty.

The Order of Events

Communication in the style of mail or email is called *asynchronous*. When activities are synchronized, they are happening at the same time—indeed, "synchron" comes from Greek words meaning "same time." So when something is asynchronous, that means the communication is happening "without same time," or more colloquially, "at different times." The underlying reality of data networking is the strange world of asynchronous communication. As was true for communication in colonial times, we simply cannot know reliably what is happening at a remote location.

In fact, the consequences are even stranger than being reduced to email. If we don't have any kind of synchrony (same-time-ness) anywhere, we don't have any way to determine if events are simultaneous in two different places. Instead, there's a different clock at every different place, which puts us into the weird world of Einstein's special relativity. Without simultaneity we can't even get a single consistent shared time line that captures all the events of interest at all the various locations. Although each place can track the order of messages sent or received locally, a collection of distant places can't establish a single consistent order of events based on only what it knows locally. A simple example makes the problem clearer.

Figure 13.2 shows a pattern of communication among four people who are far apart. We see that Alice (A) sends a message to Bob (B), Charles (C) sends a message to Diane (D), and Diane sends a message to Bob. In our ordinary experience, we might well expect that all of these players can construct the same sequencing of those events. But in a distributed system without synchronized clocks, everyone's knowledge is much more limited.

For example, assume that each of the four parties is on a different continent and running an ordinary local clock. They're not using GPS to synchronize. We'll come back to that kind of solution later. Each party can know the order of all events that happen where they are (we'll call that *local ordering*). We also know that message sending is *causal*: any time there is some message M sent and the same message M received, the event of receiving the message happens after the event of sending the message. (If we ever had a situation where a message was received before it was sent, that would imply some weird kind of clairvoyance or time travel that's beyond what we currently know how to do.) Together, local ordering and causality let us place some of the events into before-and-after orderings,

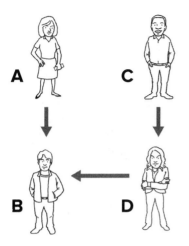

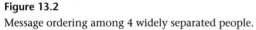

Figure 13.2
Message ordering among 4 widely separated people.

but it doesn't always tell us orderings that we might intuitively expect to know.

In this example we can walk through what each of the players knows and doesn't know. Let's first consider Alice. Alice knows:

• Bob receives the message after Alice sends it, and
• … that's pretty much all that Alice knows.

So now let's consider Charles, whose situation is much like Alice's: Charles knows:

• Diane receives the message after Charles sends it, and
• … again, that's pretty much all that Charles knows.

If we now look at Bob and Diane, we can see that they both know more about ordering, but still much less than we might expect in everyday life. Specifically, Bob knows:

• whether he received the message from Alice before he received the message from Diane, or vice versa.
• that each of those senders had to send the corresponding message before Bob could receive it.

But even though Bob knows the order in which he *received* those two messages, he doesn't know the order in which they were *sent*. Bob can't tell whether Alice sent before Diane, Diane sent before Alice, or they sent simultaneously.

Bob also doesn't know whether Diane received the message from Charles before or after she sent a message to Bob.

There is one case where it's possible to know a little more: it's possible that the message to Bob includes some information about the message received from Charles. In that case, Bob knows that Diane must have received the message from Charles before she sent the message to Bob, or else she wouldn't have been able to include that information from the Charles message. But in all other cases, Bob simply doesn't know the ordering of actions for Diane.

Finally, let's look at Diane. Similar to what we saw with Bob, Diane knows:

• the local order of whether the message she received from Charles happened before or after the message she sent to Bob.
• that Charles had to send the corresponding message before Diane could receive it.

But Diane doesn't know the ordering of the messages received by Bob, nor does she know the ordering of the messages sent by Alice and Charles.

Our everyday experience prompts us to think of the world as a linear sequence of events, with everything happening at a well-defined point that is "before," "simultaneous with," or "after" everything else that is of interest. But the world of concurrent processes and distributed systems is intrinsically not like that.

Reaching Agreement

The complex reality of asynchronous communication has some interesting consequences when we consider the actions of our counterpart (the other side of the conversation or message exchange—our correspondent, if you prefer). One consequence is that we can't reliably tell the difference between a counterpart who's slow, a counterpart who's failed, and a counterpart who's fully functional but isolated from us by some kind of communication failure. From our side of the conversation, they all look alike. We expect some kind of response, but it hasn't come.

We'll consider failure in more detail in chapter 16. Here, the core issue isn't that failures occur; it's that we can't reliably judge whether a given situation is, or isn't, some kind of failure.

Another consequence is that we can't reliably reach agreement in a distributed system without some kind of timers. Assume for a moment that we have some kind of recipe that lets a collection of distributed processes reach agreement. Computer scientists would call such a recipe a *consensus protocol*. In the absence of timers, it only takes a single faulty or malicious process to break the recipe so that the other processes can't reach agreement. This limitation is perhaps a little surprising, so let's consider what the reasoning is.

Let's assume that the participants are only trying to agree on the value of one bit—computer scientists would say 0 or 1, but we could also think of it as being a Yes/No decision. If we have a working consensus protocol for just one bit, we can build up much more elaborate decision systems. Our technique would be vaguely similar to what we saw previously in chapter 2 with being able to use many bits to represent any analog value. However, if we can't build a working consensus protocol for even one bit, then we basically can't make any decisions at all.

In a system without timers, any consensus protocol can *only* depend on steps taken by the individual players and on messages sent, because that's all there is! For any consensus protocol, there must be some particular step or message at which the decision is actually made. That is, before the crucial step or message the group could have decided either "yes" or "no," but after that particular step or message, there is only one outcome possible. Once we know what the decision point is, we can simply produce a failure right there. If that particular step or message doesn't happen because of a failure, then the protocol is stuck.

Notice that this is an argument that is mathematical in its nature, not computational. We are effectively saying (and others have proved) that for any consensus protocol, there exists *some* single failure that will cause it to get stuck…unless we have some kind of a timeout.

The argument doesn't tell us exactly how to break any particular consensus protocol. It doesn't tell us where to look for the critical step or message. But it does let us know that we have a three-way choice:

1. perfect processes and communication—no failures at all! or
2. timers, or
3. an unreliable decision process.

If we turn from this theoretical discussion to practical implementations of communication in networks with failures, we find that timers are typically included in those implementations. If you aren't aware of the theoretical issues, it's easy to see those timers as merely shortcuts that help speed up some cases where a message has been lost. But instead, theory shows that time and timers are absolutely critical so that our distributed systems can work at all.

Heartbeats

A surprisingly common reaction to the previous theoretical argument is to dismiss it, and move on to finding some practical solution to the problem. However, even simple-seeming solutions can encounter tricky problems. For example, let's consider the idea of setting up periodic "heartbeats" between communicating parties. These are just simple messages conveying "I'm here" to the other side. When the heartbeat isn't there any more, we decide that a failure has occurred and switch to a new arrangement. Computer scientists refer to making such a change as *failing over* and to the event itself as a *failover*. Figure 13.3 depicts the system before and after a failover.

The top pair shows the normal state of the system with two boxes, agreeing that the left box is the leader. The bottom pair shows the situation where the left box has failed and the right box has taken over.

If we have a heartbeat system in place, does it help? Not always. How should we interpret an absence of heartbeats? One possibility is that the

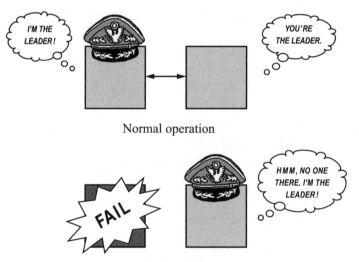

Figure 13.3
Normal operation vs. failover.

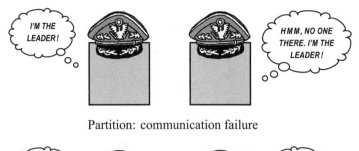

Partition: communication failure

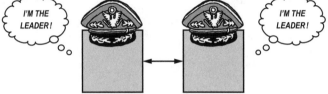

Rejoin after partition: "split-brain" problem

Figure 13.4
Bad failover caused by lack of communication.

counterpart has failed completely and is no longer operating at all. Another possibility is that the counterpart has slowed down a great deal, and the rate of heartbeats is now very slow. A final possibility is that the counterpart is doing just fine, but some part of the path to the counterpart is broken: for example, the telephone line has been accidentally cut by a backhoe, or a power failure has knocked out critical equipment along the path, or there's simply not enough capacity somewhere along the path and the heartbeat message is getting dropped. We know only that something has failed, and so nothing is getting through. Unfortunately, we cannot reliably distinguish among the possibilities.

In the worst case, we could have a communication failure so that both parties believe that the other one has failed, even though actually both parties are doing fine. Figure 13.4 shows a bad failover caused by a communication failure.

This bad failover, followed by two parallel leaders, will cause particular problems at the point where the communication failure is fixed. All the parties can now communicate with each other, but part of what they find out is that the two leaders may have both made separate and incompatible changes to the system's state and history. Depending on what else has

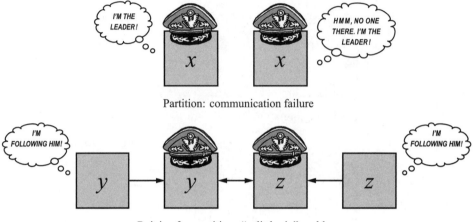

Partition: communication failure

Rejoin after partition: "split-brain" problem

Figure 13.5
Unwanted duplicate copies caused by bad failover.

happened at that point, it may not be possible to merge the different versions back into a single consistent state.

A bad failover can be a particular problem if the two parties are trying to maintain some data consistently. Both parties will assume that they are the only survivor and will set up another counterpart (so that the data will still be maintained, even if they fail). Instead of two parties cooperating to maintain a single item of data, we will have four parties (two sets of two) to maintain two separate versions of what should be a single set of data. See figure 13.5.

Do these problems mean that a heartbeat system *always* fails in these ways? No. But they do help us see that there are a number of subtle issues to consider when we're concerned with failures and communication in a distributed system.

Are Earth-Size Distances Small?

We've spent some time examining the counterintuitive weirdness of distributed systems. Distributed systems have those weird qualities because of distance, and a common view among people who work on distributed systems is that there's no way to eliminate those problems. For a large-enough distributed system, that analysis is almost certainly correct: if there really is no way of achieving synchronization among locations, then the weirdness of multiple clocks is unavoidable.

However, we have to be careful not to fall in love with analogies to physics, and the intellectual fun that can come from relating distributed systems to Einstein's special relativity. It's useful to remember that almost all interesting distributed systems are actually based on the surface of Earth—which in cosmic terms is a pretty tiny place. So we have to consider the possibility that an alternative approach to synchronized clocks and simultaneity might "only" work at planetary scale. Such an approach, despite its theoretical limitations, would nonetheless mean that essentially all practical systems can ignore distributed-system multiple-clock weirdness.

Google has built a system called Spanner that uses the Global Positioning System (GPS) and atomic clocks as a way of overcoming some of the problems of distance in a distributed system. Although GPS is most familiar as a means of identifying a receiver's geographic position, its underpinnings include a very accurate and widely distributed clock signal. That globally available clock signal makes it possible for the elements of a distributed system to operate synchronously.

In a Spanner system, there is a common synchronized clock that has some uncertainty in it. Effectively, the relativistic issues that we've previously mentioned are transformed from different local clocks into a "fuzziness" of global clock time. Each systemwide clock time is a short interval rather than a single precise instant.

In Spanner, the comparison of times is no longer in terms of exact simultaneity, but instead in terms of overlap. By being less precise about time, we can build a common clock even in a distributed system. When remote elements have common clocks, and messages can be stamped with times from those common clocks, it becomes easier to build consistent distributed systems with consistent views of shared state and events.

It's still too early to tell how much Spanner's approach will influence future systems. On the one hand, it's fairly hard and expensive work to get the GPS signals available to servers and ensure that the clock signal is accurate. On the other hand, that's work that can be shared among a large collection of servers, rather than having to be done by every different kind of application. And that work might well be worthwhile if it means that time-related problems go away for system designers. Perhaps future distributed applications will be built on a Spanner-inspired distributed operating system.

14   Packets

In the internet, communication between two parties takes place in terms of "chunks" of data, each of which is handled separately by the network. Computer scientists refer to this approach as *packet-based*. Although aspects of the internet design will surely change, this characteristic is all but certain to be preserved. It's worth taking a little time to understand why this arrangement works well and to make some connections back to our earlier discussion of the digital model (chapter 2).

Suppose that we are given some large collection of bits to communicate on a continuing basis between distant locations. There is a design choice to make: we can operate like a telephone connection or we can operate like letters in a post office. If we operate like a telephone, we establish a connection between the two communicating parties for the stream of bits to flow across. In contrast, if we operate like letters in a post office, we break the (logically continuous) stream into packets, each handled separately.

As described so far, the broken-into-packets approach just seems like extra complexity, which adds to the potential surprise in saying that this packet-based approach is the dominant means of data transmission in the modern world. In fact, even phone calls are typically handled as packets of sound (in ways that are imperceptible to the typical user of the phone system).

We should pause here to observe that there is no issue of sampling and encoding quality to be concerned about: we can always convey the bits in the stream exactly. That guarantee contrasts with some of the concerns we had in chapter 2 about analog vs. digital representation. Here, the issue isn't analog vs. digital; we're just trying to understand how the exact same (digital) bits should be handled when the task is to send them across the network.

Why would there be any advantage to breaking up the stream into packets? We can draw an analogy to roads. While it might be nice to have a dedicated

lane of highway leading from each separate house to the mall, we recognize
the impracticality of such an arrangement. While we may have a small piece
of "private road" at our house—usually called a driveway—all of the other
roads we use are shared. It's too expensive (in multiple ways) to do otherwise.

Similarly, the packet-based approach is a way of sharing network resources
efficiently. Cars can share the road in much the same way that packets can
share the network. In fact, computer scientists refer to collections of packets
on a network as "traffic."

Even in situations that might seem to involve a continuous stream of
new information, most sources of digital data don't actually deliver a continuous stream of traffic (as we will see in the next section). If the demand
is only intermittent, then it's wasteful to reserve network capacity between
the communicating parties for only occasional transfers. Establishing a
connection is like establishing a private dedicated lane—overkill unless the
traffic volume and need for special service can justify it.

Even for situations where some identifiable fraction of traffic needs
better handling than the other traffic, we can typically accommodate that
requirement within a packet-based approach: the solution is somewhat like
car-pool lanes on highways, which are not dedicated to a single user but are
instead limited to a particular class of traffic.

Compression

We mentioned in chapter 2 that audio and video can be represented digitally. We know that the analog representation of a movie is a piece of film
that moves at a constant rate through the projector. Similarly, one analog
representation of a piece of music is a segment of magnetic tape that moves
at a constant rate past the playback head; another such representation is a
vinyl disc that moves at a constant rate under a phonograph stylus. With
those examples in mind, it would be easy to assume that digitally encoded
audio or video is a constant-rate stream of bits, and perhaps the sort of
thing that could justify a "dedicated highway" style of communication.

However, most of this audio and video data isn't really a steady stream
of bits if we represent it efficiently. At an early stage of the transformation
from analog to digital there may well be a constant rate of "raw" bits. Those
raw bits are samples of continuous analog input—electrical signals derived
from sound waves or light waves. The sampling rate may well be constant.
In chapter 2, we said that we can perfectly reconstruct the original wave

if we sample at least twice as fast as the highest frequency of interest. So we might reasonably expect to be getting a steady stream of measurements at that "double speed," or perhaps even a little faster. Instead, most well-designed systems send relatively "lumpy" data: a lot of bits at one point in time, many fewer bits at another point in time. The "lumpiness" arises when the raw bits are compressed by the best available techniques.

Why does compression make the steady stream into a lumpy stream? Compression finds ways to represent the same information but using fewer bits. We have previously examined digital-to-analog and analog-to-digital transformations, and in a roughly similar fashion there can be raw-to-compressed and compressed-to-raw transformations. Whereas the analog-to-digital transformation shifts from the analog representation to the digital representation, the raw-to-compressed shifts from an "obvious" digital representation (with a simple mapping back to analog) to a "sophisticated" digital representation that is smaller.

For example, video traffic often consists of scenes in which only a small portion of the screen is moving (for example, an actor in a room) while the rest of the scene is unchanging (for example, the room itself). Various sophisticated schemes allow the compression of this traffic into just the information required to recreate the movement, while essentially reusing the image of the unchanging background. While that transformation lowers the overall size of the video stream, it also has the effect of making it variable in size: relatively few bits are required for a scene that is unchanging, while many more bits are required when a jump cut occurs to a completely unrelated setting (effectively, the data rate shifts briefly from almost zero to the full data rate of the video technology).

In the presence of compression, both audio and video traffic are unpredictable and lumpy in their demands for network capacity. The "raw" versions of audio and video consist of steady streams that suggest using a kind of digital pipeline for transport; but once that data is "cooked" with compression, it all becomes bursty and more effectively transmitted as packets.

Incompressible Data

Do all data streams turn lumpy when we apply compression? No, some kinds of traffic don't compress well and really do require the full data stream. One important example of traffic that doesn't compress well is something that's already been compressed. If we have a steady stream of compressed traffic, we typically can't get dramatic changes in its size by applying compression again. After all, if we could always compress even previously compressed traffic, we'd be able to apply compression repeatedly to keep making traffic smaller and smaller. Eventually, anything at all would be reduced so it was only one or two bits long—which we know can't be right.

If we look at the underlying reason we can't just keep compressing already compressed data, we find that it helps us understand the other main sources of incompressible traffic. A compression system finds and exploits patterns in the data being transmitted and effectively squeezes out repeating patterns. That means that the compressed data doesn't have any patterns left to squeeze out. This phenomenon is sort of like drying fruit. After we've dried some fruit (say, apple rings) we don't expect that another trip through the drier will reduce its volume the same way the first trip did—most of the water's already gone.

There are two other common ways we can encounter traffic that doesn't have any repeating patterns, and they're closely related to each other. One is that the traffic can be genuinely random, perhaps representing a sequence of coin tosses. The other is that the traffic can be encrypted, so that the underlying patterns have been deliberately hidden. The result of effective encryption looks random. The defining quality of random or random-looking data is that it doesn't have any recognizable patterns. So, naturally enough, a compression system looking for patterns doesn't find much when it's handed random(ish) data. Both random data and encrypted data will be important in later chapters when we look at security. For now, it's enough to notice that they are among the kinds of data that are typically not compressible.

15 Browsing

Web browsing is a common experience of computing. We'll consider the mechanics of a browser displaying the Google home page. When you're reading this, there might not be a service called Google any more or its home page might have changed radically. But the core of the Google home page has been stable for many years, so it seems like a good bet that it will still be recognizable in the future. We'll make two important simplifications in our description:

1. We'll just look at the behavior that's common to pretty much every browser, so we won't try to talk about special features or unusual behavior that some particular browser might have.

2. We'll pretend that all of Google is built using just a single computer. This description would have been accurate in the very early days of the web, when browsers were simple and Google was small. We'll circle back in chapter 20 to fill in a little more of what we are omitting in this initial sketch.

The simple user perspective of browsing the web is that you point your browser at Google and see the home page. Here's a step-by-step version:

1. The browser sends a home-page request to Google
2. Google sends a home page reply back to the browser
3. The browser uses the home page information received to present a visual representation of the Google home page

You might think of the web as apps or pages. Those are actually higher-level assemblies of the underlying "stuff" of the web. If we understand something about how that works, we'll have better insight into any failures that might occur. We'll also have a better idea of how we can (or can't) modify existing web services to achieve some new goal.

If we want to understand what really makes up the web at a lower level, there are two key ideas: resources and servers.

• A *resource* is a pretty flexible concept: it can be a picture, a movie, some music, some text…pretty much anything that can be stored. Importantly, a resource can also be some kind of program that executes: executing that program produces some output result like a picture, a movie, some music, some text, and so forth.

• We encountered *servers* before when we considered virtualization (chapter 12), but a server on the web is a little different. On the web, a server is just some collection of resources—it's the place where you find some resource(s) of interest.

So if we're asked "what is the web, really?" an accurate—if unhelpful— answer is "it's a collection of resources on servers."

Resources are not simply stored on servers like piles of bricks: instead, each resource acts as though it were a kind of machine itself, with some functions or buttons that we can use to get it to do something. The commands that can be applied to a resource are called *methods*. Depending on the particular method and the particular resource, there may be some kind of result from carrying out the method on the resource; such a result is called an *entity*.

Using the elements that we now know are behind the scenes, our previous apparently simple example of browsing to the Google home page can be divided into the following steps:

1. Find the server for the Google home-page resource
2. Send a "fetching" method to that home-page resource
3. Execute the method on the resource to produce an entity
4. Return the entity as the result of the request
5. Use the information in that entity to present a visual representation of the Google home page.

That sure seems like a lot of steps for just displaying a home page, when our first (simpler) list seemed like a perfectly fine solution. Why should there be all of this complexity? The extra parts and pieces don't make much difference for a simple case like getting the Google home page, but those options are a part of what makes the web so flexible. That flexibility is important for supporting billions of users and trillions of items of interest. There are a lot of stages in the browser/server interaction process at which it's possible to substitute a sophisticated choice or computation, where this simple example just does something straightforward.

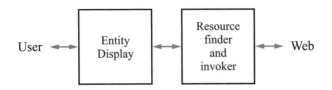

Figure 15.1
The user-facing and network-facing parts of a browser.

This example helps us start to see any browser in a different light. A browser essentially consists of two kinds of machinery stuck together. One kind of machinery knows how to display different kinds of entities and thus knows how to interpret and render the "Google home-page entity" as the familiar-looking logo and search box. The other kind of machinery knows how to interact with the networked computers of the internet so as to find resources, send them methods, and receive any resulting entities.

Accordingly, we can distinguish the user-facing "application-like" part of a browser from the network-facing "infrastructure-like" part of a browser (see figure 15.1).

Programs in Browsers

The "application-like" part of a browser even includes the ability to run programs, which is an important component in the way that many web-accessible services present themselves. Confusingly, the programs running in browsers are often called "scripts," which can leave the impression that they are somehow different from real programs. In fact, a browser functions like just another kind of step-taking machinery. So a browser is also a program for running programs, some of those programs coming from remote sites. As you might recall, "operating system" is the name we usually give to a program for running programs. Unlikely as it might seem, every modern browser has effectively stumbled into being a kind of operating system. Even stranger, the browser effectively participates in a weakly defined and evolving distributed operating system for programs that span servers and other browsers. This is not how most people think about the web—and yet that's what it has become.

However, we'll choose to focus here on the simple operations of browsing. Accordingly, we won't consider these sophisticated distributed-programming aspects further. Instead, our subsequent discussion will focus primarily on the browser's machinery for interacting with resources on the network.

Naming Resources

Returning to our simple example, let's consider naming resources. A resource doesn't really need a name: a resource can certainly exist on the web without having a name. But as we saw in our previous discussions about names (chapter 4) a name can be handy if we want to communicate the identity of something, or otherwise refer to it.

The most common way of referring to a resource is to use a *Uniform Resource Locator*, or *URL*. The URL we're interested in when we think about browsing to the Google home page is written in full as

http://www.google.com/

We'll start by assuming that a browser is just a means of fetching various things from servers, with the Google home page being one of those things.

(Naturally, focusing only on fetching the Google home page is a very limited perspective. The first thing a person would typically do with that home page after it's displayed is to type one or more search terms into it. We'll turn to the question of how that works a little later in this chapter. For now, it's simpler to just look at fetching.)

To understand how the browser "engine" converts a given URL into a corresponding entity, it's helpful to understand what the different parts of a URL mean. The URL consists of a *scheme* and a *path*. The scheme is the first part, "http:" in this case. The path is everything after the scheme. The letters "http" specify the most common web protocol, the Hypertext Transfer Protocol (HTTP). In networking, a *protocol* is a set of message formats and their associated meanings. The protocol is the shared vocabulary for how the browser and server will talk. We'll encounter many more protocols when we look more at networking in chapters 18 and 19.

Even if you have been paying close attention to URLs, most likely you've only ever seen ones that start with "http:" or "https:" as the scheme. You may not even have noticed the single-character difference between those two. Historically, "https:" schemes were used on pages that involve information that must be kept secret, like passwords or credit card numbers, while "http:" schemes are used in other places where there isn't as much concern about hiding information. But after the Snowden revelations about activities of the U.S. National Security Agency, many websites shifted to using the more secure approach for more kinds of information. In addition to the protocol, the scheme also determines how the remainder of the URL (the path) is interpreted to identify that server and some resource on it.

We can separate the interpretation of the path into two pieces: how the path is used as a name for a resource, and how the server for that resource is contacted. As it happens, the "http:" and "https:" schemes have the same rules for how to interpret the paths, but they differ in how the browser contacts the server. The "https:" scheme uses a more secure (but also more costly) mechanism to send information across the network. We examine the issues of protecting information in chapter 24. For now, we'll look only at ordinary "http:" URLs. We know from the scheme that we'll eventually contact a server using HTTP, and we haven't yet examined what that means; but before we learn what it means to "speak" HTTP, we have to figure out what we're "speaking" to, and that requires understanding the path.

Recall that we're considering the URL

http://www.google.com/

Now let's look more closely at the path (that is, the part after the "http:" scheme):

//www.google.com/

The two slashes at the beginning mark the start of the name of a server. So this path effectively says "a server named 'www.google.com' then the resource named '/'." As we'll see in a while, the server name and the resource name have some interesting similarities and differences. We'll start by looking at the resource name ("/") since it's smaller; we'll use what we learn in that examination to help explain how server names work.

Hierarchical Names

Our first observation is that "/" seems like a strange name for a resource. However, that name makes sense once you understand the naming system. There are levels that are "higher" or "bigger" and levels that are "lower" or "smaller." The levels are separated by slashes. The bigger things are on the left, the smaller things are on the right:

/Biggest/Big/Medium/Small/Tiny

Computer scientists refer to this kind of naming as *hierarchical*. We often use hierarchical naming systems in everyday life without thinking about them in those terms. For example, if you were sending a letter to the U.S. President, you would need to write a postal address like this on the envelope:

1600 Pennsylvania Avenue, Washington, District of Columbia, United States

We could take that same mailing address and render it into the "path vocabulary" like this:

/UnitedStates/DistrictOfColumbia/Washington/PennsylvaniaAvenue/1600

Our original postal address had spaces separating the words. One of the quirks of the path vocabulary in URLs is that it doesn't allow spaces, so our converted postal address leaves them out. That change makes familiar phrases look SortOfAwkward, but you soon get used to reading that style of writing.

Figure 15.2 shows this address, as well as some other things we could talk about in this example micro-world.

In addition to the "DistrictOfColumbia" we also have "Ohio" and "California" as elements below "UnitedStates." And within California we have the cities of "SanFrancisco" and "LosAngeles."

Although this example uses street addresses, the slash-separated hierarchical names are applicable to many different settings. In principle, such a name can be as long as you want. Any time you want to make some finer distinctions, you can add another level of names—although in practice it starts to get tedious to use really long names with many different levels.

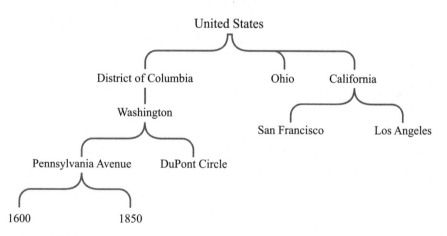

Figure 15.2
A hierarchy identifying some American locations.

Shorter Names

One of the merits of hierarchical structuring is that we don't have to always use the full version of a name. If we have some environment that defines a large, more general part of the name, we can identify specific items in that environment by only providing the other (small, more specific) part of the name.

For an example of one of these environments, we can shorten the hierarchical name we used before, leaving off the specific address of the White House. This form instead identifies all the addresses on Pennsylvania Avenue:

/UnitedStates/DistrictOfColumbia/Washington/PennsylvaniaAvenue/

or we can use something even shorter to talk about all the addresses in the District of Columbia:

/UnitedStates/DistrictOfColumbia/

Importantly, we can change our starting point for understanding names. We can think in terms of navigating the diagram. The very beginning of this addressing scheme is also the very top of the branching diagram, but we can start further down—as though we have already followed one of these shorter names from the top. For example, if we already know that we are concerned only with names of entities in Washington, DC, we can omit the first part of the path (/UnitedStates/DistrictOfColumbia/Washington). We can think of starting at the "Washington" spot in the earlier branching diagram, rather than starting at the very top. If we know that we're starting at Washington, the address of the White House becomes

PennsylvaniaAvenue/1600

while a different address otherwise on the exact same street is

PennsylvaniaAvenue/1850

Notice that both of these addresses *don't* start with a single slash.

The single slash on its own "/" is a name for the top starting point—what computer scientists would call the *root* of the hierarchy. In this particular example of postal addresses, "/" roughly corresponds to "Earth."

Editing URLs

You might have found a particular book called *Widgets* at a publisher's web-site and seen that the URL was something like:

//example.com/books/Widgets

If you're curious about other books published by this same publisher, it's reasonable to try the shorter URL:

//example.com/books

It might not work, or it might produce something different from what you expect. But it works the way you expect often enough to be useful. The defining standards for URLs say that any URL should be *opaque*, handled as just a bunch of characters with no internal structure or meaning. You aren't supposed to see or take advantage of the hierarchy that we just described. But I use this URL-shortening and editing all the time, and that behavior is widespread. When you navigate to some hierarchical URL and you find that you're interested in more than that single item, it's handy if you can shorten the URL and try to fetch something there.

Genuinely opaque URLs that just have some long unintelligible string of characters are much less helpful when you're trying to find some-thing. Technically, a URL should still operate in exactly the same way if it included characters mixed up from completely different character sys-tems like Greek, Chinese, and Hindi—but no human user would find that convenient.

When the web was first invented, URLs were assumed to be opaque with the idea that searching would be used to find relevant URLs. With the ben-efit of years of experience, we can say that that theory is correct but incom-plete. We do search to find relevant URLs, but we also sometimes use URL construction or modification.

Naming Servers

Now, let's return to the double slash "//" and what immediately follows it: "www.google.com." We've said that's the name of the server; but what does it mean to be the name of a server, and how does this naming work? Let's first look at the syntax of server names, and then we can examine the way that names lead us to servers.

Recall that in this context a server is a computer that's prepared to answer a request for a resource. There are many different servers on the web, so we need to identify the one of interest—typically by using its name. The name may be ambiguous: with people, there might be more than one "John Smith," and similarly for servers there might be more than one "www.google.com." In spite of those possible ambiguities, a relatively short, readable-by-people textual name is still the handiest way to refer to someone or something with relatively little chance of confusion.

Why does the server name have dots, and why are the "www" and "com" parts there? In some ways those elements seem unnecessary. We can already tell that the main distinguishing part here is the "google" part, and indeed many people are fairly good at taking a company's name and guessing that the likely corresponding website has "www." at the beginning, ".com" at the end, and some version of the company's name in between.

The structure of a server name comes from another kind of hierarchical naming, somewhat like what we described with the slash-separated part of the path. But in a server name, the elements of the hierarchy are separated with dots instead of slashes. And making it extra interesting, the order of the hierarchy is *reversed*. We previously saw that a resource name narrows left-to-right: the rightmost element is the smallest, and the leftmost element is the largest. In contrast, server names narrow right-to-left: the rightmost element (in this case, "com") is the largest, and the leftmost element (in this case, "www") is the smallest.

So just to be completely clear about this slightly goofy and illogical situation: We refer to resources in terms of URLs. Each URL consists of three main parts (scheme, server, resource) that have completely different naming systems; two of those systems (server and resource) use hierarchical structuring while one system (scheme) doesn't. The two hierarchical naming systems use different special characters to separate the parts of the hierarchy ("." for servers, "/" for resources) and the hierarchies go in opposite orders. What a mess!

Finding Servers

Fortunately, naming is not as confusing in practice as it might sound from this description. The structuring of the server name reflects an ingenious system that allows many different organizations to control how those names

work locally. The underlying "trick" is that each level of the hierarchy logically identifies a directory that contains the meaning of the name immediately to the left. In figure 15.3, "com" is the name of a directory service
that knows the identity of "google.com"—that is, there is an entry in the
"com" directory for the name "google," and that entry potentially represents another directory to be consulted.

Similarly, the directory service identified by "google.com" has an entry
for the name "www" and that server has the full name "www.google.com"
(see figure 15.4).

So now we know in principle how to find the server named
"www.google.com":

1. Ask the server for "com" where to find "google.com"
2. Ask the server for "google.com" where to find "www.google.com"

The quick-witted reader will recognize this as a recursive process, as previously described in chapter 5. This recursive approach to definition and lookup
allows us to make names with any number of levels separated by dots.

The directory service for naming servers is called the *Domain Name System* or *DNS*. Each "level" of the long name is actually called a *domain*. Since
each domain has total control of the meaning of its own names, a domain
is both a kind of directory and a kind of kingdom. Accordingly, the name
"domain" seems quite appropriate.

DNS allows the delegation of naming control to diverse organizations,
which are then in turn allowed to delegate some or all of their naming powers
to other organizations. This decentralized approach to naming was defined
in the early 1980s, well before the invention of the web. It has survived the
enormous growth of the internet without changes to its fundamental model.

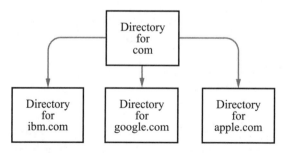

Figure 15.3
The directory for com.

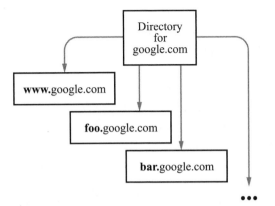

Figure 15.4
The directory for google.com.

DNS is perhaps insufficiently appreciated by the average user, exactly because it is pervasive and reliable.

When we finally succeed in walking our way through the directory hierarchy to find a particular server, what do we actually get as a result? We get a number—sort of like a zip code or postal code for a single server. The number uniquely identifies the server of interest, and lets us establish communication with it. Even if DNS isn't working, you can still browse to the Google home page if you know the right number for one of its servers—you can type one of those numbers into the URL box of the browser, taking the place of the server name "www.google.com." For example, as I am writing this chapter, I can replace "www.google.com" with the number "74.125.226.16" in a browser bar and get the exact same page. (Your results may differ, for reasons that we explain later in the book.) In chapter 20 we'll take a closer look at how the number actually allows us to communicate with a particular server. For now, we just assume that the right number has quasi-magical powers that allow us to communicate with the corresponding server.

We explained the recursive lookup process: look in a parent directory to find a child, repeat as necessary. However, we haven't yet explained how to find "com" to get started—we need a base case for this recursive lookup process, and it comes down to a kind of "hard-wired" system. Certain *root servers* are special. Their addresses are widely published and changed rarely, if ever. In addition, special efforts are made to protect the integrity of the data that they hold, since that information serves as the basis for the naming system. To find a directory service for a top-level domain like "com" or "edu" or "org," you contact a root server. At this writing, there are thirteen different root servers around the world, each run by a different organization—some nonprofit, some government, some for-profit.

However, this arrangement is only a shared convention, not a law of nature. One of the interesting governance issues for the web is control of the root servers, which carries with it the power to determine all naming. Creating new top-level domains (rightmost names, like com) offers new opportunities for profit, since the new names in the domain can be sold to people and organizations that want those names. Placing top-level domains under control of national governments offers new opportunities for control: "com" (and, therefore, "www.google.com") might mean something different in Iran or China from what it means in the United States, if those other countries each had their own version of "com."

Caching

DNS is remarkably effective. It provides as many names as anyone needs, divided as finely as needed, with independent control of the generation and meaning of those names. It's all quite elegant! However, as we've described it so far, this hierarchy is potentially very inefficient. We don't really want to repeatedly consult various directory services across the internet just to figure out what some particular name means. Simply finding a server shouldn't require lots of possibly expensive directory lookups.

Is there a way to avoid doing repeated directory lookups? Yes, by saving and reusing the results from previous lookups.

When we considered computation in chapter 4, we observed that although it's technically correct to say that the value of $(237 + 384)$ is $(237 + 384)$, most people find it more useful to say that the value of $(237 + 384)$ is 621. If we have an even longer expression, like

$(26 + 89 + 9 + 20 + 49 + 38 + 83 + 22 + 10 + 3 + 77)$

which has the value 436, it's even more useful to keep around the final value rather than recomputing it every time it might be needed. In this particular case, a simple way to record that result is to write it on the page where we can read it later. However, if a similar situation arose that wasn't an example in a book and we nevertheless had to remember the

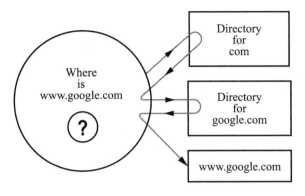

Figure 15.5
Looking up www.google.com.

result of a computation, we'd want to write it down or otherwise save it somehow.

We can take these observations as simple examples of a general principle: rather than redo a computation, we can keep the result around and save ourselves the effort of redoing the computation. Naturally, this strategy becomes considerably more powerful as the computations become more complex and expensive, instead of this rather simple example of addition. Computer scientists refer to this strategy as *caching*. Correspondingly, they refer to a *cache* as the place where some previously computed results might be stored for reuse.

When we have a lookup problem where the answers don't change very often, and we can easily tell when an answer is wrong, that is a great setup for caching previous answers. For example, having once done the full-scale lookup for "www.google.com" to figure out the numeric address of the server, we can then keep a local copy of the result, perhaps in our own little directory. Figure 15.5 shows the full lookup process we'd go through to find "www.google.com":

- The first step consults the top directory for "com."
- The next step consults the middle directory for "google.com."
- And the last step actually contacts the server identified as www.google.com.

The next time we need to know what that particular name means, we can simply assume that it's the exact same server as before. Figure 15.6 includes the same elements as before to show how we would use a cache as a shortcut on the process.

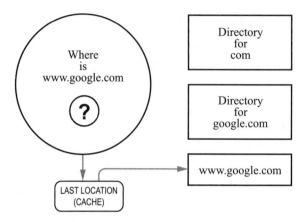

Figure 15.6
Using a cache for faster lookup.

Instead of doing all the lookups again, we can use the previous result to just go straight to www.google.com. If we're wrong, we can tell without any harm being done. Being wrong doesn't happen very often, because the association between a particular name and a particular server is pretty stable. We need both those properties (no harm on error, *and* errors are uncommon) to use caching well. If either of those properties isn't true, then caching is probably not going to work well. A cached copy is not guaranteed to be accurate, so we can't use caching if an occasional error would be a serious problem. And the speedup that we get from caching only happens when there's no error, so we won't get any benefit if errors are common.

A great feature of this caching trick is that it can be applied at every level of the naming hierarchy. So in addition to the browser potentially caching the meaning of "www.google.com," it can also cache the meanings of "google.com" and "com." Why is that useful? Because we expect that even when some specific server is changed, it's likely that much of the rest of the naming hierarchy around that change is still unchanged and reusable.

So if we're contacting our "usual" servers, we don't generally start from the root server and walk down the whole collection of dictionaries: instead, we go straight to the cached location of the server (www.google.com). If that "educated guess" is incorrect, we next make another similar guess to contact the parent google.com directory at its last known (and cached) location. Only for an entirely new server name—no overlapping elements with previous server names—would we need to do a full-scale lookup start-ing from a root server.

Talking to the Server

At this point, we know how to understand the server part of the URL. That knowledge lets us find www.google.com by consulting DNS. Further, we know roughly how the browser/server conversation will go: the browser will ask the server for a particular resource. How does that conversation with the server actually take place?

The conversation between the browser and the server is broken up into packets (chapter 14), each of which crosses the network independently. The packets aren't just any old packets—instead, both browser and server agree to communicate according to the rules of yet another protocol. That protocol is called TCP, which stands for Transmission Control Protocol, but that name doesn't illuminate much. Just as no one refers to IBM as "International Business Machines," no one ever calls TCP anything except TCP.

TCP hides most of the messiness of packet-based networking, and we will examine it in some more detail in chapter 19. So by using TCP, rather than working with packets, the browser can simply write some text across the network to the server, and the server will get it just the way the browser sent it; likewise, the server can write some other text over the network to the browser, and the browser will get it just the way the server sent it. (There's no choice or negotiation involved in the use of TCP here—you can't do web browsing any other way.)

The "http:" scheme in the URL means that the browser will establish a TCP conversation with the server using a particular numeric indicator (80). That value signals to the server that the conversation will use HTTP, which is both the specific web-browsing vocabulary used on top of TCP and the first protocol we mentioned in this chapter. The browser has to include that indicator because the server might be handling lots of different kinds of TCP conversations—not every use of TCP is web browsing!

TCP involves some setup work—back-and-forth messages—between the two parties. Once that setup is complete, the two parties (browser and server) can each send text to the other. Then the browser "speaks" a par-ticular command from the vocabulary defined by HTTP. Specifically, the browser sends "GET /" which means "send me the resource named '/'." The server responds with a relatively long message that includes information about the layout of the Google home page.

The browser then takes all of the material returned in the server's response, and uses that data to render a visible version of it as the familiar Google home page.

Structure vs. Presentation

Even an apparently simple web page may include many different parts. The Google home page prominently includes the Google logo, a box for typing some words to guide the search, and two buttons for selecting the kind of search. (We're choosing to ignore some of the additional features that Google sometimes adds—substitute versions of the logo including animation, or various other buttons and messages around the edge of the page.)

The information received from the server specified all of this information: the appearance of the logo, the number and placement of elements on the page. The elements of the page and their relationships are described in a somewhat elastic way—the goal is to ensure that the result still looks good and works correctly when presented on a wide variety of display sizes. Such elasticity is quite challenging: different people may well look at the exact same web page using a tiny mobile-phone screen or an enormous desktop display, and design choices that make sense for one setting may well look ridiculous or be completely unusable in the other.

In principle, web pages are organized so that there is a separation between *structure* and *presentation*. The structure consists of the aspects that are included regardless of how the page is presented—we could think of structure as the bones of the page. The presentation is how the page actually looks—the flesh on the bones, if you like. Pages are described in a language called HTML, the HyperText Markup Language. That language makes it fairly easy to produce an adequate if unimpressive result—what you might think of as a generic person with generic clothing. However, it requires a completely different level of effort to achieve something that is widely adaptable and aesthetically striking. Such high-end design usually requires considerable sophistication, experience, and testing.

Forms

Throughout all of this discussion about understanding the URL and contacting the server, we've focused only on displaying information that the browser is fetching from the server. Now we will briefly consider what happens when the flow of information is in the opposite direction, from user to server. For example, we can look at what happens when a user types some text into the Google search box and hits "return." We'll start with the simple version of how this mechanism worked at Google in the early days of the web, since that's how many parts of the web still work; then we'll describe a little about how Google works differently now.

The Google home page is one particular example of a more general web page structure called a *form*. A form describes a mixture of information to be displayed, empty fields to be filled in by the user, and buttons that can be pressed by the user. A single form may be very large and complex with many fields, and a single web page may include multiple forms. However, the "classic" Google home page that we are using as our example consists of only a single search box and two buttons. The search box is specified to accept text—whatever the user feels like typing in. In general, both text fields and buttons may have actions associated with them; and in the case of the Google home page, all of those elements—the search box and the two buttons—do indeed have actions associated with them.

How does the browser know what buttons to display, and what actions to perform? All the necessary information was included in the reply that came from the server. Part specified the look of the page, part specified the actions, and part specified the associations between parts of the page and the actions. Effectively, the server sent the browser a kind of program that the browser then runs to provide the relevant page to a user, with the resulting page having additional little programs embedded.

Whether the search is triggered by hitting "return" on the keyboard or by clicking on one of the buttons, the browser constructs a request to a server. In some ways this is just like the process that we already saw for fetching the Google home page. The main difference is that in the previous interaction we started with a fairly simple URL that was typed in by the user; in contrast, now the URL is constructed by the browser. How does the browser construct the URL? It's following rules specified by what the server sent down to build the form on the Google home page. In this particular case, those rules involve taking the text in the search box, processing it slightly, and embedding that processed text in the path of the constructed URL. That URL is then used for another fetch like the one that brought down the information about how to present the Google home page.

Interacting with the web via a dynamically constructed collection of little programs, each of them downloaded on demand from a remote server—that sounds pretty exotic and futuristic! But that's an accurate description of how even a simple form-based page works.

Returning now to the URL constructed by the search box, you can find the search terms in the path following a special marker. Depending on how you typed the search terms into the browser, that marker will show up as "#q=" or "?q=" The following search terms themselves are tweaked so that they can be represented within the URL rules. For example, a space between words becomes "+" since a URL can't contain spaces. So if you type "Barack Obama" in the search box, it becomes "Barack+Obama" in the URL.

We already know something about how a URL is interpreted and a server contacted. Once the request is received by the server, the actual search takes place. As far as the browser is concerned, the server just miraculously returns one or more entities as results; we won't attempt to explain how the search is performed, or how the database is built.

Escaping

You might well wonder, if "+" means a space, how can you represent a "+" in this URL-encoding? An actual plus sign "+" that appears in the search box is instead transformed into "%2B" – which might seem arbitrary, but is actually another way of writing the particular sequence of bits that is used to represent "+." So if you write "3+4" in the search box, it shows up in the path as "3%2B4."

This substitution is an example of what computer scientists call *escape codes* or *escaping*: the "%" is used as a marker that "what comes afterward is special," and various hard-to-represent symbols or characters are translated into a different representation. There are a number of places in computer systems in which data needs to be similarly "escaped" so that unconstrained data can be transferred through some mechanism that treats particular data elements as meaningful.

There is a comical version of this problem in a classic short Monty Python sketch, "Gestures to Indicate Pauses in Televised Talk." The announcer is trying to distinguish pauses in his speech from the end of the announcement. To that end, he introduces both a gesture to indicate a normal pause that shouldn't end the sketch, and a separate gesture he'll use to indicate the end of the sketch. He then struggles to remember to use the "pause" gesture every time he pauses, as well as having difficulty with demonstrating the "end" gesture without inadvertently ending the sketch prematurely. It's handy to realize that you can readily see a practical example of this need to mark things the right way: in your browser bar when you search at Google.

Searching Searches

The Google search page is actually a little more sophisticated than what we've described so far. Even when we narrow our attention to just the text box, there is also a "prompting" or "completion" feature that we haven't yet described.

The search box has another action attached, in addition to the "search" action that we have described. This additional action takes place after every single character typed by the user. Originally, this kind of action was intended for validation of what the user types. On each keystroke, the triggered action can check whether the input character is acceptable, and reject or correct it if it is not.

The Google search page ingeniously repurposes that input validation to produce quite a different effect. The per-character action takes the partial search string (including the newly typed character) and hands it to the server for a search. But the browser is asking for a different kind of search from the ones we previously described. Instead of searching the web for corresponding results, there is a search of popular Google searches. Why is that helpful? Many other people may have previously searched for something similar to what you've typed so far. The set of all information on the web is inconceivably huge, but there is only a much smaller set of currently popular phrases resembling what you've typed so far. Accordingly, it's possible to do a useful search of popular relevant phrases much more rapidly than is possible for searching the whole web.

The top few results of the search are supplied as possible choices that are displayed adjacent to the search box. Each such choice has an associated action to perform the corresponding search. Effectively, each character typed is triggering a program. That program contacts a Google server to run another program. That server program in turn sends back snippets of text each associated with its own little program. The user experiences all this as the service making helpful suggestions. Meanwhile, the underlying mechanism is doing a surprising amount of surprisingly complicated work in response to every single keystroke. Once again we see the possibilities that arise from the sheer number of steps that modern computers can take during an interval that seems quite short in human terms.

III   Unstoppable Processes

16 Failure

In parts I and II, we considered computations running on perfect step-taking machinery. That doesn't mean we've considered only perfect computations: we've been concerned with flaws, especially wrong specifications or wrong implementations, and we've also been concerned with not having enough resources for a computation. But so far we haven't been concerned with what to do when the machinery breaks, or just doesn't work correctly any more.

By thinking about how systems fail, we can build systems that tolerate or overcome failures. We need to understand something about the likelihood of failures, and the shape or form of the failures, so as to be able to build systems that can keep working in spite of those failures. We can move our systems toward being unstoppable.

Reliability vs. Availability

Assume that we have some valuable service like the Google search service, and we'd like for it to have this unstoppable quality. There are two often confused issues involved, which computer scientists call reliability and availability.

Reliability refers to the integrity of the service—correctness of the answers we get, durability of any state that's maintained—but doesn't say anything about whether the system actually provides the service. Having a service that is only reliable is like having a very trustworthy friend with an unpredictable schedule—you're not quite sure whether you'll be able to get hold of them, but you know that they will absolutely be able to give you the right answer if you can find them. In figure 16.1 we show the trustworthy friend present in some boxes and absent in others.

Figure 16.1
High reliability, low availability.

Figure 16.2
High availability, low reliability.

In the context of the Google search service, reliability means that the search results are high quality and not subject to losses or strange variations every time some component has failed. However, the service might be completely unable to give an answer, in which case its theoretical reliability is not very relevant.

In contrast, *availability* refers to the likelihood of getting service, while saying nothing about the quality of the service—like whether the answer received is correct. Having a service that is only available is like having a friend with poor judgment who nevertheless keeps a very predictable schedule; you always know exactly when and where to find them, but whether they can help you with your problem is hit-or-miss. In figure 16.2 we show someone present in every box, but most of the time he's kind of goofy and not very helpful.

In the context of the Google search service, availability means that the service is always willing to answer search requests. However, those answers might be dubious or just plain wrong, in which case the service's conspicuous availability is not very relevant.

Table 16.1 is another way of summarizing the difference between reliability and availability.

Table 16.1
Reliability vs. Availability

	Likelihood of getting *some* answer	Likelihood of getting a *good* answer
Reliable	?	High
Available	High	?

Figure 16.3
The ideal: high reliability and high availability.

Ideally we would design systems to be both reliable *and* available in all cases—like a trustworthy friend with consistent habits. That's what we show in figure 16.3 with the "good" version in every box.

Unfortunately, in the presence of failures we often have to trade off one characteristic against the other.

Fail-Stop

In the most common approach to handling failure, we assume that each component either works correctly or fails completely (falls silent, dies) – nothing in between. A computer scientist would call this approach a *fail-stop model*.

In this model, it doesn't matter how simple or complex the machine is; it's either working or broken. The fail-stop model is essentially a variant of the digital model that we saw in chapter 2. The digital model separates all real-world variability and fuzziness into just the two values "0" and "1." Correspondingly, the fail-stop model separates all of the messiness of possible operating conditions into just two distinct states, which are usually called "up" and "down." "The system is up" means that it's working, while "the system is down" means that it's failed. In much the same way that a digital model doesn't recognize the validity of a halfway extended state for a counting finger, the fail-stop model doesn't recognize any sort of "mostly working" or "limping along" situation for step-taking machinery. Sometimes people talk about a computer, program, or disk *crashing*. For example, "my laptop crashed," or "the mail server crashed." That terminology is usually an indication that they are referring to a system built around a fail-stop model.

A fail-stop model acknowledges that the universe is imperfect—things do fail unpredictably. However, a fail-stop model implies that apart from those unpredictable failures, the universe is pretty well behaved. There are other failure models that allow for a more pessimistic view—seeing the universe as more hostile. We'll mention one of these other models in chapter 17.

Spares

In a fail-stop world, we need to have multiple copies of computers and storage if we want to have an unstoppable system, because any single copy can fail; and the failure might be permanent. For example, a computer can simply stop working—either because it has no power, or because something else has gone wrong that effectively looks like losing power. Similarly, a storage device can simply stop working, which means that we've lost whatever was stored there … unless we kept another copy of that data somewhere else. So in a fail-stop world, we need to assemble multiple computers and/or multiple storage devices in ways that allow the system to tolerate failures.

Computer systems aren't the only place where we might encounter multiple redundant copies. The most familiar version of this same principle in everyday life is to simply have a *spare*. For example, most cars carry a spare tire mounted on a spare wheel. If one of the car's tires is damaged so that it can't work anymore (for example, it's been punctured so that it can't hold air), then the bad wheel is removed and the spare wheel replaces it. Similarly, a car rental location typically has more cars available than are actually committed to renters at any given time. If you're picking up a rental car and the first car assigned is unsatisfactory for some reason, it's usually not too hard to swap in another car as a replacement.

The idea of spares and recovery can also be applied at much finer granularity, and in particular we can have "spare bits" to help recover from "failed bits." Just as words can get garbled or lost by noise in ordinary conversation, and papers can get lost or decay in storage, we can be in a situation where some particular bit is unclear, and we can no longer tell whether the value of that bit should be 0 or 1.

Using spares to solve this problem may seem a little weird—we can't just literally supply a single "spare bit" like a spare tire, of course. We don't know in advance what the bit value is that we'll have to replace. And keeping two spare bits so we have both values available isn't an improvement! If we have two spare bits, one 0 and one 1, we know in an annoying-mathematician way that we definitely have the right replacement value available. We just don't know which one it is, which is sort of useless. So using spare bits is not quite like the spare tire approach.

Error Correction

Instead, we can think of supplying enough additional information so that we can reconstruct the lost bit. The situation is like a tiny detective story in which we figure out the original value by examining the clues left in the aftermath of the failure. In contrast to a typical detective story, we're not trying to figure out the identity of the perpetrator; instead, we're trying to figure out the identity of the victim, the missing bit.

Here's a really simple and inefficient version: if we knew in advance that we would only ever lose one bit at a time, and we weren't very worried about costs, we could simply use two bits for every original bit. That is, instead of transmitting/storing "1" we would transmit/store "11." Likewise, instead of "0" we would use "00." Table 16.2 summarizes that information.

If we're using this scheme, then when some bit was garbled or noisy so we couldn't understand it (which we'll write as "?") we would wind up with a 2-bit sequence like "1?" (1 followed by not-sure) or "?0" (not-sure followed by 0). In either of those cases, we would be able to rebuild the right value by using the bit that didn't get garbled. Table 16.3 summarizes the value reconstruction by the receiver.

Table 16.2
Simple bit-doubling code: sender's actions

To send...	Actually send...
0	00
1	11

Table 16.3
Simple bit-doubling code: receiver's actions

When we receive...	It really means...
00	0
0?	0
?0	0
11	1
1?	1
?1	1

This bit-doubling is a very crude example of an *error-correcting code*. In practice, this particular code has two problems: first, it takes up twice as many bits as the information that we are actually transmitting, so all of our storage and transmission costs double. Second, even after taking up twice as many bits, the code will only work correctly if a single bit at a time changes, and only to a "not-sure" state. If there is ever any scenario in which more than one bit can change at once, or a bit could change to its opposite value, this simple code doesn't help. It could either leave us unsure about the value (a pair like "??" could represent either 0 or 1), or worse it could flip a bit undetectably (producing a pair like "11" when the original value was "00," for example).

Fortunately, there are more sophisticated codes that perform much better, requiring only a small "tax" of extra bits to handle larger and more complex failure cases.

Error Detection

We've just looked at a simple example of an error-correcting code. It's also possible to have a weaker kind of "spare bit" scheme called an error-*detecting* code. An error-detecting code only lets us know that something has gone wrong, but doesn't supply the right answer.

For example, our simple bit-doubling code works as an error-correcting code if we know that only one bit can be wrong. However, if we use that exact same code in an environment where there could be two errors in a row, the code is no longer able to correct all errors that occur. In particular, when two errors produce the code "??" we can tell that's not a good answer—but we can't tell what it should have been.

In general, we would prefer to get the right answer rather than just knowing there's been a mistake. So why is an error-detecting code ever interesting? There are two basic reasons. One possibility is that a correction isn't useful; the other possibility is that a correction isn't possible. We'll explain both these cases a little further.

We might think that a correction is always useful, but sometimes a low-level failure requires a high-level reset or restart. It's not always useful to fix the immediate problem. For a real-life analogy, consider booking travel. If your desired flight is sold out, it may or may not make sense for you to be booked onto an alternative. Under some circumstances, another flight may be a fine substitute; in other cases, the inability to get a particular flight may mean the whole itinerary needs to be reworked, or the whole trip needs to be scrapped. An "error-correcting" travel agent who *always* gets us from point A to point B regardless of the date, time, or airline may be unhelpful or even aggravating.

Likewise in a computation: if some or all of the preceding steps need to be redone, there may well be completely different data being handled, and the recovery of the garbled data is pointless. Under these circumstances, it may be useful to perform error *detection* just to be aware that the data is not correct. However, it would be unwise to incur any additional cost to achieve local error *correction*. We will encounter a more-general version of this line of thought in chapter 18, where it is an important design principle for reliable communication.

The other reason for wanting error detection is that it's an improvement over having nothing, in cases where error correction is not possible. Any error-correcting code has some limit on the number of errors that it can correct. Any error-detecting code likewise has some limit on the number of errors that it can detect. However, in general it is easier to detect errors than to correct them, as we have already seen with our simple bit-doubling code: it can still detect a kind of error that it can't correct.

To understand these levels of difficulty, let's look again at a concrete example. Assume that errors never flip 0 directly into 1 or vice-versa, but always go through "?" first. How does our bit-doubling approach perform for error correction and detection in that environment? It's a code that can correct one bad bit, can detect two bad bits, but can't detect three or more bad bits. Any single error can be one of the following four changes, where we use a right arrow → to mean "becomes":

$0 \rightarrow ?$

$? \rightarrow 0$

$1 \rightarrow ?$

$? \rightarrow 1$

but a single error cannot be one of the following two changes:

$0 \rightarrow 1$

$1 \rightarrow 0$

Under these assumptions, our simple bit-doubling code offers different "levels" of capability, depending on how many errors have occurred. We can distinguish the following four levels in terms of a sequence of flips applied as we try to transmit the single bit value "1":

• 0 errors: Normal operation, correct result decoded
  Example: We send "11" which is received as "11" and correctly decoded as "1"
• 1 error: Error-correcting operation, correct result decoded
  Example: We send "11" which is corrupted to "1?" but still correctly decoded as "1"
• 2 errors: Error-detecting operation, result may be incorrect but is known to be flawed
  Example: We send "11" which is corrupted to "1?" and then further corrupted to "??" which can't be reliably decoded. But the receiver knows that an error has occurred.
• 3 or more errors: Erroneous operation, result may be incorrect and may not be known to be flawed
  Example: We send "11" which is corrupted to "1?" and then further corrupted to "??" and yet further corrupted to "?0" which is incorrectly decoded as "0"

Keep in mind that this simple bit-doubling code is intended to be easy to understand, not to work efficiently. More realistic codes work differently. However, this overall pattern is typical: increasing the number of errors shifts the system successively from normal operation to error-correcting operation (if possible), then to error-detecting operation (if possible), and finally to erroneous operation.

Storage and Failure

Ideas about error correction and error detection are not only useful for the transmission of data; they are also applicable to the storage of data. This similarity is not surprising if we engage in some big-picture thinking: after all, storage is effectively just a transmission to some future recipient (possibly our future self), while retrieval of stored information is just receipt of a transmission from a past sender (possibly our past self).

In addition to error-detecting and error-correcting codes, there are other kinds of spares or redundancy that we can use to build reliable storage systems. Before we look at those approaches, it's worth understanding a little about what's happening in storage and what's failing.

At this writing, large-scale, long-term storage is typically on magnetic disks. They have a thin layer of material that can be selectively magnetized so as to encode information in the patterns of magnetization, and the pattern of magnetization can then be sensed to read back the information that was encoded there. The underlying magnetic technology is similar to what was used to record music on audio cassettes and 8-track tapes—formats that were once popular but are now obsolete. However, the similarity is only in the use of magnetic techniques. Those old music formats used magnetic storage to record music in analog form. In contrast, we want to record digital data (recall that we looked at analog vs. digital models in chapter 2).

In principle, magnetic storage is not very different from what you can do with paper, pencil, and eraser: making marks and reading them later. That said, there are some useful differences. It's handy that the magnetic "marks" being made are tiny, which means that a small device can store a very large number of them. It's also handy that the "pencil" and the "eraser" are combined. The effect is a little like having one of those pens that lets you click among different points with different ink colors—except that instead of having one blue point and one red point, here one point marks and one point erases. Finally, magnetic writing and erasing causes far less wear than the corresponding operations with pencil and eraser, so a magnetic storage device can still be working fine long after a cycle of repeated writing and erasing that would wear out even the best paper.

Although they're superior to writing and erasing paper, magnetic disks are usually the least reliable elements of computer systems. This is not because the manufacturers are incompetent, but because magnetic disks involve a kind of mechanical brinksmanship. People want magnetic disks to have both fast operations and high density (many bits of storage per device). It's expensive to build the mechanism that reads and writes bits magnetically, so that element is just a small read/write head that operates on only a tiny fraction of the total storage at any one time. To read or write something on a part of the disk far away from the current position of the read/write head, the head and/or the disk has to move so that the head is directly over the area of interest.

Although we're currently focused on magnetic disks, we can note in passing that there's a similar structure to both vinyl phonograph records and optical CDs or DVDs. In all of these systems, there's a relatively large rotating disk containing information of interest, but only a relatively small area where the "action" happens.

In fact, it's useful to pursue this comparison a little further and consider what's happening "up close" with a record, a CD/DVD, and a magnetic disk.

In figure 16.4, we see a section through the playback mechanism using vinyl records. The stylus actually rests on the record. Although this wears out the vinyl, the stylus is very light and the record doesn't move very fast.

In figure 16.5, we see a similar view but now of a CD or DVD. The read/write mechanism is optical, based on lasers. There is no longer any need for physical contact, and instead there's an emphasis on moving the disk quickly. To achieve fast operations, there needs to be only a short time between when a request is made and when the read/write head is in the right part of the disk. To minimize that delay time, the disk needs to spin rapidly. A rapidly spinning disk moves the relevant areas quickly under the read/write head where the "action" occurs.

Figure 16.4
Cross section of vinyl record in use.

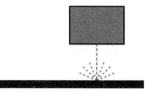

Figure 16.5
Cross section of optical disk (CD/DVD) in use.

Figure 16.6
Cross section of magnetic disk in use.

Similar reasoning applies to a magnetic disk, but there is an additional constraint. To achieve high storage density, the units of magnetization that represent bits must be very small. Using small units means that the magnetic force to be sensed is small, which in turn means that the read/write head must be positioned very close to the magnetic material, as shown in figure 16.6.

Fast operations *and* high density mean that we have to have the disk spinning as fast as possible, with the head as close to the disk as possible. The combination of a fast-moving disk and a very close head means that there is no room for mechanical error or wear.

Flash

Magnetic storage is not the only way to store a large number of bits so that they can still be read days, weeks, or years later. Especially in phones and other mobile devices, it is more common to use *flash* or *solid state drives* that have no mechanical moving parts, just as the other elements of most computer systems have no mechanical moving parts. Instead of "marking" tiny magnetic areas, these technologies "mark" an array of tiny transistors. Instead of using magnetization as the marking and erasing, these devices use electrical charge: each transistor is configured to be like a holding bin for a small amount of electrical charge, and the presence or absence of electrical charge is used to encode bits.

This approach is faster, more reliable, and requires less power than using magnetic disks. At this writing, it's also currently more expensive, which is part of the reason why magnetic disks are still popular. Although solid-state storage is more reliable than magnetic storage, it's still not perfect—it is still vulnerable to failures that can permanently lose data. In fact, its problems are more like writing on paper than like magnetic disks: solid-state storage can wear out from repeated marking/erasing cycles. So even with this newer technology, we still need to consider how to make storage more reliable and available.

Injury vs. Death

In considering how to make storage failure less likely, there are two key hazards to consider. We can think of these two hazards as "injury" and "death" for the data being stored. The data suffers an "injury" if we have some kind of failure in the middle of writing to permanent storage. For example, there might be a temporary power failure or a physical problem with writing a particular part of the disk. After such a failure the device can recover to a mostly functioning state again; but although the device is operating, some of the data on it may be corrupted or unreadable.

The data suffers "death" if its containing device fails permanently. The data is not economically retrievable or recoverable. It is worth distinguishing here between different ways in which data goes missing. The very common problem of "data recovery" after mistakenly deleting a file is quite different from the problem of reconstructing data from a nonfunctioning disk.

Typically a deleted file on a computer has not actually been destroyed, only removed from the directory used to locate files. In much the same way that a library book that is missing from the catalog can be "lost" even though it's just sitting on the shelf where it's always been, the deleted file may very well appear to be gone even though all of its contents are still unchanged on the disk. File recovery tools perform an operation somewhat like looking through library stacks for a "lost" book—once the relevant book is found, a new catalog entry is constructed and the book is now "found" again, even though it may have remained undisturbed through the whole process.

Physical damage to a disk or a device's mechanical breakdown, in contrast, may be more like a fire in a library—some books may be readily salvageable, some may only be partially recoverable even with the best efforts of the most capable experts, and others may be a total loss.

Sometimes it's easy to think that all data is recoverable. There are software tools and services that help recover deleted files. Even when files have been deliberately erased, experts may be able to read remaining traces—there are various claims about the ability of the CIA or other intelligence agencies to read data even when someone has attempted to overwrite that data. But the reality is that both accidents and deliberate destruction can put data out of reach. So although we may well note that many files are readily recoverable from loss, and also that intelligence agencies have remarkable capabilities for reconstructing deliberately erased materials, we should nevertheless categorize these observations as "true but irrelevant." There are still situations in which data can be lost forever if there's only one copy. We need redundancy to avoid those situations.

Logging vs. Replication

So far, our approach to writing information in a cell has been to replace an old value with a new value. That's not a wise approach when we are concerned about surviving these hazards we've identified; if something goes wrong with writing the new value, we don't want to have lost the old value.

Figure 16.7A shows how a conventional cell with conventional write replaces the old value (x) with the new value (y). There are two techniques that avoid overwriting the only copy of an item: logging and replication.

With *logging*, there is still only one copy but there's no overwriting of old information with new information—instead, any new or updated information is always written at the tail end of the log.

Figure 16.7B shows that a write of y to the log simply appends y to the previous value x, rather than overwriting it.

With *replication*, there is still overwriting but there's no single copy—instead, there are multiple copies. New or updated information overwrites any old value in each place.

Figure 16.7C shows that the two cells are each written with new values. This might not seem to be any kind of improvement over the original

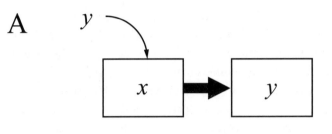

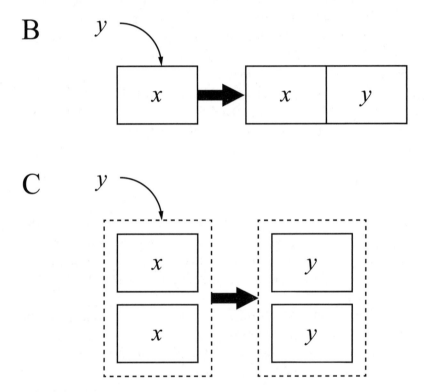

Figure 16.7
Different kinds of updating.

single-cell write—but we can arrange the multiple cells so that they are unlikely to fail at the same time or in the same way. Let's look at that next.

Stable Storage

One simple form of replication is called *stable storage*. Stable storage works just like an ordinary disk, but with better failure properties: whereas an ordinary disk mostly works but occasionally crashes, stable storage keeps working even when an ordinary disk would have failed. However, as we'll see, stable storage is also more expensive than ordinary storage.

We can build stable storage from two separate unreliable storage devices by always following a careful sequence of steps for reading and writing. For example, suppose that we want to write some value X and be sure that it's really safely stored. We have two disks that we'll call disk 1 and disk 2, and they operate independently. We can then take the following steps, shown in figure 16.8:

1. write X to disk 1
2. read back X from device 1
3. write X to device 2
4. read back X from device 2

At the end of that sequence, we know for sure that we have put a good copy of the data on both devices. We've not only written the two copies,

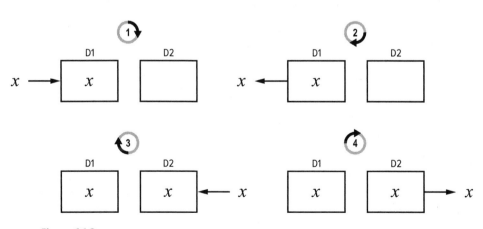

Figure 16.8
Writing stable storage.

we've also read both copies to ensure that both values are what we wanted them to be.

Later, to read that same data item, we can read it from both device 1 *and* device 2, then compare their contents. It's possible that some failure of a disk or another part of the system will corrupt or lose data. But even in this very simple version, we can see that it's unlikely that we will read a bad value without knowing something is wrong. In the diagram we wrote the value X. We know that it's very unlikely that the value X could turn into a different value (call it Y) *identically* on both independent disks. So we might:

- read two identical copies of X and know the read is fine; or
- read an X and a Y and not be sure if either is the correct value

Notice that this careful two-disk approach is more reliable than a single disk, even though we aren't using any of the error-correcting or -detecting codes that we considered earlier. If we also use such codes, it's possible to devise schemes that reliably determine which copy is correct in the case of a failure. The careful two-disk approach also makes no assumptions about how disks fail, other than assuming that they crash cleanly (a fail-stop model). If we assume slightly better behavior by disks, we can omit the separate reads entirely, and also do the two writes at the same time.

This simple approach to stable storage lets us store data more reliably than a single disk can. In contrast to a single disk, the stable storage system can only lose data if *both* of the component disks fail at the exact same time. When we consider two entirely independent devices doing completely different actions, their simultaneous failure is very unlikely. If we have genuinely independent failures of the different disks, we can multiply their likelihood of failure. So the combination of two disks with an annual failure rate of 1 percent becomes stable storage with an annual failure rate of $1\% \times 1\% = 0.01\%$. If we need even higher reliability, we can repeat the trick with more disks.

RAID

However, this stable storage is paying a high cost to purchase increased reliability: what the user of the stable storage sees as a "simple single write" of X actually requires two writes and two reads, plus some comparisons to make sure everything worked. Likewise, what looks like a "simple single read" actually requires two reads, plus some comparisons. So everything related to storage just slowed down considerably. Depending on exactly what needs to be stored and/or read, this stable storage would take somewhere between twice as long and four times as long as storing/reading the same data on a single (unreliable) disk. Since disks are often the slowest part of a computer system, this slowdown is a problem.

We mentioned that there are many error-correcting and error-detecting codes that are more sophisticated and effective than the simple bit-doubling scheme that we described earlier. Similarly, there are many ways to arrange multiple disks that perform better than the simple disk-doubling approach to stable storage we've described. The broad class of multidisk schemes is often called RAID, an acronym for Redundant Array of Inexpensive Disks. There is a substantial menagerie of different "RAID numbers" like RAID 0, RAID 1, and RAID 5, where the different numbers refer to different schemes for combining disks and operations on those disks to support the logical read and write operations.

The "RAID number" phrases are worth recognizing, even though the details and differences are unlikely to matter to a nonspecialist. The important part for our purpose is that it's possible to group disks in various nonobvious ways to achieve fault-tolerance. The different schemes have different trade-offs of performance and failure characteristics. Our simple disk-doubling stable storage scheme is not far away from what's called RAID 0. (The main difference is that in RAID 0 the writes and reads to the two devices happen at the same time, and there's no need to reread after a write.)

Independent Failures?

Now that we see that there are ways to overcome diverse kinds of failures, we might start to wonder about the limits of these approaches. Can we always build a system to be unstoppable? Can we overcome all failures? If not, why not?

Our approach to surviving failure has depended on redundancy and spares. We've asserted that the redundant elements fail independently. It's useful to consider whether this assertion is correct in the real world. Certainly, two disk drives look like different objects—you can have yours, I can have mine, we can perform different operations on them—so they don't have any obvious linkage that would cause them to fail at the same time.

If we imagine a spectrum of same-failure-behavior, on one end we have completely unrelated devices (say, a tractor and a disk drive) doing completely different things. We wouldn't expect there to be any similarity at all in their failures. At the other end of the spectrum, we can imagine two apparently separate devices that actually have a hidden mechanism so that a failure in one causes an identical failure in the other. Any two real devices fall somewhere on the spectrum between these two extremes. Clearly the first extreme of unrelated devices isn't useful for building an unstoppable system, since we can't substitute a tractor for a disk drive even though they fail independently. Likewise, the second extreme of perfectly matched, identically failing devices isn't useful for our purposes, since both elements will fail at exactly the same time even though one would be substitutable for the other. Let's consider the potentially useful middle ground.

Common-Mode Failure

Even if we take two different devices of the exact same kind, and run them side by side starting at the same point in time, we don't usually expect them to fail at the same time. There is still some independence between the otherwise-identical situations, because of the slightly different physical characteristics of each manufactured device. In many uses of multiple disks, part of the difference between devices is that we expect them to be used for slightly different purposes: they have different workloads. However, that assumption of different workloads may not be true if we are using a multi-disk scheme involving identical reads and writes, like the ones we saw for stable storage and RAID. Since the different disks may have to do identical work in such a scheme, we might reasonably expect them to have very similar wear patterns. Intriguingly, we find that this problem of identical devices wearing out identically becomes worse as we become more precise in our manufacturing. A more sophisticated device may require tighter tolerances (more precise matching to specifications) simply to function correctly, and a better-run manufacturing process may produce less variance within acceptable bounds. In both respects, an unintended consequence of increasingly sophisticated manufacturing may be an increasing similarity of failure characteristics.

So one source of linked failures is when identical devices are subjected to identical load. Failures in which otherwise-independent components fail in the same way are called *common-mode failures*. Common-mode failure under-cuts redundancy—if all the potentially spare components fail at roughly the same time, the system fails despite its apparently redundant design.

Another important source of common-mode failure is *design failure*, in which every disk might fail in the exact same way. We usually assume that there is some randomness in the failure process. However, sometimes a failure is due to the device being designed wrong—every device will fail in exactly the same way when the "wrong thing happens."

For example, if a house light switch is wired incorrectly, the wrong light will turn on *every* time the light switch is flipped—it's not a question of the light switch, wiring, or light bulb somehow wearing out. If the incorrect wiring was actually designed that way on the blueprints used by a developer for building many identical houses, then every one of those houses will have the exact same (wrong) behavior when the light switch is flipped.

Similarly, a disk drive can have a design error that means that *every* disk of the same model fails identically. The failure might not be as obvious or as quick as the wrongly wired light—but it can be just as consistent.

Failure Rates

How often do components fail? Even the least-reliable elements in a modern computer are pretty reliable when viewed as individual items. A common measure of reliability is the Mean Time Before Failure (MTBF). This is a statistical measure like the average height of a group of people, rather than a precise measure like the width of your kitchen table. Accordingly, it's important not to treat it as a guarantee, but more as a guideline. MTBF expresses the average time of operation before something fails—but it can be wildly misleading if used incorrectly. A single disk drive can easily have a MTBF of more than a million hours, which is a very impressive length of time: a million hours is more than a hundred years of continuous operation. So if a disk drive is specified to have a million-hour MTBF, does that mean that every such disk drive will run for a hundred years? No. After all, we know that having an average height of 5' 10" for a group of people doesn't rule out having a particular person in that group who is only 4' 8" tall.

Similarly, it's entirely possible to drown while walking across a river at a spot where the average depth is only 6 inches (figure 16.9). Wide shallow banks can combine with a relatively narrow, deep channel to produce

Figure 16.9
Misled by average depth.

a reassuringly small average that is completely unrelated to the potential hazard of being in water over your head.

A different statistical measure is more helpful in making realistic estimates: the Annual Failure Rate (AFR) expresses the likelihood that a component will fail in the course of a year. A single disk drive often has an AFR of 1–3 percent. If the AFR is 1 percent, then we would expect roughly one failure each year in every group of 100 disk drives.

However we measure, it's clear that the overwhelming majority of disk drives don't fail. We mentioned earlier in this chapter that disk drives are usually the least reliable hardware components. So there's only a tiny chance that you will ever encounter such a failure on a single disk. This is one reason why people have such trouble with backing up their data: *most* people get away with not having backups *most* of the time. It is an unusual experience to have a disk crash on a modern computer. Of course, the rarity of such an experience is little comfort to a person who is nevertheless having that experience, and all the associated disruption (figure 16.10).

Although individual disks may seem incredibly reliable by these measures, they seem almost hopelessly flawed when they are used in very-large-scale computing systems. For example, suppose that we build a disk in which the expected failure rate is only one in a hundred years (3.1 billion seconds)—that might seem like a sufficient level of reliability that we could stop worrying

Figure 16.10
"This hardly ever happens."

about the issue. But then consider a facility that includes a million of those disks.

Some failure will happen somewhere in that facility about once each hour. Far from being something that we can simply forget about, now the failures of these systems (and dealing with the consequences) has probably become someone's full-time job. A million disks and their associated failures are not hypothetical extrapolations, they are a present-day reality: Companies like Google and Amazon run multiple data centers, each of which has an enormous array of computing and storage devices. In each of those data centers there is a full-time crew working on replacing and upgrading those devices. When people talk about computing or storing "in a cloud," it's useful to keep in mind that there does need to be something real underpinning the "cloudy" abstractions. Those actual underpinnings include not only acres of machines, but also a team of minders.

Suppose now that we're letting one of those cloud providers take care of all the hardware reliability and availability problems. They may have to do lots of work to provide unstoppable step-taking machinery for us, but that's no longer our problem; we need to be concerned only about software issues. We take those up in the next chapter.

17 Software Failure

Software doesn't fail physically. It doesn't wear out. Since software doesn't wear out, its behavior is unchanging (although we noted in chapter 7 that changes in the environment often feel like "bit rot" in software). Unfortunately, wrong behavior by software is also consistent and unchanging. Can we use some kind of redundancy to lessen the impact of a software failure?

We have had some kind of "spare stuff" in each of our previous efforts to survive failure. Some researchers have likewise attempted to avoid common-mode failures in software by using multiple different realizations of the software. These are not identical copies of the same program—identical copies would succeed or fail identically, and so wouldn't provide any advantage. Instead, the different realizations are deliberately designed to be *different* ways of achieving the same effect. The multiple versions are spare computational approaches, rather than spare bits or spare disks. The multiple realizations each compute their own independent version of an answer, and then those answers are compared to determine the single right answer. At one level this sounds like a straightforward generalization of error-correcting codes, stable storage, and RAID—but it's actually a much harder problem and suffers from some difficulties that may not be obvious.

Specifications Revisited

Recall that a specification tells us *what* software should do. In contrast, the implementation provides all the details required about *how* the software works (we first encountered this distinction in chapter 3). Conceptually, we want a single specification that allows us to build multiple distinct implementations. Because they have the same specification, the multiple versions will all produce the same results; because they have different implementations, they will fail independently.

The first difficulty is that it is hard to develop the specifications for such multiversion software, even beyond the problems we saw previously for specifying any computation (chapter 6). In addition to the usual challenges for a specification, the specification for multiversion software must allow multiple competing realizations to be developed. Multiple distinct implementations are crucial to avoid common-mode failure. Accordingly, the specification cannot be overly prescriptive. If it is too detailed, it may effectively allow only one implementation, even if those implementations are written independently.

However, it is not enough to write a very "loose" specification so as to ensure that there can be multiple different implementations. The specification must also ensure that all implementations are in fact computing the exact same result. If the specification isn't sufficiently strict, the different versions may compute different results. Then, comparison of the results reaches an incorrect conclusion—not because of detecting errors in individual implementations, but simply because of ambiguity in the specification.

So, overall, building multiversion software requires specifications that are "specific enough" but not "too specific." In general, getting this "just right" or "Goldilocks" balance in the specification is hard. In fact, getting the right flexibility in a specification for multiversion is probably harder than just writing a single correct implementation of a simpler specification. So despite the theoretical attraction of having spare software versions, in practice it may not work any better than just producing one good version.

Consistent Comparison

There is an additional subtle problem for the construction of the independent versions: the *consistent comparison problem*. To understand the consistent comparison problem, we need to understand something about arithmetic as it's performed in computers.

Computer arithmetic is a digital version of the analog arithmetic mathematicians use. Accordingly, as we know from our previous look at digital vs. analog (chapter 2), computer arithmetic has a "stepped" quality that's not true for the perfectly smooth, infinitely subdivisible numbers that are familiar from mathematics. That stepped or gritty quality to computer arithmetic means that two different ways of computing the same logical value may actually wind up with values that differ by small amounts, because the step-size differences between a digital version and the smooth analog version accumulated differently in the two computations.

You can see a simple example of this kind of glitch in finite decimal notation by considering what it means to divide 1 by 3 and then multiply that result by 3. Logically, the division produces 1/3, and then the multiplication produces 1 again. But the decimal representation of 1/3 is:

0.3333...

where the "..." captures the idea that the sequence repeats infinitely. Since we've said we're using a finite decimal notation, we can't represent that infinite sequence. Instead we have to use a finite approximation like:

0.33333

but that doesn't work quite right. When we multiply that by 3, we get 0.99999, not 1. That result is very close, of course—but if we don't know how to manage these small gaps and errors, we can get into trouble. Computers don't usually use decimal representations for calculations, so the specific values that cause problems are different from this example, but the nature of the problem is the same.

Suppose that a program is testing whether a particular value is larger than zero, and its output is simply "yes" or "no." It's easy for one version of the calculation to wind up with a very tiny value that is positive while the other version of the calculation winds up with a very tiny value that is negative. Our different approaches have produced results that are quite close, and perhaps the differences are not significant—but the nature of the comparison to zero means that the similarities are lost. Of course, we could fix this particular case now that we have identified it: this particular test with these particular computations can produce a misleading result. But although it is possible to fix specific cases of this problem that are identified, in general it is not possible to avoid them or detect them.

In fact, there is a lurking contradiction here that threatens to foil our best efforts. First, we recall that the only reason these comparisons even arise is that we are trying to build multiversion software. Then we also recall that to do multiversion software correctly, the specific implementation details of algorithms are *not* part of the specification.

Consequently, we have a paradox. On one hand, to implement multiversion software successfully we must avoid actions that could introduce common elements in different versions, since those common elements could fail identically, undercutting the value of multiversion implementation. On the other hand, to dodge the consistent comparison problem we must understand and identify places in the separate implementations that produce meaningless differences in what are logically identical results.

Comparing Results

In our earlier exploration of limits (chapters 6 and 7), we repeatedly identified a limiting factor and then set it aside to ask what else was a limit. In a similar fashion, we will now choose to ignore the expense and difficulty of specifications for multiversion software, assuming instead that we can somehow get past that problem. We'll also assume that we aren't troubled by issues related to consistent comparison. Can we then build multiversion software with the desired reliability? No, because there is still a potential common-mode failure when the different results are compared. In multiversion software, there comes a point at which the collection of programs somehow combine the separate results into a single decision or course of action (figure 17.1).

If we simply write a single program that combines the different values, that single program becomes a critical risk for design failures. We can't mitigate that risk by writing multiple different versions of the combining mechanism, because those different versions would still need some single combining mechanism of their own. The most common solution to this problem is to accept that the single combining mechanism has a high risk

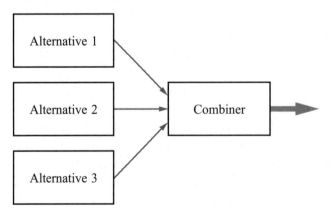

Figure 17.1
Combining diverse computations to produce a single result.

of being a source of design failure, and to design it accordingly: it has to be as simple as possible, so as to reduce the likelihood of errors.

It is also possible to build multiversion systems without using a single piece of software to combine results. Human spaceflight is an area in which it is critical to have reliable systems despite component failures. The designers of the U.S. space shuttle included multiple redundant computers for navigation of the shuttle, and they had to find a way of reliably combining the outputs of those multiple computers. They didn't even try to combine the results in software. Instead, each of the computers is physically connected to a shared control lever (think of it as a kind of joystick). Each computer uses its available force to move the lever in the "correct" direction. The resolution of any disagreement among the navigation computers is effectively arm-wrestling: by design, a majority of computers can overpower a minority of computers.

Let's consider whether we have identified a successful way forward for using redundant computations. In figure 17.2, the "?" at the bottom represents the uncertainty about whether diverse implementations are an improvement overall.

The underlying problem here is that we need to replicate goodness but not replicate badness. But we already know from an earlier chapter that one of our limitations is that we cannot reliably distinguish good software from

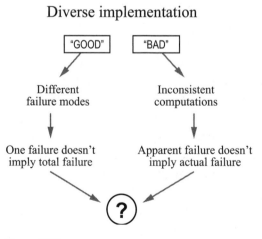

Figure 17.2
Are diverse computations valuable?

bad software (chapter 7). After all, if we were able to reliably distinguish good software from bad software, we would only build or select good software. Then we would have no need for any of this multiversion complexity.

Byzantine Failure

Instead of supplying "spare computations," we can use a completely different failure model. Rather than using a fail-stop model, it's possible to design systems around a *Byzantine* model of failure. In a Byzantine model, failed elements might not stop cleanly, but instead may cause further problems. In particular, a Byzantine model means that failed elements are free to perform in precisely the most damaging and confounding ways, no matter how unlikely those sequences of actions might seem to be.

The Byzantine failure model gets its name from the "Byzantine Generals" problem that was first posed in 1982. There, the problem was one of treachery among military leaders, and the question of how a cohort of loyal generals could reach successful agreement on whether to attack or retreat despite the efforts of some number of traitorous generals that were undercutting them.

Intuitively, it might seem that it is impossible to survive Byzantine failures—how can a group continue to function with members that are deliberately choosing to behave in the worst possible way? And yet a contrary intuition suggests that a single traitor in a large group might not be enough to undercut the group's ability to reach agreement. Both intuitions are correct but incomplete. The crucial issue is how many generals are loyal vs. how many are traitors. In a systems context, we would view that in terms of how many elements are good vs. how many have failed. Some of the time we are pretty sure that the system can survive the failed component; some of the time we are pretty sure the system can't survive with most of its components working against it. Where is the crossover?

Computer scientists have determined the answer to this question. Although the details depend on the specific arrangement of elements and the problem to be solved, a reasonable high-level summary is that a system can survive these malicious failures as long as only about 1/3 of the elements misbehave. Meanwhile, the other 2/3 of the elements behave properly and cooperate despite the efforts of the misbehaving elements. This is a useful result to keep in mind when considering other domains of decision making and governance. It is worth noticing how far away this threshold is from the common idea of majority rule: if we have only a bare majority of well-behaving elements, we are in trouble.

It is not yet common to build systems to tolerate Byzantine failures, but they are practical. We will look at Bitcoin in chapters 25 and 26, and Bitcoin is effectively built around a kind of Byzantine agreement. The system allows for the possibility that some participants will behave badly and try to cheat others; nevertheless, the system still functions well as long as there are enough honest participants.

18   Reliable Networks

In chapter 16, we saw how the transmission of data could be protected by error-correcting codes, so that information could be received accurately in spite of occasional noise. Such codes are an important ingredient in getting reliable communication, but not the whole story. Although such codes can correct or detect a small number of bits lost or garbled, often there's a bigger failure to be overcome. In a typical packet network, a whole packet (of many bits) can be lost all at once. What can we do to ensure that communication still succeeds despite that kind of loss?

Guaranteed Delivery?

We could try to build the network so that it guarantees delivery of every message, but that approach doesn't work out as well as we might hope. Let's consider what would be required for guaranteed delivery. The network is handling various messages that are sent at unpredictable times by different sending parties, traversing the network to reach various other parties. Because we don't know in advance who will send a message or to whom they'll send it, we could have a situation where an unusually popular destination or path exhausts its resources—for example, it could run out of space for holding messages.

If we're building a network that guarantees delivery, we can't allow any situations in which the network runs out of resources. So guaranteed delivery also requires guaranteed space at every step along the delivery path. To have guaranteed space at every step we have to both determine a path and reserve resources all the way from sender to receiver.

What's strange about those requirements is that we already considered and rejected this path-reserving approach when we first looked at data networking (chapter 14). So did we make the wrong choice when we argued in favor of packet networks instead of end-to-end connections? No. Packet networks are a better overall choice, especially if the communications are bursty rather than constant—and as we noted previously, bursty communication is very common. The end-to-end reservation is expensive: effectively, each transmission from sender to receiver may require crossing the network *twice*. The first network crossing finds a suitable path and reserves the needed space, and the second network crossing actually transmits the data.

Worse is that building a network with guaranteed delivery is not only expensive but also ultimately futile. Even with all of those reservations, we still can't really guarantee delivery. After all, it's still possible that a component along the reserved path might fail. In any of those occasional failure situations, all of the carefully arranged reservations won't make any difference.

Redundant Messages

What can we do instead of guaranteed service? Can we build an error-correcting code so that it could replace a whole lost message? Yes, but it's often not an attractive approach. If we want to be able to recover hundreds or thousands of lost bits, the error-correcting code will involve sending hundreds or thousands more bits. That error correction will take a substantial fraction of the communication capacity available, in a super-cautious effort to recover in case some message is lost. Although there are systems that work this way, most of the time this approach is wasteful. The loss of a packet occurs only occasionally, while the overhead cost of the extra bits is a burden all of the time.

What we really want instead is to send a second or third copy of a message only when it's needed. It's still a redundancy strategy, but now, instead of sending redundant information all of the time, we're just keeping one extra copy on hand to resend as needed.

The End-to-End Principle

We assume that the network will at least try to deliver each message—this is what is sometimes referred to as a "best effort" service—but there's no guarantee of success. How should we think about organizing communication to achieve reliability? Computer scientists have a term for this approach: the *end-to-end principle*. We can put this principle into some everyday terms: if someone is asking you whether you received a phone call, they ask you—not the phone company. Or if someone is asking you if you received a letter, they ask you—not the post office. If you didn't receive a call, it doesn't matter what the phone company says about the call. Likewise, if you didn't receive a letter, it doesn't matter what the post office says about getting it to somewhere near you.

The phone company or post office might have relevant information if there is a disagreement about whether you have received a call or letter, but their view of success can't be substituted for yours as the ultimate recipient of a call or letter.

For example, in a postal service there are "return reply" postcards that may be signed by the recipient—not by the post office!—and returned to the original sender. Such a postcard conveys that the sent item was actually *received*, not just delivered.

The lesson from these examples is the principle that applies to data networking in general: even if the network were completely reliable in its task, that still wouldn't guarantee reliable delivery to the recipient. There could still be a failure between the network service itself and whatever or whoever is using the network.

If we require an end-to-end mechanism to achieve real reliability, is there any point to having any kind of guaranteed delivery? Yes, but the value is a little different from what we might have thought. It's possible—but by no means certain—that a guaranteed-delivery network offers improved performance. Resending a message all the way from sender to recipient may take a while, and it may be smart to avoid that cost. But that possible performance benefit is quite different from a reliability guarantee.

Acknowledgment and Retransmission

So far, we've concluded that a guaranteed-delivery network is not the same as reliable end-to-end communication; indeed, a guaranteed-delivery network is arguably an expensive way of solving the wrong problem if what we really want is reliable end-to-end communication. Instead of a guaranteed-delivery network, we need to add two elements:

1. Acknowledgment of received messages, and
2. Retransmission of lost messages

Actually getting these two elements to work typically requires some additional machinery. In particular, the sender needs some way to figure out when a message has been lost. The lost message doesn't announce itself. Instead, just like when a letter is lost in a postal system, the sender has to judge when a message is lost.

As in a postal system, the key input for the judgment is elapsed time since sending. The sender needs a timer to estimate a reasonable span of time for the message to be sent and the corresponding acknowledgment to be received. If a message is acknowledged within the expected time, that is success (for that particular message). But if a message has not been acknowledged within the expected time, it has to be declared as lost. Then the message is retransmitted.

Getting the timer right can be hard. If the timer is too long, then the sender wastes time waiting whenever a message is genuinely lost. If the timer is too short, the sender will resend messages unnecessarily. Each unnecessary resent message causes no confusion for the receiver, who can easily discard it. But sending the extra message wastes time and network capacity that could have been used for sending useful messages.

Multiple Acknowledgments and Negative Acknowledgments

Once we've seen how a single-message system works, it's not hard to see how we could send more than one message at a time. There has to be some kind of labeling of the different messages and their corresponding acknowledgments, so we can tell which acknowledgment is for which message. A really simple system that allows up to three messages in flight might call them "red," "green," and "blue." Each time we send a message, we'd say which color slot we were using, and we'd have different-color timers and matching-color acknowledgments.

Or instead of using colors, we could use numbers like 1, 2, 3. If we use numbers, that makes it easier to see how we could keep expanding the number of slots in use—we could just add the next-higher number if we wanted to use an additional slot.

Using numbers, it also becomes easier to have a single acknowledgment indicating that multiple messages have been received. Usually, messages don't get lost. (In environments where we expect to lose lots of messages we might well return to the error-correcting code approach we previously considered too wasteful.) So rather than sending an acknowledgment for 1, followed by an acknowledgment for 2, followed by an acknowledgment for 3, we could send an acknowledgment for 3 that implicitly acknowledges the receipt of 1 and 2.

In a system where a particular acknowledgment implicitly acknowledges all of the previous numbers, we need a different way of handling a situation in which we have received most of the messages but are missing some. The solution is to use *negative acknowledgments*. Whereas ordinary acknowledgments signal that the receiver has successfully received the corresponding message(s), negative acknowledgments signal that the receiver has found a "hole" in the received message sequence and is requesting a resending of what's missing.

Even as we increase the sophistication of our acknowledgments, the underlying strategy remains the same:

1. The sender retains a copy of each message until it's acknowledged.
2. If any message remains unacknowledged within a reasonable time, the sender assumes that the message is lost.
3. The sender retransmits a message if it seems to have been lost.

In practice, this work of reliable transmission is almost always handled on the internet by the protocol called TCP. We encountered TCP already in chapter 15. When you use the internet, TCP is just another piece of the invisible plumbing, rather than something that you're likely to interact with directly. But it's worth being aware that TCP is the underlying mechanism used for web traffic, email, and many other less common uses of the internet. In the vast majority of cases where it's important to be sure that all of the packets get across the network, TCP is involved.

Congestion Collapse

When we looked at reliable storage, we overcame individual component failures by using groups of components. Then, when we looked at reliable networking, we overcame individual message loss by using multiple messages as needed. This pattern might leave an impression that groups are always better for reliability, but that would be an incomplete picture. To better round out our understanding, it's also worth looking at a problem that arises only from groups.

We have already seen one kind of group-only problem. We previously mentioned gridlock as one kind of failure that arises in non-computer settings (chapter 8). Gridlock simply can't occur when there's only a single entity taking actions—there's no one else to "gridlock with."

Another kind of failure that requires multiple players is called *congestion collapse*. To understand it, let's start with a simple model: a single sender/receiver pair and some external, otherwise-unspecified source of interference. The sender and receiver communicate easily in the absence of interference but have increasing difficulty as the level of interference increases. As interference increases, more messages are lost and need to be retransmitted. As the loss rate increases, there is a corresponding decrease in the efficiency of the transmission between sender and receiver. We can still get reliable communication by retransmitting lost messages. But that communication is both slower (because of the delay caused by retransmission) and less efficient in the use of capacity (because some messages are transmitted more than once). The more likely a loss is, the longer it takes for any single message to be successfully transmitted. So far, this is just a simple statement of the problems for a single communicating pair, as interference increases.

We start to get an inkling of the problem of congestion collapse when we realize that in a shared network, each transmitting process is not only trying to communicate—it is also, from the perspective of every other transmitting process, a potential source of interference. If the sender/receiver pairs were completely isolated from each other, they wouldn't affect each other. But since they are using some of the same resources in the shared network, they are competing and potentially interfering. As we increase the density of attempted communication, we are not only increasing the number of sources of traffic—we are also, intrinsically, increasing the number of sources of interference.

Congestion collapse is an unintended consequence of our otherwise sensible system for achieving reliable delivery. The hold-message-until-acknowledged approach works fine as long as losses are relatively rare. If losses don't happen very often, then the retransmissions typically succeed. However, we can run into trouble as losses happen more often. More losses cause more retransmissions, which in turn cause more losses. What is an individually sensible strategy becomes madness when applied by all parties.

In congestion collapse, everyone may be very "busy" but they are not accomplishing anything. Like a cocktail party in which everyone is talking but no one is listening, it is loud but not useful. It is the networking equivalent of thrashing, which we previously encountered briefly in our discussion of coordination (chapter 8). Everyone's transmitted traffic is dropped and has to be retransmitted. But since every other sender's traffic is likewise being dropped and then has to be retransmitted, nothing much happens. Congestion collapse is not a merely theoretical concern—it was a real-world problem that affected the internet in October 1986. That incident led to the urgent study of the problem and a search for solutions.

Congestion Control

How can we avoid congestion collapse? As with the cocktail party where everyone is talking at once, we have to create some space for real conversation by reducing interference. Congestion collapse occurs because everyone is eager to talk, creating a situation in which no one actually succeeds at being heard. Avoiding congestion collapse requires that everyone be prepared to stop talking, creating a situation in which some communication succeeds. To avoid congestion collapse, a reliable-communication protocol like TCP needs to include some kind of *congestion control* mechanism that causes it to do three things:

1. send at a slow rate initially;
2. build up communication speed gradually; and
3. sharply reduce its communication speed at the first sign of congestion.

Most TCP implementations use an *implicit* form of congestion control. With implicit congestion control, the sender assumes that the loss of a message means that the network is congested; the sender then reduces its sending rate.

However, not all message failures or losses are caused by congestion. Depending on the kind of network being used, there may be other reasons why a message could be lost. For example, a mobile telephone may be in an area with no wireless service. Attempts to send messages fail, but that kind of loss just happens because of circumstances of geography—it's completely unrelated to any kind of congestion in the network.

In environments where noncongestion losses are frequent, TCP implementations with implicit congestion control don't perform very well. A TCP implementation that interprets every message loss as congestion will tend to slow down when it doesn't really need to. Alternative protocols have been designed for those environments: some are variants of TCP, while others are completely unrelated protocols. A common feature is that they don't consider a single packet loss to be a signal of congestion. Some protocols rely on explicit signals of congestion from the network, while others perform a more sophisticated analysis on the patterns of loss to better infer the presence or absence of congestion.

Cheating on Congestion Control

In an ideal world, everyone sharing a network would implement congestion control consistently. Consistent use of congestion control means that everyone's results are better than without congestion control. Unfortunately, communication over a network typically happens between distant, autonomous parties. Accordingly, congestion control requires cooperation among those independent entities. Getting the right result is not like changing the laws of a single country. It's more like negotiating an international treaty.

Consider what happens if only two senders cheat on the convention by not implementing any congestion control. That deviation from the norm can be sufficient to induce congestion collapse, even if everyone else implements congestion control. The two cheating senders can potentially grab all the available resources and more, interfering with each other and all the other senders.

That might be the end of the story, with the moral that everyone needs to implement congestion control. But it's a little more complex than that. Curiously, a single cheater won't induce congestion collapse, and the cheater will get unusually good service as a result of grabbing more than their fair share. After all, if there's only one blabbermouth at a party, they are clearly heard by everyone else.

Accordingly, a chronic problem in real networks is convincing senders not to cheat on congestion control. Many people who are reasonably familiar with networks in their everyday life don't know about the risk of congestion collapse. A possible comparison would be to people who operate a ferry and don't understand the risk of sinking; they might be tempted to discard all that "useless bulk" of life vests and rafts.

Sometimes the discarding of congestion control shows up as a networking vendor who has "invented" a great new way to improve performance.

Other times, it shows up as a user who has "discovered" that they can adjust their local settings to get dramatically improved performance. The problem is hard to prevent entirely, because each initial attempt at cheating yields excellent results for the first single cheater. However, the apparent success produces a widespread failure if others do likewise. What initially seems to be a promising business model or brilliant insight turns out to be a catastrophe when used more widely.

19   Inside the Cloud

In previous chapters we have discussed the sending of messages between parties that are far away from each other, but so far we have been pretty vague about how the message transport really happens. This vague approach actually has its own name: we call this nonspecific network a *cloud*.

In figure 19.1, boxes represent the two communicating parties. They each communicate with the cloud, and the cloud somehow gets the message across to the other party. There may be lots of communicating parties that are interconnected "somehow." The cloud provides that interconnection without specifying exactly how things work. One party sends a message into this network cloud, and somehow the message comes out to the right recipient. This network cloud is different from cloud computing, although the two ideas are related—we'll encounter cloud computing in the next chapter.

This data-network cloud is not so different from a postal system or telephone system. In those more familiar systems, we likewise don't really need to know the details of how a letter gets from sender to receiver, or how a phone call is set up. Although we don't have to know those details, it can still be helpful to have at least some idea of the sorting stages in a postal

Figure 19.1
Two communicating endpoints and a network cloud.

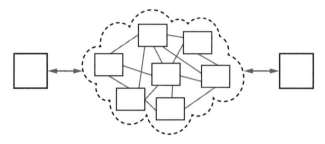

Figure 19.2
Two communicating endpoints and various network devices.

system, or the switching stages in a telephone system. With that knowledge, we have a better understanding of the ways in which the system might break down, or otherwise not meet our expectations.

The communicating entities outside the cloud are typically computers of various kinds, possibly including phones and tablets. Although we've referred to them informally as communicating parties or counterparts, a better technical term is *endpoints*. We've previously talked about clients and servers—both clients and servers are endpoints. Endpoints are different from all the various cooperating devices that are operating inside the cloud, implementing the network's delivery machinery. We'll refer to those devices inside the cloud as *network devices*. Network devices usually look quite different from endpoints; they go by different names and come from different manufacturers. In spite of those surface differences, it's worth keeping in mind that under the covers they are all step-taking machines running various kinds of programs. Like other kinds of step-taking machines, they can fail in different ways. Fortunately, the network includes mechanisms so that messages can be delivered in spite of those failures. We'll examine those mechanisms further in this chapter.

Figure 19.2 depicts the same situation as the previous picture, but it replaces the cloud with a collection of network devices. This view is closer to what really exists as the communication mechanism between the parties.

Wires and Jacks

We can think about communication as a fairly abstract process of transferring a message from one endpoint to another, but we can also think about the network at a physical level. At that physical level, we can think of the network as providing a wire to each endpoint. In the modern world, lots of computers are actually using wireless connections or shared wires of various kinds. However, we'll ignore those complexities. For our purposes, those are just like different kinds of wire, and the overall flow of communication works much the same way regardless of those details.

So we can think of an endpoint as having a single wire on which it can send and receive messages. Then we can think of a network device as having multiple wires on which it can send and receive messages. A network device has to be prepared to receive a message on more than one wire, whereas an endpoint only ever receives a message on its one wire. A network device may also have to decide which one of its multiple wires to use when sending a message, whereas an endpoint only ever sends a message on its one wire. The problem of sending a message from endpoint A to endpoint B is to somehow get it from A's wire to B's wire. Unless A is wired directly to B, getting the message from A to B will involve some number of intermediate devices passing the message along and making the right choices among their multiple wires.

Router

Let's look at a typical simple router, the sort of device that might be used in a home or small office. It most likely has an internet connection, some wired connections, and the capacity to operate as a wireless access point. With the right configuration of information in the router and the right arrangement of connecting wires, such a router allows endpoints to exchange messages both locally and remotely (across the internet).

For simplicity, we're going to ignore both the internet connection and the wireless network. Instead we'll focus only on the wired connections, because they're easier to understand. (Despite that simplification, we'll work our way back to the internet by the end of the chapter.)

We'll draw a router as a simple box with 4 ports or jacks along the bottom edge (figure 19.3) A single router like this allows communication among endpoints connected to the jacks. It works like a little cloud for those connected endpoints. (A networking professional might get fussy and say this is a *switch*, not a router. For our purposes that distinction isn't important, but it's worth being aware that people will sometimes be picky about whether something is dealing with mostly local destinations or mostly remote

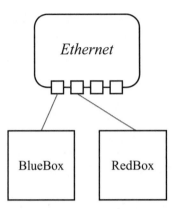

Figure 19.3
BlueBox and RedBox are connected to the simple router.

destinations. They will then tend to call a mostly local device a switch, and a mostly remote device a router.)

Consider the case of two devices that we'll call BlueBox and RedBox, attached to the router by wires. In figure 19.3, the wires are shown as simple connecting lines. Physically, the wires we would use in this situation look a little like telephone wires. We'll treat them as though they were phone lines. Like telephone wires, these wires plug into jacks on the router. However, if you find yourself hooking these devices up, it's worth knowing that these aren't phone lines. Instead, they're like super phone lines. They have a couple of additional wires inside the insulation, and slightly wider jacks and plugs accordingly. They're also built more carefully so they don't distort the high-speed digital signals used on networks. With appropriate adapters, you can use networking cable to carry phone signals; but you can't generally use ordinary phone lines to wire up data networks.

On our example router, each of the jacks is numbered. We can distinguish among the multiple otherwise-similar jacks by referring to jack 1, jack 2, and so on. Now assume that we have attached the endpoint we're calling BlueBox to network jack 1 of the router. We've also attached the endpoint we're calling RedBox to network jack 2 of the router. We'd like to have a way for BlueBox to send messages to RedBox and vice versa.

The router itself has some kind of ability to receive messages on jack 1 and send them to jack 2, and vice versa. But even if RedBox knows something about BlueBox, it doesn't necessarily know which jack it's using. In fact, BlueBox might get unplugged from jack 1 and plugged into jack 4, so we don't want the communication to be in terms of the local jack numbers.

Ethernet

This interbox communication problem is not so different from what is familiar in the telephone system. In our everyday conversations, we might think of a telephone number as tied to a particular address (for a landline) or tied to a particular device (for a mobile phone). However, we also know that telephone numbers are portable—within some limits, they can be transferred across telephone companies or geographies, or moved from an "old" device to a "new" device.

Calling the exact same phone number can ring a phone at one house one day, and then ring a phone at a completely different house the next day. So we know that the telephone number is not attached permanently to the wires at the first house. Instead, there must be some kind of a table with entries about phone numbers and their corresponding wires. When a phone number is moved from one house to another, or from one mobile device to another, it's really the entries in that table that are changed.

The local communication problem between RedBox and BlueBox uses a similar kind of table lookup. When you plug two different endpoints like BlueBox and RedBox into the two different jacks, each endpoint provides the router with its own unique identifying number—a little like a telephone number—and the router builds a little table matching those numbers with the jacks. (A networking professional might quibble here that there are other ways for the routing to happen that don't involve the router building a table—but this explanation is good enough for our purposes.) The identifying numbers are most often related to a particular local-network technology called Ethernet.

In Ethernet, the counterpart of a phone number is called an *Ethernet address*. However, Ethernet addresses are "baked into" the devices that use them, which is pretty different from phone numbers. Every device using Ethernet communication has its own unique Ethernet address. Every manufacturer of devices using Ethernet communication gets a batch of unique numbers and uses each one only once. If RedBox and BlueBox know each other's Ethernet addresses, and communicate in terms of those addresses, then it doesn't matter which jack each one is using. The router can sort it all out.

Interconnecting Networks

The router is using this Ethernet addressing scheme locally, and we've said that all Ethernet addresses are distinct—every different Ethernet device has its own unique address. An obvious question here is, Why can't we just use those Ethernet addresses to get messages around between any two devices in the world? The answer is that we might be able to do that if every device in the world used Ethernet; but there are many other ways of performing local addressing and communication. In fact, for both short distances and long distances, there are lots of different choices of communication technologies. It might seem simpler to just pick one single technology and insist on using it everywhere, but that would be a little like saying there should only be one kind of motor vehicle. Instead of having only a single type of motor vehicle, we know that there are cars, trucks, and motorcycles, with further divisions within each category. With motor vehicles we recognize that the different kinds of vehicles, and different models within each category, reflect real differences in capabilities and value. And so it is with networking technologies.

Let's consider some other networking scheme that's not Ethernet—call it "Othernet." It has its own wires and ports and addresses that are different from Ethernet. Let's also assume we have two other endpoints GreenBox and YellowBox that can plug into Othernet but not Ethernet. In much the same way that RedBox and BlueBox were plugged into an Ethernet router, GreenBox and YellowBox plug into some similar little router and communicate with each other via Othernet.

But now consider what it means for RedBox to communicate with GreenBox, or BlueBox to communicate with YellowBox. RedBox "speaks" Ethernet, but GreenBox doesn't. Likewise YellowBox "speaks" Othernet, but BlueBox doesn't. Even if we could move the endpoints between routers, or plug them into both routers at once, that seems complex and expensive. And if the RedBox/BlueBox/router group is in Massachusetts on one side of the country while the GreenBox/YellowBox/router group is in California on the other side of the country, those kinds of manual swapping or double-connecting approaches can't work at all.

We might imagine that we can have the two routers talk to each other, but what do they speak in terms of? The Ethernet router doesn't understand Othernet, and vice versa. The solution is to interconnect the networks—to build an *internet* (figure 19.4).

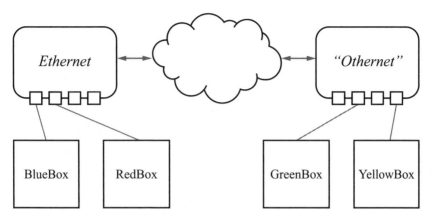

Figure 19.4
Connecting the routers to form a simple internet.

Internet Protocol (IP)

Almost everyone has heard of the internet, even if they might be a little fuzzy about what it really is or why it matters. For many people, it's the most familiar and most important example of a computer data network. When we consider communicating between our Ethernet router and our Othernet router, we can see where the name "internet" comes from. In much the same way that "international" means crossing national boundaries, "internetwork" means crossing network boundaries. The *internet protocol* or *IP* serves as a common language—a lingua franca, if you prefer—of networking across technologies and across distance. IP ensures that endpoints can communicate identically regardless of whether they are near or far, and regardless of the local-networking technology in use by each endpoint.

One important feature of IP is that each endpoint is numbered. The number of an endpoint serves to distinguish and identify the specific endpoint. That number is called an *internet address* or *IP address*. In some ways, this scheme is just like what we saw with Ethernet: Ethernet communication happens in terms of Ethernet addresses, and likewise IP communication happens in terms of IP addresses. But unlike what we saw in Ethernet, the IP address isn't permanently baked into the device. Indeed, in IP it's possible to reuse the exact same number for a completely different device. That might seem kind of weird when compared to the way that Ethernet works, but it's not so strange when we realize that it's like the way that phone numbers work. Sometimes this flexibility of IP addresses can be useful for sophisticated purposes, where one device intentionally takes on the role of another one—we'll see a little of that later in this chapter. But sometimes, reusability of IP addresses just means that there are occasional glitches in network operations, in which two different devices are simultaneously trying to use the same IP address.

At one level an IP address is just an integer, and that's where we'll focus for the moment. So let's assume that we assign the number 3782 to BlueBox and 2901 to RedBox. There's a special way to write IP addresses, which we'll learn shortly—in practice, it would be strange to write an IP address in this way, as "just" a number. But for the moment, it's enough to say that Blue-Box and RedBox each have their own special IP address number.

Internet Routing

As with our previous Ethernet example, we now have two endpoints communicating in terms of identifying numbers, although now those numbers are IP addresses instead of Ethernet addresses. The problem of working out the right path of wires from the relevant IP addresses is called *internet routing* or *IP routing*. In this particular case, communication between BlueBox and RedBox will be pretty easy. When we compare IP-based communication to Ethernet-based communication for the case of BlueBox and RedBox, there are differences in the details but not much difference in the big picture. The merits of IP become more apparent, and routing gets more interesting, when we start considering communication between devices that are *not* attached to the same network device—like when RedBox is communicating with GreenBox.

To begin, we'll look at the internet as it was originally designed—with one distinct IP address assigned to each endpoint. (We'll refine our understanding to be more like the modern internet in a later section.)

Routing as a Network Service

To understand how and why IP routing works as it does, it's helpful to think of a kind of network growth story. The point here isn't that any particular network developed in exactly this way, but more that thinking about this mythical network helps us understand the issues.

At a small scale, IP routing is not very complicated. Let's first assume a handful of different endpoints that want to communicate. Let's further assume that these endpoints are all quite near each other, and that changes to the group of communicating endpoints don't happen very often. Under those circumstances, it's possible to do routing by just keeping track of which endpoint corresponds to each address in some kind of local table—like the one that we already considered when thinking about how the phone company keeps track of phone numbers, or like how a router matches Ethernet addresses to jacks.

Computer scientists call this kind of information a *routing table*. This particular type of routing table is organized by IP address; for each IP address, the entry stored in the table is some kind of choice. At a minimum, that choice is just how to get one step closer to the destination from the current location. Alternatively, the entry might be the whole series of steps to get to the destination. Either way, the information in the routing table is useful for reaching the specified IP address from the current location.

In simple cases, it's not clear why it's worth bothering with IP addresses and IP routing at all—they're just an extra layer of work. It seems like we might as well just identify each possible destination endpoint directly, perhaps by listing out the sequence of wires required to get there.

But now consider what happens as the number of different endpoints starts to grow. It becomes harder for each endpoint to maintain one of these routing tables for itself. Each table is larger, and thus consumes more space at each endpoint.

In the first part of figure 19.5, A and B each have a routing table that lists the two possible destinations on the network. We don't show any detail of what information is in the routing table for each destination, since that doesn't much matter for this discussion.

In the second part of figure 19.5, there are lots more destinations on the network, and so these routing tables are getting very long. Although we aren't showing it in the picture, each of the new destinations C, D, etc., must also have a routing table of similar size.

Eventually, it's too much trouble for the endpoints to keep the routing tables. Instead, the endpoints hand over that bookkeeping and lookup work, leaving them to the network itself. In the last part of figure 19.5, the destinations are no longer trying to keep their own copy of a routing table. If the network is doing the lookups and routing work, each endpoint needs

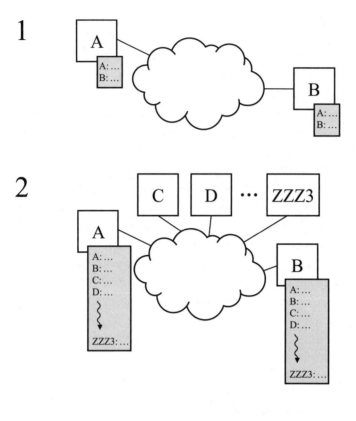

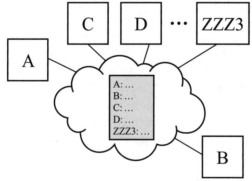

Figure 19.5
The evolution of routing tables.

to know only its own IP address and the IP addresses of any other endpoints it wants to contact. The network now handles any work required to transform IP addresses to paths through the network.

We can see the attraction of such an arrangement for an endpoint, but why would the network agree to take on the work of routing? The network can take advantage of a trick that's not available to the endpoints. The network can operate as a single logical entity with a common shared view of routing, while maintaining only relevant fragments of the total routing table in different locations. This fragmented or federated approach to the routing table can be more efficient than the maintenance of separate tables per endpoint. Indeed, the advantage of this network trick grows as the size, complexity, and volatility of the network increase.

DHCP

In a simple view of routing, every device needs to know its IP address and give it to the network. Since those IP addresses aren't baked into each device when it's manufactured, that means that at some point someone had to assign IP addresses consistently to all the various devices on the network. Manually assigning those addresses is a hassle and a frequent source of errors, particularly if two different devices are accidentally given the same IP address. Can we do better?

Yes, we can avoid many of these problems, at least for client endpoints. Recall that clients initiate connections to servers; client endpoints are typically the mobile devices or laptops of users, while servers are providing some kind of service(s) to those clients. There's an important difference between clients and servers in terms of IP address usage. Clients have to know server IP addresses somehow, so the clients can start the conversation (by doing the network equivalent of saying "hi"). Typically clients find those servers via names stored in DNS, as we already examined for browsing (chapter 15).

In contrast, servers don't need to find clients. Servers can just sit and wait for clients to ask for services, and each such request from a client already includes the client's IP address. So whereas the server's IP address may need to be relatively stable and relatively well known (so that clients can send requests to the server), any client's IP address can be assigned on the fly as long as it doesn't conflict with other clients.

Who does this assignment of IP addresses? Typically, the requester's closest router does the assignment. (A network professional might insist here that the address assignment is actually a specialized service that's unrelated to carrying network messages—and that's correct. However, in most environments that service looks like a part of the router.) The device and the router have a conversation using yet another protocol, this one called *Dynamic Host Configuration Protocol (DHCP)*. A successful DHCP conversation ends with the device and the router agreeing on the new IP address of the device, and a period of time for which that assignment is valid. After that time ends, the router takes back the IP address—the router is effectively "leasing" the IP address to the device for a limited time, not letting the device "own" it. This leasing arrangement is why you can sometimes fix a networking problem by restarting or resetting your device's network service: your device has drifted out of synchronization with the local address assignments, but getting a "new" address brings you back into alignment with the current arrangement.

Advertising

At this point we know that each router knows the IP addresses of any attached endpoints. Each of those endpoints can give the router messages for other endpoints, identified by IP address. We can see how this message exchange works at a single router with endpoints that are directly attached, but we haven't yet explained anything more. So at this point, using IP is no improvement over what we already had. With Ethernet, we already had the capacity for the router to send messages among locally attached endpoints. But how do we expand or modify that approach, so the router can help send messages among endpoints that are not locally attached?

The broad solution is that routers share addressing information with each other. The first step is to think in terms of routers sharing only their locally attached addresses. Earlier, we saw that an individual endpoint declares its (single) IP address to its (single) local router. We can have each router do a kind of multiple-address version of that same address-declaration operation, which we'll call *advertising*. In the same way that an endpoint has some kind of physical connection to a local router, each router has some kind of connection to another router, like a telephone line. (In the early days of the internet, these connections literally were a kind of telephone line. Now they are digital data lines—but they're still often supplied by a telephone company.)

Instead of advertising only a single IP address, the router advertises *all* of the IP addresses of locally attached endpoints. It sends that advertisement to all of its immediate-neighbor routers—those that are separated from it by only a single connection.

Let's give the name OurRouter to the router with BlueBox and RedBox attached. This name is just for our convenience in explaining; nothing about the operation of the network requires the router to have a name. When it's speaking to another router, OurRouter doesn't bother to advertise which jack BlueBox or RedBox is attached to—that's not useful information for other routers. What it does advertise is that it knows how to get traffic to the IP addresses 3782 and 2901. Any other router that needs to send traffic to either of those addresses knows to send it to OurRouter.

Longer Routes

This advertising scheme greatly increases the flexibility of the network, but it doesn't quite give us the right solution yet. Our first IP routing mechanism only let us communicate with other endpoints on the exact same router—what we might call "one router away." With this second mechanism, routers are advertising their directly connected endpoints. That arrangement means that endpoints can communicate with other endpoints that are attached to a different router—as long as that router is directly attached to our router. So we now know how to communicate with a party that is "two routers away." But as soon as there are three or more routers between endpoints, our local router won't know how to reach that endpoint.

Fortunately, it doesn't take much more to get the right solution. For both senders and receivers, it doesn't matter (much) if an advertised IP address is directly attached to the router that's advertising it.

We know in our example that OurRouter has both RedBox and BlueBox directly attached. But now assume that we move BlueBox (with IP address 3782) to a different router (let's call it YourRouter). That doesn't necessarily mean that OurRouter has to stop advertising that it knows how to get traffic to IP address 3782. As long as OurRouter still knows what to do with that kind of traffic, it can still be advertising that it knows how to get traffic to 3782.

Of course, OurRouter has to change its behavior when it receives traffic for 3782. When BlueBox was directly attached to OurRouter, then OurRouter sent 3782's traffic to jack 1. When BlueBox moves to YourRouter, then Our-Router sends 3782's traffic to YourRouter. But OurRouter's advertisement doesn't need to change.

And note that BlueBox might move again to YetAnotherRouter. Our-Router might find out about that change, in which case it would update its routing table so that 3782 traffic is sent to YetAnotherRouter. Alternatively, OurRouter might be left knowing only that YourRouter knows how to reach 3782; so it would continue to send 3782's traffic to YourRouter, which would then need to send it on to YetAnotherRouter. As you can probably already see from this small example, there are some tricky issues like avoiding loops. We will just note that as another area where computing professionals earn their pay.

Scaling Up

Although this simple scheme lets endpoints reach each other with any number of routers in between, it doesn't work very well at large scale. As we've outlined it so far, every router has to provide every other router with a list of every distinct address that it knows about, even if it's only an indirect path. That would lead to two problems: first, there are lots of addresses; and second, most of the available paths aren't very good.

How many addresses would need to be considered? To answer that question, we first note that there are two different kinds of IP addresses. The "old" style is called IPv4 (that's version 4 of the IP protocol) and the "new" style is called IPv6 (for version 6 of the IP protocol…and no, there is no IPv5).

There is general agreement that there aren't enough of the older IPv4 addresses, which is a large part of the reason why a transition to IPv6 has been slowly taking place. Even so, there are roughly 4 billion different IPv4 addresses. The scheme we've sketched so far would potentially mean that every network device is potentially sending updates about any of those billions of addresses. That might be possible, but it doesn't seem like a very smart approach. And then when we look at the newer IPv6 addresses, we find the scale is mind-numbing. Not only can you assign billions of IPv6 addresses, but there are enough addresses so that every one of those billions of addresses could be communicating with its own distinct collection of billions of devices…and there'd still be addresses left over! That's a great feature in some ways, because it means we aren't likely to have a problem with running out of IPv6 addresses—but it does mean that the routers have to be smarter about managing these updates.

IP Address Notation

Although we've talked about an IPv4 address as though it were just an integer, it's more typical to think of it as a sequence of four bytes. A byte is eight bits, which is enough to represent numbers from 0 to 255. So each of the four bytes of an IPv4 address can be any value from 0 to 255. The bytes of an IPv4 address are written separated by dots, so the lowest possible IPv4 address is 0.0.0.0. Similarly, the highest possible IPv4 address is 255.255.255.255. Writing it this way doesn't change the meaning or value of the address. You can think of it as being a little like saying that the phone number 6175551212 is more easily understood when written as 617–555–1212. We haven't changed the numbers provided to the telephone network when you dial that number, we're just viewing and presenting it differently.

This notation lets us write a single endpoint's IP address. What if we want to write the addresses of two different endpoints? One solution would be just to write out two separate addresses, like when we wrote 0.0.0.0 and 255.255.255.255 above. But a different trick is available if we confine ourselves to groups of addresses that are adjacent—that is, sequential numbers.

Our approach is essentially the same as what we can use for printing part of a multipage document. We can list multiple individual page numbers like "3, 7, 22" or we can talk about a page range like "7–22." The page range has the nice property that our specification of the pages can be similar in size, whether we are talking about only a few pages or a very large number of pages. For example, the page range "1002–1003" and the page range "1002–5003" are the same length in this sentence, even though the second range refers to thousands more pages than the first.

In the same way that we can refer to a sequence of adjacent pages, we can refer to a collection of adjacent addresses. But instead of listing the starting and ending page numbers, we provide an IP address and a *netmask*—a notation that indicates how many of the IP address bits must have exactly the values provided. What's a little weird about netmask notation is that it mixes two different ways of thinking about the IP address. The dotted notation like "192.163.7.1" represents the 32 bits of an IP address as four decimal numbers, one for each of the four 8-bit bytes. The netmask written with a slash like "/31" is also a decimal number, but refers to the *binary* representation. To understand what /31 really means, we can't somehow apply "31" to one of those numbers in the dotted address, like "192" or "7." Instead we have to think about the address "192.163.7.1" written out as 32 bits:

11000000.10100011.00000111.00000001

(the dots are included only for clarity)

The netmask /31 means that we hold the left 31 bits fixed, but let the remainder (only 1 bit in this case) vary. Similarly, a netmask /8 would mean that we hold the left 8 bits fixed and let the remaining 24 bits vary. Again, this may seem esoteric—but it's basically accomplishing the same effect as specifying a page range of "7–22" in a document, just within the different world of network addresses.

The simplest examples are ones that no one would really use, but they're worth examining just to understand the notation. If we write 255.255.255.255/32, that means the same as just writing 255.255.255.255— that is, it's a single IP address where all four bytes have the maximum value. The /32 at the end says that all 32 bits must match exactly.

What happens if we change the netmask to be /31? That means only the top 31 bits need to match exactly. So 255.255.255.255/31 means two addresses: 255.255.255.254 and 255.255.255.255.

We're not limited to doing this only at the top end of the possible IP addresses. For example, 192.128.7.0/31 is also a pair of addresses: one address is 192.128.7.0, and the other address is 192.128.7.1. If we use the next smaller netmask number, we double the number of addresses represented. So 192.128.7.0/30 is a quartet of addresses:

192.128.7.0

192.128.7.1

192.128.7.2

192.128.7.3

and similarly, 192.128.7.0/24 is the set of 256 addresses from 192.128.7.0 to 192.128.7.255.

Summarizing and Filtering

Instead of sharing every individual detail, routers summarize their routing information. Rather than sending information about every individual IP address, a router will group the addresses into *subnets*. Subnets are specified by the netmask notation we just introduced. All of the IP addresses in a subnet are "routed alike," at least until they reach the router that has been summarizing them in its advertisements.

Summarizing means that routers can advertise a lot of contiguous addresses with only a small amount of information. That's one part of how the network can manage a lot of routing information. In addition, a router is not obliged to advertise everything it knows; so routers don't just summarize, they also filter their routing information. Although a router may be able to reach a particular destination, it may not want to advertise that ability if it doesn't want to receive and handle traffic for a destination. In addition, it may not be helpful to advertise destinations for which the router is a poor choice.

Distributed Management

We now understand something about how the network does routing at large scale. A further wrinkle is that the management of routing tables is not performed centrally. We can imagine what would happen if we did manage the tables centrally: we would collect advertisements from all of the network devices, mush them all together in some kind of global routing table, and then distribute the relevant pieces. Unfortunately, we would find that the computation of new routes was getting slower and slower as the network got bigger.

Instead, the routing computation is distributed across the routers. Each router makes local decisions based on what it knows locally and what it learns from its neighbors. Those local decisions determine both how the router handles traffic that it receives, and also what information it shares with its neighbors. The distributed computation can scale up in a way that the centralized computation can't. But the trade-off is that decisions have to be made with less information. Each router is making decisions based only on its local knowledge, not a full global view.

Network Address Translation (NAT)

We initially made a simplifying assumption that every endpoint has a unique IP address, but we also noted that there are only about 4 billion IPv4 addresses. However, there have been more than 4 billion internet-connected devices for a long time—indeed, estimates for the count of internet-connected devices were already in the neighborhood of 10 billion in 2014. Obviously we can't give each of those 10 billion devices a different address if there are only 4 billion total addresses. So how does IP communication work if we have to somehow share and reuse IP addresses?

The solution is a technology called *network address translation* or *NAT* (pronounced like "gnat" or the first syllable of the word "natty"). NAT is a little like forwarding postal mail: we can cross out the original address and write in a new one instead. However, we can see that there must be something more than just crossing out one 32-bit address and writing in a new 32-bit address: that won't solve the problem that a 32-bit address only lets you reach 4 billion different destinations.

Crucially, there's a kind of subaddressing at each endpoint. A connection goes between two IP addresses, but that's not the whole story of addressing. In addition to the IP address, there is a *port* number at each end of the connection. A port is an integer that just serves to distinguish among connections at each end. We mentioned ports previously when we were explaining the mechanics of browsing (chapter 15), but now we're looking at the more general usage of ports. Broadly, we use ports to ensure that when there are two or more connections between the same IP addresses (say, Alice and Bob) neither end gets confused about which messages belong to which connection.

If we just want to distinguish the connections, we could simply increment the port number on either side to make sure that it's different from other connections. That might mean that the first connection from Alice to Bob is actually marked as "Alice:0" (Alice's IP address, port 0) for its sender while the second connection from Alice to Bob is marked as "Alice:1" (still Alice's IP address, but now port 1). Once we have that arrangement in place, we don't have to worry about confusing the two connections on Bob's side, because even though they have identical IP addresses for their source, Bob actually distinguishes connections based on the combination of IP and port.

The actual port assignment rules are a little more complicated than this example, but not by much. In general, the party starting the connection (the

Source address	Source port	Destination address	Destination port

Figure 19.6
A quad.

client) picks a number that is locally unique for its client port. However, the client also picks the port number for the other end of the connection, choosing a number that indicates what kind of service is desired. For example, port 80 usually means "I would like a web server to respond."

Once the connection is set up, each packet has four different items of addressing information. Two of them relate to the source (sender) of the packet, while the other two relate to the destination (receiver) of the packet. This set of four items (source address, source port, destination address, destination port) is sometimes called a *quad*. See figure 19.6.

The trick of NAT, then, is that there really isn't (only) a 32-bit space of IP addresses, even if we confine ourselves to the older IPv4 scheme. Each end of a conversation is really identified by the combination of a 32-bit IP address and a 32-bit port. Whereas 32 bits only let us have 4 billion different addresses, each additional bit doubles that number (we saw the power of successive doubling with the emperor and the chessboard in chapter 7). As we mentioned earlier, a 64-bit address space is really huge. So if we're willing to do some bookkeeping, we can use this larger address space by translating between quads at convenient boundaries.

In an IP network, messages with the same quad are treated alike. If there are multiple messages with the same quad in the network, they must be different parts of what is logically a single flow of information between the communicating parties. The game of NAT is to shift the traffic from using one quad to another without inadvertently colliding with any other quad in use.

Effective use of NAT usually requires us to distinguish between public IP addresses and private IP addresses. A public IP address must be globally unique and can't be reused, but private IP addresses are visible only inside an organization and can be reused by many different organizations. For a private IP address to connect outside the organization, its connection goes via a public IP address. Outgoing traffic from a private address is translated ("natted") to a public IP address and port. Correspondingly, incoming traffic to that public IP address and port is natted back to the private address and port.

Routing Failure

The last layer of interconnection is easiest to understand in terms of routing failure. Is routing failure a real issue? Yes. One famous problem in the early days of networking happened when a router partly failed. Each of the routers maintained a table of costs that it used for making routing decisions. Unfortunately, one router's hardware failed in a very particular way: that table of costs always seemed to contain zeros. The faulty (all-zero) information in the local routing table meant that the router had faulty (all-zero) costs for reaching every other known destination.

When the router advertised that zero-cost information to its neighbors, they updated their routing tables accordingly. The broken router's neighbors then forwarded that information to their neighbors in turn. Soon the entire network had learned that this one defective router was the best route to every network destination. The natural, if unfortunate, result was that every other router sent all of its traffic to that one router. And the further natural, if unfortunate, result was that the defective router "crashed" due to overload, so no one's traffic reached its destination. The network would have recovered if the defective router had stayed down—if it had conformed to a simple fail-stop model. Instead, this is a vivid real-world example of a Byzantine failure. The router restarted and again tried to participate in the routing protocol with its neighbors: it again advertised that it had zero-cost routes to everywhere. A single failure in a single router meant that the entire network failed to deliver any traffic. Network service was only restored when the faulty router was identified and turned off.

Although this particular network failure was an unusual case, it does point to the next level of challenge in building networks. So far we have assumed that the routing is distributed but homogeneous. But the global internet is actually composed not only of distinct technologies for local networking, but also distinct technologies for routing. As a result, even a routing failure like the one we described will typically only affect a part of the internet, rather than the whole internet at once. Although the internet is an extremely complex system and parts of it have failed from time to time, it's unlikely that an internet-wide failure would ever eliminate networking service for everyone. The internet is actually structured as a federation of autonomous networks, and we examine that structure next.

Interconnecting Different Routing

Looking inside a particular single network, we will find that all the routers of that network participate in the same kind of computation. Looking inside an entirely different single network, we will again find that all the routers participate in the same kind of computation. But looking across those two networks, we often find that a router in one network is behaving very differently from a router in the other network. To build an internet, we have to do more than bridge between different local-networking technologies. We also have to bridge between networks that are using different kinds of routing. As with local network technologies, we don't expect that the different routing mechanisms can talk to each other directly. Instead, we need to have special devices that know how to "talk" to both sides (see figure 19.7).

If we think of the two networks as being like fenced fields, a router with two different sides facing the two different networks is like a gate. A router operating in this way is sometimes called a *gateway* to distinguish it from an ordinary router.

Although this is a conceptually simple solution, it's expensive and complex in practice. In fact, we encounter much the same problem here that we had a little earlier when we wanted to communicate effectively across different local-networking technology. In the case of interconnecting local-network technologies, we concluded that it was foolish to build a collection of two-way gateways, and instead we would have a single consistent bridging format. In the case of the local networking technologies like Ethernet and "Othernet," that bridging format is IP. In a similar fashion, when we want to

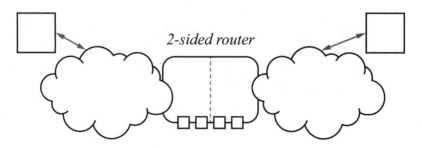

Figure 19.7
Connecting networks with different routing mechanisms.

interconnect differently routed networks, we have them communicate via a consistent bridging layer. So just as we saw that IP is a common layer that bridges among local-network technologies, so we now want to have a common layer that bridges among routing technologies. The common layer is a sort of "inter-internet protocol," if you like.

That common layer between differently routed IP networks is actually called the *Border Gateway Protocol*, or *BGP*. An IP network may contain a huge number of nodes and different local-network technologies, spread all over the world; but from the perspective of BGP that whole network is a single entity if it is operating under a single shared routing computation. In BGP, such a single entity is called an *Autonomous System* or *AS*. BGP defines how an AS shares routing information with another AS. At this point you will likely not be surprised to know that each AS is identified by a unique number. For example, one of MIT's networks is AS number 3; Microsoft controls a network with AS number 3598; Apple controls a network with AS number 714; and so on. There's no system to the number allocation, they're just assigned in the order that organizations requested them. Figure 19.8 shows a three-AS network.

In roughly the same way that a router advertises the endpoints that it can reach, an AS advertises the endpoints that it can reach. But BGP advertisements typically contain much less detail than what a router advertises

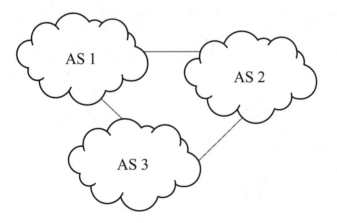

Figure 19.8
Three interconnected Autonomous Systems.

for routing, because the advertisements summarize an entire network as a single entity.

Within an AS, a router is constrained to cooperate closely with its peer routers; it is not free to pick and choose what it does, or else the routing computation becomes unreliable. In contrast, each AS is free to choose its degree of interaction with another AS. Thus the reason why the "A" of AS means "autonomous"—BGP is the level of networking at which choices can be made for pure economic or policy reasons, and no other entity's cooperation or agreement is required.

At the BGP level, the question of what to advertise is related to commercial considerations. For understanding these kinds of issues, it's useful to keep three general guidelines in mind:

1. Networks are generally happy to accept traffic to or from their paying customers.
2. Networks are generally OK with accepting traffic to or from other networks with similar volumes of traffic.
3. Networks are generally unhappy with being asked to deliver lots of traffic for some other network's customers.

Networks typically adjust what information they advertise, and to whom they advertise that information, so as to reflect these principles.

What determines the boundary of an AS? An AS could reach around the world (in a multinational network provider, like one of the big telecommunication companies) or it might be just a few machines in a lab. A particular network belongs in an AS if it shares control and routing policy with the other networks in that AS. Correspondingly, a particular network does not belong in a particular AS if that network's control and/or routing policy are distinct from that AS.

In much the same way that we worried about possibly running out of IP addresses, we might worry about running out of AS numbers. Fortunately, as with IP addresses, there is a useful distinction between public and private AS numbers. Public AS numbers are globally visible and carefully allocated, while private AS numbers are reusable in many different private networks because they can't be seen on the wider (public) internet.

The simple-seeming network cloud thus turns out to have at least three different layers of standardized formats and protocols. Over short distances, a local-networking technology like Ethernet allows messages to be sent among devices—even if a device is unplugged from one jack and then plugged into another one. Over long distances and across different local-networking technology, IP allows messages to be sent regardless of the physical distances and local-network details. And finally, BGP allows multiple autonomous IP networks to cooperate (or ignore each other) despite differences in their routing algorithms, commercial goals, or policies.

20 Browsing Revisited

In chapter 15, we described how a web service answers a request. However, we made a simplifying assumption in that description: we assumed that the web service was built using only a single server to answer all requests. This structure is not how any widely used service (such as Google search) actually works, for two important reasons:

1. The number of requests coming from across the world is far larger than what any single computer could actually handle.
2. Even if we miraculously had a single machine that was fast enough, we would prefer to use multiple computers for fault tolerance.

We'd like to replace the single server we assumed previously with the effect of a single massive server that is unstoppable. Our ingredients are large collections of real (smaller) servers that fail independently. Those servers can be placed in different specialized facilities—the *data centers* that we have mentioned previously. Like different servers, we expect that different data centers fail independently.

We know that multiple servers will be required, but how do we organize them? There are three essential approaches:

1. Use multiple copies of functionally equivalent servers in a single location
2. Use multiple layers of functionally distinct servers in a single location
3. Replicate the resulting multicopy, multilayer collection of servers across multiple distinct geographic locations.

Spraying Requests

The first step is to be able to distribute requests across a collection of servers, where the servers are all equally able to provide the necessary service. This

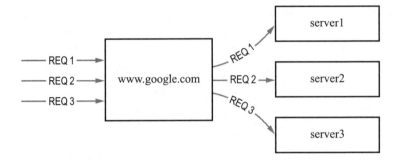

Figure 20.1
Spraying requests.

distribution is sometimes referred to as *spraying* the requests. A single "front-end" server sprays the traffic, acting as though it were the only server.

In figure 20.1, all of the clients issuing search requests are off to the left. We don't see the clients, just some of their requests—labeled Req 1, Req 2, and Req 3. All of the clients interact with the front-end server, labeled as www.google.com in the diagram. That single server appears to provide all the service to them. Unknown to the clients, the front-end server actually maintains a list of real "back-end" servers. In the diagram, those servers are labeled as server1, server2, and server3. The front-end server sends every request it receives on to one of the back-end servers. The front-end server operates as a switching point sending traffic on, but never tries to do any meaningful work on a request.

Because the front-end server is only touching the traffic long enough to redirect it, some other (back-end) server has to do all of the real work that's required for any particular request. When a back-end server has a result, it sends that result to the client. The back-end server will usually send that information in a way that looks as though the front-end server produced it.

There are special-purpose systems for doing the front-end traffic-distri-bution tasks. Such a special-purpose system is called a *content switch, load-balancer,* or *application delivery controller*—those are all basically the same kind of thing, just going by different names. Sometimes such a special-purpose system includes special hardware; more often, it is simply a specialized piece of software running on an ordinary server.

Whatever device or software is used, the effect is still similar: the back-end servers are presented as though they constitute a larger, more-powerful, more-fault-tolerant single server. The resulting *virtual server* is more capable than any of the individual servers can be. When we previously saw virtual memory and virtual machines (chapter 12), the "magic" came from the raw speed of the step-taking machinery. That speed made it possible to rearrange limited resources fast enough so that they looked unlimited, or at least much larger than they really were. In some ways the mechanisms involved in a virtual server are the reverse. Instead of a limited resource trying to look larger, we now have a large collection of servers trying to look like a single server.

Let's pause to consider what's solved and unsolved so far. This arrangement lets us build a "team" of multiple servers, where each one is able to take the place of another. We can now expect to handle many more requests than any single server could, by spraying the requests across multiple servers. However, we are still vulnerable to the failure of a single back-end server once it's started working on one of those requests. The server might simply not give an answer; or it might fail in a way that has a bad effect on other requests. For example, the server might fail while holding a lock on some shared data (recall locks from chapter 10). Or the server might fail after only doing a part of some set of changes, which would leave shared data inconsistent. So spraying the traffic across servers isn't enough; we also need some way of making sure that an activity that fails "in the middle" of something complicated doesn't leave behind a mess.

Fortunately, there are such mechanisms in the form of *transactions*. Transactions are a powerful approach to build all-or-nothing changes to data. If a failure occurs partway through a set of changes, the transaction mechanism has recorded enough information so that the changes can be undone or redone to get back to a consistent state. Transactions are a fascinating subject in their own right, but the crucial summary for a nonspecialist is that they provide the right kind of selective reversibility or time travel; they allow for complex partial changes to be automatically canceled out if there's a failure.

What if we aren't concerned about a partial failure muddling the data, but a complete failure of the front-end server? As described so far, we've increased the capacity of the system but we're still vulnerable to a failure in that one component. It seems like we want to have multiple front-end servers, but we'll have to do something different to distribute traffic across them: it clearly won't improve anything to just put another front-end server in place to spray requests across multiple front-end servers. We'll solve this

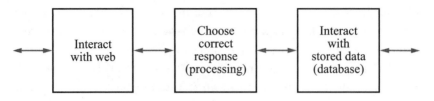

Figure 20.2
Three tiers between user and stored data.

problem later in the chapter. First we'll take up another way of increasing the capacity of those multiple servers.

Tiers

We know that we want to build a web service that is more powerful in terms of capacity and resilience than what we can do with a single server. Grouping multiple servers to look like a single server was the first step, but there are additional techniques we can apply to build large services.

We can think about dividing the service into stages, as in figure 20.2.

We've divided a typical application into three different kinds of activities. On the left is the work required for interacting with web clients: maintaining the conversations with clients, and translating between the vocabulary of the web and the data structures of the application. In the middle is the work of determining what to do with a particular request. That work might be pretty straightforward, or it might require a lot of computation. On the right is the work of interacting with various kinds of stored data. For typical applications, this "three-tier" framework works well—although it's not *always* the right choice.

To really take advantage of a multitiered structure, we don't just think about a logical division of the application as we did above. Instead, we actually use multiple servers to implement each separate tier. Within a tier, all of the servers are able to provide the same function; so within a tier, it doesn't matter which of the servers we use. As a result, the number of servers in a tier can be adjusted to match the demands of that tier, independent of what may be required in other tiers.

The next diagram replaces the simple three-tier structure from a logical view of three stages to a physical view of tiered servers, with multiple servers per tier.

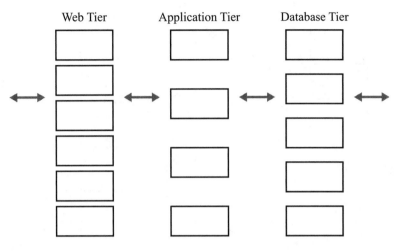

Figure 20.3
Each tier may have a different numbers of servers.

In figure 20.3, all three tiers consist of multiple servers, but the tiers are not the same size. The boxes in each column represent servers in a tier. In this particular example, the web tier has the most servers, and the application tier has the least. This is just an example—there is no particular rule that governs their relative sizes. The number of servers in a tier is determined by the workload of that tier.

This diagram still uses the same simple arrows that we showed previously connecting the three logical stages. However, a more accurate diagram would be more complicated, with many more arrows. Traffic within each tier may be balanced independently of any other tier's actions. If we consider the path of a single request through the servers (figure 20.4), it's entirely possible that the request would be handled by a server in a quite different place in each tier.

As shown by the dashed arrows in figure 20.4, the server shown at the top of the web tier handles the request, then passes it to the server at the bottom of the application tier, which then passes it to the server in the middle of the database tier.

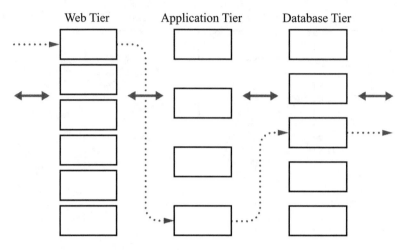

Figure 20.4
A single request may have a complex path.

Geographic Distribution

We first saw how we could spray traffic across servers, then we saw how we could divide processing into stages using tiers. Those were two approaches that spread the work across multiple machines. Spreading the work lets us build high-capacity, high-resilience multiserver systems.

There is a third ingredient we can add to the mix: we can divide up these servers geographically, rather than having them all in one area. Even if we are only concerned with fault-tolerance, it's often useful to have some servers in one data center and some other similar servers in a different data center. We know from our previous musings on separation (chapter 13) that we don't want to have distance just for the sake of distance. But some geographic distance can help the system to tolerate a local natural disaster like an earthquake or hurricane. To gain resilience from geographic diversity, there are two requirements. First, the two data centers must have enough independence that one can continue functioning even if there's some kind of catastrophic failure in the other one. Second, the servers in each data center have to be able to provide similar services even if the other data center is unavailable.

Is resilience the only reason for dispersing servers geographically? No, there are at least two additional reasons: regulations and speed.

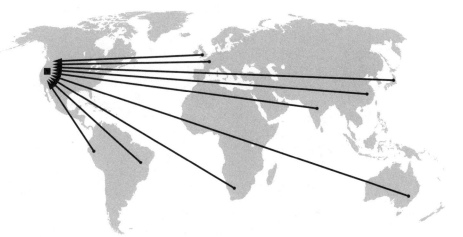

Figure 20.5
Serving global clients from a single site.

Let's first consider regulations. Sometimes there is a legal requirement to keep certain kinds of information in one country and other kinds of information in a different country: for example, information about German customers might have to be stored in Germany, while information about French customers might have to be stored in France. So some geographic spreading of servers is driven primarily by reasons of law and regulatory compliance.

Next, let's consider speed. The spreading of servers across geography is sometimes prompted by performance requirements. As we mentioned in chapter 13, light is not actually very speedy for certain kinds of interaction across long distances. If an application has demanding performance requirements *and* its users are spread out across the world, it becomes important to spread servers out as well—not so that they fail separately, or are in particular countries, but so they are closer to those users.

In figure 20.5, we show a variety of requests from around the world interacting with a service that is delivered from a single site in California. It's worth noting both the length of the arrows and the density of lines near that data center.

In contrast, figure 20.6 takes the exact same traffic but now sends it to three data centers—there is still one in California, but now there is also one in London and another in China. Many of the longest lines have become

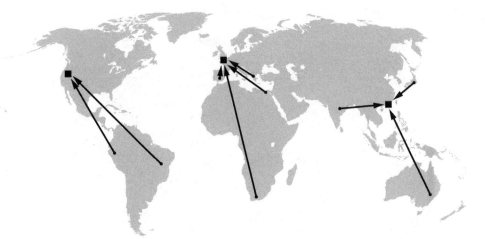

Figure 20.6
Serving global clients from multiple sites.

much shorter, which probably translates into better performance for the users issuing those requests. And now the global service is less vulnerable to a catastrophe that affects the California data center.

This geographic distribution typically arises from cunning use of DNS, which we previously examined in chapter 15. Nothing about DNS requires that every client looking up a name be given the exact same answer. So it's possible to arrange for clients in different parts of the world to be sent to *different* servers. In addition, that same trick solves the problem that we saw earlier in this chapter, where we had multiple back-end servers but also wanted to have multiple front-end servers. In a single data center we are not concerned with geographic distribution, but we can still use DNS to spread traffic. We might think that if we can spread traffic using DNS, why did we bother with introducing those front-end servers earlier in the chapter? It turns out that cunning use of DNS is quite a bit weaker than a front-end server in terms of the level of traffic control possible. So we'd choose DNS for that purpose only when we can't do something better.

Some specialists have built their own networks of servers for reaching widespread clients. The networks they have built, and sometimes the companies that run them, are called *content distribution networks* or *CDNs*. The business of a CDN is effectively renting out some or all of its servers in "slices" for different applications. If you could benefit from having your application on lots of different servers, but it doesn't make economic sense for you to set up and run all those servers yourself, you are a good candidate for a CDN.

To summarize: building a large-scale version of a web service like Google search may include geographic distribution of servers. A part of that geographic spread is to improve fault-tolerance, but there may also be reasons connected to law and to system performance.

Cloud Computing and Big Data

All of these server-side structuring tricks are effectively invisible to the browser. From the client's point of view, all of this complexity is hidden. The client's activity is unchanged from what we described previously: the client (still) simply converts URLs to entities and displays them. The server side may be organized using geographic distribution, multiple physical servers to implement a logical server, and/or the layering of servers in tiers—but the client doesn't need or want to know about that structure.

Since the client is unaffected by the structure of the implementation, there is a tremendous opportunity for adjusting the scale of a multiserver system. If there's high demand, more servers can be added: more capacity but a higher cost. If there's low demand, some of the servers can be taken away: lower cost but a lower capacity. When we take advantage of this kind of flexibility, we can apply the term *cloud computing*. Where we previously had a network cloud that let us wave our hands about how messages traveled from one endpoint to another, now even some endpoints are being pulled into the cloud and turned into computing services rather than identifiable machines. In cloud computing, the supply of computing and storage is treated as a metered utility, like electricity or gas. With such a metered model, you use more or less as you need it, and you are effectively renting the underlying machinery rather than owning it.

You and your household likely neither know nor care how your electricity is generated. Likewise, the typical cloud computing user is largely indifferent to the exact physical implementation of the computing being performed. Instead, the cloud computing user supplies one or more virtual machines to perform the computation, along with identifying the computing and storage to be used. The cloud computing supplier responds to these demands by allocating or deallocating servers and storage to be used by the virtual machine(s).

Cloud computing is interesting in its own right as a way of building flexible large-scale services. In addition, the cloud computing approach is a crucial ingredient for most uses of *big data* techniques. In those big data approaches, large collections of computing power are briefly brought to bear on large collections of data to produce useful insights in ways that were not previously feasible. The key change that enables big data is more economic than technological: cloud computing allows for the short-term rental of large collections of computing resources.

A roughly similar situation arises when considering cars and transportation. If we own a single car, we can effectively lend it to a different friend on each of a dozen different days; but if all dozen friends are coming on the same day, perhaps to attend a special event, our single car is not very useful. It's more powerful to be able to rent a dozen different cars for a single day in the case where all dozen friends are coming to town simultaneously. Entertaining all dozen friends simultaneously might be very appealing, and would be impossible if we were limited to what we could do with a single car.

In a similar fashion, it can be useful to apply a large collection of computing simultaneously to get a result quickly. The cost may be the same as applying a smaller amount of computing for a long time to get the result. The appeal of big data techniques largely center on this rearrangement enabled by cloud computing: it's possible to get results much faster for roughly the same cost.

IV Defending Processes

21   Attackers

In the first two parts of the book, we considered how computer systems work. Then, in the third part, we considered how computer systems fail. Knowing that failures are inevitable, we then looked at ways to tolerate failures by incorporating redundant resources. With appropriate arrangements of those resources, we can ensure that the system continues working despite occasional failures.

In this last part of the book, we take up problems and solutions related to deliberate attacks. Whereas before we were concerned with "natural" failures—the impossibility of creating perfect components—now we are concerned with "artificial" failures, caused by attackers seeking to take down otherwise healthy systems. This chapter looks at the nature of deliberate attacks. The remaining chapters elaborate on some of the issues identified—the profound vulnerability of software and the crucial role of cryptography. Then we bring several threads together into an explanation of how the Bitcoin system operates.

Defending: An Overview

Defending against attacks is much less satisfying than the previous topics, in both economic and philosophical terms. When we are considering either normal operation of a system or operation of a system within an expected failure model, we can make useful statements about the system's expected costs and behavior. However, our analysis is subject to a kind of implicit footnote, saying roughly "as long as there's no terrible unanticipated development." When we are focusing on normal operation or tolerating ordinary failures, we can still count it as a success (of sorts) if the system behaves well except in some unusual, completely unanticipated, strange circumstances. In contrast, when we shift to a concern with attacks and deliberate bad behavior, we are essentially taking on that disclaiming footnote as our primary concern. The problem then is twofold:

1. We can't really anticipate every kind of attack that could be mounted;
2. Even if we could somehow anticipate every attack, we don't typically have the resources to defend against every single one of them.

In some ways we can see the situation as comparable to being a gladiator in a Roman circus. We can choose weapons and armor, and we can train ourselves, but we cannot be invulnerable. Too many weapons or too much armor makes us heavy and slow-moving; but speed and agility require giving up protections (whether weapons or armor) that we may dearly wish we had chosen instead.

We are necessarily in the uncomfortable position of choosing which attacks we can deflect, and accepting that we will fail if attacked in other ways. We also have to accept that the end goal is not perfect security. Most houses are vulnerable if a burglar is determined; the usual goal of a homeowner is not to have zero risk of burglary, but rather to have an acceptably low risk. Mechanisms like locks, lighting, alert neighbors, and police patrols all help to convince burglars to look for easier pickings elsewhere. As the old joke goes, you don't have to outrun the bear—you only have to outrun the other potential victims in the vicinity.

Viruses

Why are there misbehaving programs? Sometimes the misbehavior is an inadvertent flaw: as we've considered previously, it's hard to get programs right (see chapter 6). However, sometimes a program is intentionally written to misbehave. Such a program might be "correct" in achieving its author's goals, even though it is not being a well-behaved program from the perspective of an ordinary user.

One example of an intentionally misbehaving program is a *virus*. A virus acts primarily to propagate itself, and secondarily to achieve other effects. Some viruses can be very destructive, wiping out data or rendering computers unusable; others have essentially no effect other than persisting and spreading in ways that ordinary programs don't. One cause for concern is that even an apparently benign virus could do something destructive at a later point, when some triggering condition occurs or some triggering signal is received. (We might think of the oddly unpredictable "exploding program" we considered in chapter 6.)

As with biological viruses, hygiene is an important defense against computer viruses. Here, hygiene takes the form of avoiding exposure to unknown programs, and particularly the execution of an unknown program. That in turn requires knowing what actions allow a program to execute, and avoiding those unless you actually want to execute a particular program. The challenge for a non-expert is that so many innocent-seeming actions—clicking a link, opening an email—can initiate program execution, sometimes without any visible sign or warning of that effect.

A number of common viruses recruit the infected computer into service as a part-time slave, executing computational and network tasks on demand. A collection of such recruited machines is called a *botnet* and is often used by criminals and vandals to carry out large-scale attacks in ways that are hard to counter and hard to trace. That means that antivirus hygiene has benefits even apart from the obvious protection it offers your own machine: even if some virus lurking on your machine doesn't cause problems for you, it could cause problems for others. Your fellow users benefit if you practice appropriate antivirus hygiene, and keep yourself from being an unwitting participant in stealthy criminal activity.

Viruses and their "ecology"—hygiene practices, antivirus tools, and the like—seem like a strange aspect of using personal computers (PCs). We have many other kinds of electronic devices in our lives, many of them with some amount of software involved—and yet we don't typically worry about viruses or protection against viruses for those other devices. Where does the virus problem come from, and can it be eliminated?

Single-Purpose vs. Multipurpose

It's crucial to distinguish between a single-purpose device and a multipurpose device, because much of the vulnerability comes from the nature of being multipurpose. A PC is intended to be a kind of universal machine. Each of the different applications makes the computer behave differently. By changing among different programs, we are able to achieve the effect of dozens of special-purpose devices. Indeed, we are not limited to merely having multiple programs: we can also have complex ways in which programs affect other programs.

There are programs that create other programs, such as the programming-language translators called compilers (we will say much more about compilers later; see chapter 23). There are programs that modify other programs: one such program, called a *linker*, combines different components into a new larger program, fixing up the connections as needed. Another such program, called a *debugger*, inserts "hooks" into a program so that it's possible to follow the flow of a program's execution to understand what that program is doing. Finally, we already learned (chapters 8, 11, and 12) that operating systems are programs that control or switch among other programs. All of these program/program interactions are easy to take for granted, but they would actually be quite difficult to achieve if the machinery accepted only a single program or a small fixed set of programs.

A multipurpose device has an additional vulnerability if it supports multiple operating systems. In normal operation, the operating system is in charge of deciding what program runs next—but the operating system itself is a kind of program. The operating system can't be the mechanism that starts up the operating system, because the operating system isn't yet running. So how does an operating system start? There is usually a specialized program called a *boot loader* whose role is a little like a starter motor in an internal combustion engine. Just as a starter motor gets the engine running and then gets out of the way, a boot loader gets an operating system running and then does nothing more. The boot loader only understands how to load the operating system into the computer, and then hands control to that operating system. The operating system then starts its own activities of loading additional services and applications.

In terms of fighting viruses, part of the problem is that the operating system can't be in charge of trust and security until it's running. If a virus is able to affect the boot loader, or the data that the boot loader uses, then it won't matter how well the operating system defends itself against viruses—because the virus will have control before the operating system is even on the scene.

Computer scientists often use the term *code* as shorthand for "data that is intended to be a program." The power of a universal machine partly comes from the ability to read or construct ordinary, passive data that is then interpreted as active code. In particular, a program can grab a chunk of "data" produced by someone else and execute it. That's exactly what the boot loader does, and that's exactly what the operating system does. The newly executing program might transform our computer to do something far beyond what we could build or even envision ourselves. Converting passive data to active code is a marvelous capability, but it's two-edged. Being open to all the great and wonderful programs that can be built by other people also means that the system is open to all the awful and horrible programs that can be built by other people.

Extensibility and Viruses

In an earlier time, we didn't have to worry about viruses in our TV or other electronics. The distinction is not as simple as saying that devices now use more software. Even if the older devices were running software to control their functions, they weren't very extensible. Each electronic device was designed for a relatively narrow use case, and was not attempting to be anything like a universal computer. Any software involved was just an implementation "material," like the silicon chips or copper wires. Accordingly, in those older times there were no "apps" to download and run for a TV or stereo.

Because of the risks inherent in a multipurpose device, it is often wise to stick with a single-purpose device whenever that is workable. For example, some vendors sell various kinds of network "appliances" for corporate computing: each such appliance is marketed as a single-purpose device. One kind provides a particular kind of file storage, another kind provides a particular kind of filtering of network traffic, and yet a third kind provides a particular kind of "spraying" of traffic among multiple servers (as we saw previously in chapter 20). In spite of the name "appliance," these devices are not really appliances like your refrigerator or stove—built from the ground up for a single purpose. Instead, these network "appliances" are actually built as software running on ordinary PC—the same kind of hardware that anyone could go buy, not something exotic and unusual. As we have mentioned previously, a PC is very much a multipurpose device. It has no intrinsic function, but it can do a wide variety of tasks depending on how it's programmed.

In principle, a network appliance that is built on PC hardware could operate in much the same way if it were packaged as software to be loaded onto a PC. All of the interesting capabilities are in the software. Nevertheless, there is value to selling hardware and software together. When the software and hardware are bundled together as an appliance, the manufacturer can also modify the operating system on the PC to match the appliance use case, and thereby reduce vulnerabilities. For example, the manufacturer can remove the capability to load additional programs onto the PC. Such a restriction protects the primary function of the appliance: misbehaving "neighbor" programs running on the same hardware can no longer interfere with the primary program, because there simply are no such neighbors! Likewise, the manufacturer can also disable general-purpose communication mechanisms that might be avenues for virus attacks but are not actually needed for the appliance's primary function.

Packaging software into an "appliance" is an example of shrinking vulnerability by removing generality and programmability. We can also see an opposing trend of making devices "smart"—more flexible and more programmable, with more customization, downloadable apps, and the like. As a device becomes more programmable, it becomes more vulnerable to viruses and other kinds of deliberate misbehavior. There is no sure way of eliminating this risk except for eliminating the benefit. One possibility is to simply remove or disallow programmability. Another possibility is to allow programmability, but only via a trusted gatekeeper. In either case, an improvement in safety comes at the cost of reducing flexibility.

Preventing Viruses

Most of our single-purpose devices are not PCs that have been converted into appliances. Instead, they are devices like simple TVs or calculators that are only designed and built to serve one purpose. Such a single-purpose electronic device typically doesn't allow any conversion of data into processes once it leaves the factory. If it does allow such conversion, it typically has only a very tightly controlled update mechanism. In contrast, the whole point of a PC is to be the engine powering a wide variety of useful programs, most of which could not be anticipated by the people producing and selling the PC. Using a similarly narrow "update" mechanism for a general-purpose PC would reduce its value considerably, even if such a restriction might also reduce that machine's vulnerability.

Is it impossible to have a virus-free system? No, but it might well be impractical. Programmers know that it's possible to build a very small program that's correct. It's hard to do much better because it's easy to exceed the programmer's cognitive limits (see chapter 6). Those cognitive limits seem to be a part of what it means to be human. Techniques exist to build software well despite those cognitive limits, but they are expensive; except for systems whose failure can kill people, it's generally uneconomical to do better.

In the same way that it's possible to build a small program that is correct, it's also possible to have small systems that allow the conversion of data into processes without flaws. The challenge is in keeping such systems small. In principle it might be possible for each user to write the exact applications and operating system they need, with no extraneous features at all. However, that would be a very different world from the one in which we actually live. Everyone would be a programmer, and everyone would construct their own software environment from scratch. There would be no commonality of computing environments and no reason to share programs. As a result, there would be no virus problems. However, we would all have to do a lot of work on building and maintaining our own personal software—which might well be a bigger problem than viruses.

In contrast to the expense of producing the first copy of a correct piece of software, the production of an additional copy is essentially free. Recall that software is so evanescent that sometimes we have trouble deciding if it's real (chapter 2). The "manufacturing" of software is not at all like the manufacturing of other goods. Indeed, the usual problem for a software vendor is that it's too easy to produce copies of software that haven't been paid for. A radical analysis of the software and information business argues that the very notion of property and trade needs to be rethought when applied to software. After all, if I can give you the software that I have without giving up anything myself, that's quite different from a conventional exchange. In more typical (non-software) settings, selling you my widget means that you now have it—but I don't.

Since the production of the first copy of correct software is expensive, but its subsequent duplication is extremely cheap, there are strong economic forces working against our hypothetical world in which everyone programs their own systems. Instead, those economic forces steer us into a world where there are only a small number of different implementations for generally useful functionality. In practice, it is much more economical for operating systems and applications to be shared among many users.

Detecting Viruses

At this point we've come to understand that if we have a multipurpose (extensible, programmable) system, it's vulnerable to viruses. So if we can't *prevent* all viruses, can we at least *detect* them? Can we build some kind of guaranteed-reliable virus detector? Not really. Once again, it may be possible to solve the problem on a very small scale, but not on a large scale or for general cases.

The problem of determining whether a given program misbehaves is just a form of the halting problem that we previously examined (chapter 7). The halting problem in its narrowest form says that there are circumstances in which we can't build a program to predict another program's behavior. Now, from a philosophical perspective it is important to note that this limitation could be meaningless. The existence of *some* programs that are unpredictable doesn't necessarily imply anything about whether the programs we care about can be handled correctly. It's possible that all interesting programs can be analyzed successfully, and the theoretical limit would then have no impact at all on our ability to find problems. The philosophical argument here is like learning that blueberries might be a carcinogen, but also learning that the lowest dose that might cause cancer requires eating only blueberries continuously for 20 years. The possible carcinogenic impact might still be interesting information, but it's not likely to have any practical effect on our lives.

But in reality, the halting problem is important guidance. The reason it's important is not so much because we know for certain about the characteristics of interesting programs; instead, it matters because we're in an adversarial situation. We are attempting to find viruses, while the attackers (people writing viruses) want to hide them from us. If they're smart, the virus-writers will exploit whatever opening(s) they can find. The existence of the halting problem says that the virus-writers are pretty much guaranteed to have some avenues open for exploitation. The underlying theory here says that there are some things the good guys will miss, no matter how hard they work.

To review, problems with viruses arise because:

1. our computers are generally programmable,
2. we use software that we didn't write ourselves, and
3. no trust mechanism is 100 percent reliable.

We can reduce or eliminate virus vulnerabilities if we use devices without general programmability—like single-purpose appliances without upgrade or extension capabilities. We can also *completely* eliminate virus vulnerabilities if we are prepared to write *all* of the software ourselves, including all of our programming tools. But as soon as we trust another person's software, it's hard to be sure of what's in it. Even innocent-seeming software tools can be instruments of subversion, as we will explore further in the next chapter.

Ken Thompson is a famous computer scientist with many accomplishments, but we are interested in him primarily for what he did to teach the world about the problem of trust in software systems. Among his achievements, Thompson was one of the inventors of an operating system named Unix that has been very popular and influential. In 1983 that work won him the Turing Award, often described as the "Nobel Prize of computer science." That might not seem very relevant to our story, but here's where things get interesting.

In his Turing Award acceptance speech, Thompson disclosed that he had deliberately created a weakness in Unix—he had built in a secret mechanism that computer scientists would call a *back door*. Specifically, Thompson had arranged it so that *any* Unix system allowed him to sign in. Every Unix system in the world would allow him this privilege, even though system administrators would not see any indication that he could do this—for example, he did not appear in any lists of authorized users. Further, Thompson had built the back door so that it was extremely well hidden. Without knowing his specific trick—which we will examine in this chapter—it is unlikely that even the most careful scrutiny would have found it.

The scene must have been strange indeed when Thompson gave his talk. When dignitaries assemble to confer a major annual award—even in a young field like computer science—one expects a certain bland predictability to the event. A few people stand up to speak, there are various polite rounds of applause, the awards are handed over, photographs are taken, and then everyone goes home. The audience is emphatically not expecting to learn new information, and they're certainly not expecting to hear a borderline confession of borderline criminal behavior. But that's what they got at that particular Turing Award convocation.

Although Thompson did not use the word "hack" in his Turing talk to refer to his construction, the mechanism is most commonly referred to now as Thompson's Hack or the Ken Thompson Hack, or KTH for short. The word "hack" has been used with both positive and negative connotations. Among engineers, "hack" is often a positive term for an ingenious trick. In the media, "hack" is usually a negative term for an attack on the integrity of computer systems. What Thompson described is a hack in both senses, and it is eye-opening when properly understood. (In my experience, even many computer professionals do not really understand its significance.)

Translating High-Level Language

To appreciate the mechanism Thompson used, we must be aware of two aspects of programming that are important in practice but have not yet appeared in our discussion of computer science concepts.

1. The steps taken by computer hardware are *very* small and simple: they are so tiny and repetitive, and so many of them are required to get anything useful done, that they are a poor match for human cognitive capabilities. Instead of working at the machine's level of tiny steps and mechanisms, humans generally program in terms of *high-level languages*: more comfortable languages that express the computation with fewer, more sophisticated operations.
2. Operating systems can be—and usually are—written in terms of these high-level languages.

The Thompson hack cunningly takes advantage of these two aspects of the computational landscape.

Before we go further, we should consider a concrete example of a high-level language vs. the machine code that's really executed. A very simple case is the kind of thing that we've written before in talking about fragments of programs, like

$y \leftarrow x+1$

We can understand this easily enough: something called y is going to be updated to contain the result of adding the value of x and 1. But the instructions actually available on the machine don't allow for abstract variable names like x and y. Although the machine instructions do let us add one to a value and store it somewhere, using those instructions requires relentless attention to concrete details, such as exactly where each of these variables is stored. Instead of talking about x and y, the machine instructions need to specify particular memory addresses.

Working in machine instructions is roughly as annoying as if we had to refer to people by globally unique ID numbers instead of names. Instead of introducing John to Jane, we have to introduce 492–93–2901 to 937–01–3874, and continue to use those numbers consistently thereafter.

Worse is that the machine's addition operations can only be applied to special locations called *registers*. So not only do we have to talk about the abstract values in terms of concrete locations with long numbers, we also have to move things in and out of these special registers. To return to our example of John and Jane, we not only have to introduce 492–93–2901 to 937–01–3874, but we first have to escort each of those people (as identified by number) to a particular room before the introduction can take place. And afterward, because there's only a limited number of such rooms available, we have to be prepared to escort both of them back to where they came from after we've introduced them to each other.

What has finally been accomplished after all that shuffling and bookkeeping? Only the addition of two numbers, which might seem kind of trivial.

The great thing about a high-level language is that it lets the programmer write something simple, that's similar to the way they want to think about the calculation. Then those high-level expressions are translated into all of the necessary numbers, moving, and bookkeeping required to get the real work done. But a key consequence is that the "human-friendly" programming language must be translated into "machine-friendly" instructions before the originally written program can actually be executed by the computer.

Thompson's Hack: Simple Version

Returning now to Thompson's Turing lecture, there were two elements to his attack. We'll first identify the concrete elements of his hack, then extract the general principles.

The Unix operating system is written in the programming language called C. Computers can't run C programs directly; instead, those programs have to be translated into simpler machine instructions. This process is much like the one we outlined for the expression "$y \leftarrow x + 1$."

The program that translates C into machine instructions is itself a program written in C, and then translated into machine instructions for execution. It's called cc (for "C compiler"). We'll use the terms "compiler" and "translator" interchangeably in this chapter. A computing professional might quibble that not all translators are compilers, but that distinction doesn't matter for our purposes.

Figure 22.1 shows how a simple program is processed by the compiler cc. All we're really doing here is introducing a diagram to match the narrative we gave before about the need to translate from a C version to a machine-code version. Notice again that the C compiler is itself machine code: the computer has to execute it to perform the translation.

Next, figure 22.2 shows how cc executes to translate itself. The executing cc (in the center, heavy lines) takes in a version of cc written in C (on the left) and produces a version of cc written in machine code (on the right).

One element of Thompson's hack is a high-level language that is translated by a program in the same high-level language. The other element is that the operating system is also written in the same high-level language. The operating system is itself a program—albeit a special kind of program—and like other high-level-language programs, it must be translated into machine instructions before it can be executed.

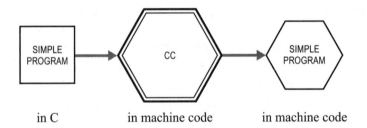

Figure 22.1
Compiler cc translates an ordinary program.

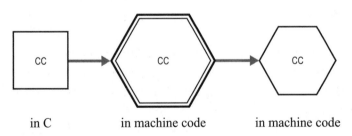

Figure 22.2
Compiler cc translates itself.

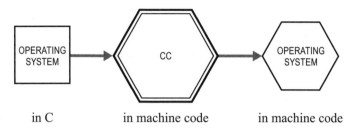

Figure 22.3
Compiler cc translates the operating system.

Since the operating system is also a C program, it has a similar diagram (figure 22.3).

In ordinary situations where we're not concerned about Thompson's hack, there is nothing very interesting about the relationship of the operating system to cc. However, as we mentioned before, Thompson's hack hid a "back door" in the Unix operating system that allowed him to log in. The C compiler is a part of the attack, as we'll see.

We'll start with a simplified version of the attack. In this version, we change the C compiler (cc) so that it can detect when it is translating a particular program. The program to be detected is the operating system. It doesn't matter to us how the translator does this detection—in a relatively large and stable program like an operating system, there are almost certain to be distinctive features that would let the translator identify it as the program of interest. The crucial part is that the translator behaves in a special way when it has figured out that it's translating the operating system.

Let's call our modified (naughty) translator "HackedC," or HC for short. We can use HC just like we used cc previously. For the moment we aren't going to think much about HC translating itself, although that will be important a little later. We mostly want to note that it's possible to modify the C compiler so that it does something naughty. In particular, something interesting happens when HC is translating the operating system (figure 22.4).

When HC translates the operating system, it does not do a straightforward translation: instead, it first detects (somehow) that this input is the operating system. Then, it (somehow) inserts the back door. In particular, when it sees a relevant part of the operating system, it not only translates as it is supposed to, but it also inserts some additional machine instructions that allow Thompson to login with his name and password.

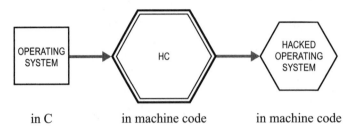

Figure 22.4
Compiler HC translates the operating system, naughtily.

We haven't really explained how the detection and rewriting happen, and we're not going to try to make that more detailed. For our purposes, it doesn't much matter *how* those happen, just that they can happen. The central point here is that there is a translation step involved in getting from *programming* the operating system to *executing* the operating system, and that the translation can be creatively subverted.

The full version of the hack gets more elaborate, as we'll see in the next section; but even with this simple version of the attack, there is a substantial security problem. The operating system has a back door that is not apparent from reading the C version. There is no back door in the C version—instead, the translation process of going from C to machine instructions inserted the back door.

However, the attacker built HC by modifying cc, which means that the defender can read the C version of HC to find the unusual behavior. Somewhere in HC there is a part that looks roughly like this:

If (modifying the operating system) then insert back door

There is nothing like this section in the original cc. So the defender can examine the system's C compiler, looking for this rather unusual behavior. The defender can find and remove the relevant operating-system-modifying instructions, converting HC back to cc.

Thompson's Hack: The Real Thing

Putting the back door attack into the translator instead of directly into the operating system made it harder to find. Repeating that trick produces a particularly devilish attack, and is the real version of Thompson's hack.

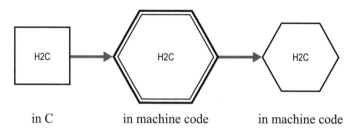

in C   in machine code   in machine code

Figure 22.5
Compiler H2C translates itself.

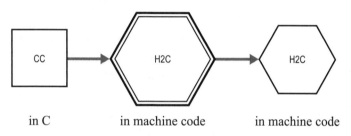

in C   in machine code   in machine code

Figure 22.6
Compiler H2C translates cc, naughtily.

In this refinement, we'll have yet another modified translator called "DoubleHackedC" or "H2C" for short. As we saw with its predecessor HC, H2C looks just like cc for most purposes, and we can show a diagram where it "produces itself" after translation (figure 22.5).

Like its predecessor HC, H2C detects when it's translating the operating system and inserts the back door. What's more interesting about this new version is that it also detects when it's translating the *translator*: the original, unhacked compiler cc.

So in roughly the same way that the translator could detect the operating system being translated and insert the back door, the translator H2C can instead detect that the original translator cc is being translated and insert the back-door-inserting instructions (figure 22.6).

Let's put that another way: H2C can detect when it is being asked to translate some version of the C compiler cc. What the user expects is for H2C to produce a straightforward machine-instruction version of what it's handed. But what H2C actually does is to produce a machine-instruction version of *itself*. It effectively substitutes itself for the translator program that it was asked to translate.

The Invisible Attack

This is all a little mind-scrambling, so let's pause briefly and consider the implications. Go back one step to where H2C is converted into a machine-instruction version. After that, the hacked part that does the sneaky rewriting can actually be removed (!) from the C version of H2C. The attacker doesn't need it in the C program anymore, because the corrupted translator will insert it.

Even though the translator-hacking trick doesn't appear at all anywhere in the C version of the translator, the functionality of creating a hacked translator will happen every time the translator is translated! Even if you get suspicious of the translator you're using, and you retranslate it from the correct-looking C version, you'll *still* get the hacked version as the output.

How could we get rid of this hack? Once it's in the translator, it's almost like an infection that we can't easily wipe out. We haven't said much about how the translator detects that it should play the trick. Depending on how that works, it might be possible to fool it, or to change the program so drastically that it no longer triggers the trick. But any ordinary process of rebuilding the translator and operating system is now thoroughly corrupted. Only a radical change might have a chance of eliminating this hack. Unless someone goes to the trouble of rebuilding little by little from a clean program—what computer scientists would call bootstrapping from the source code—the attack-inserting trick will stay in the translator almost regardless of how the translator is changed.

We may be able to improve our chances of detecting this problem if we maintain multiple independent C compilers. By carefully comparing what happens when a compiler translates itself vs. what happens when a compiler translates a completely different compiler, we can get indications of when this kind of back-door-inserting trick is happening. Unfortunately, that approach is expensive and probably unworkable in most cases, for all the reasons we already identified as problems when we previously considered multiversion software (chapter 17).

Assessing the Danger

Why is Thompson's hack so dangerous? We can analyze the problem informally in terms of "levels of trouble" from a back door or other attack. We start with the idea of a correctly functioning system, with no back door.

• The first level of attack simply puts the back door into the operating system directly. That creates a vulnerability, but one that is easily seen in the operating system program itself.
• The second level of attack has the *translator* insert the back door into the operating system. That creates a vulnerability that is invisible in the operating system but is still visible in the translator program.
• The third level of attack is to have the translator insert the back door-inserting instructions into the translator itself. That creates a vulnerability that is invisible in both the operating system *and* the translator.

What is the significance of all this fooling around with programs translating programs and inserting other programs? It helps delineate another limit of what we can do in the digital world. In chapter 6 we pointed out that the sheer size and complexity of programs, with their many discrete states, make it hard to ensure that a program functions correctly. We can now see that the problem is not only that a program may contain errors or mistakes that impair its function; but also, it can have carefully hidden mechanisms that subvert it undetectably. As much as we may want to think in terms of using mechanisms to protect us from untrusted code, there are some ways in which using someone else's software is inseparable from trusting them.

The style of subversion in Thompson's hack is not limited to software: its effects can occur in any system that has been touched by software. In the modern world, essentially any complex artifact is touched by software. For example, the step-taking machinery of modern computers is built by using elaborate design tools, made of software. Accordingly, an attacker using these ideas could put undetectable elements into those design tools. The subverting elements would then insert misbehaving components into the hardware being designed. A checking or analysis tool for the hardware could likewise be subverted. Subverted hardware could potentially be carrying out a version of this hack on all the instructions executed, making it literally impossible to avoid the subversion without replacing the hardware. The implication is sobering: you can't really trust anything that you didn't build yourself from the ground up—which is impractical. So in a practical sense, all of us are exposed all the time to systems we cannot really trust.

23 Secrets

So far, all of our discussion about enforcing trust has assumed that the problem is local. When we are dealing with a single step-taking machine, we can build trust mechanisms that are based on some aspect of that machine's physical implementation. For example, we have described ways in which an interrupt causes the execution of a particular piece of (local) trusted interrupt-handling code (chapter 11). It's also possible to load trusted programs into a particular part of the computer's (local) storage, so that attempts to write into that trusted area are very carefully checked. It's still not possible to avoid all attacks—for example, we have mentioned problems like viruses (chapter 21) and Thompson's hack (chapter 22)—but when everything is local, it is at least easy to distinguish the privileged operating system from an unprivileged ordinary application.

As we know from chapter 13, distributed systems create new problems for functionality, correctness, performance, and fault-tolerance. So it's really no surprise that distributed systems also create new problems relating to trust. In the world of distributed systems, there is nothing that corresponds to a privileged address or privileged section of memory. Instead, we have different entities separated by distance, operating autonomously, and communicating only in terms of messages.

Within any one of those messages, there are numbers (network addresses) that identify different machines for communication. It would be easy—but incorrect!—to think that those network-addressing numbers are like the memory-addressing numbers that identify different storage locations within a single machine. The difference is in how easy it is to forge network addresses. As received in a network message, each network address is just another kind of data. There is nothing to stop a rogue computer from forging those network addresses. So even if we were to decide that a particular unique machine would be the only one we would trust to give us special commands, we don't yet have any way to keep an attacker from pretending to be that special machine. In contrast, if an attacker tries to forge a special memory address, the local operating system's memory protection causes an interrupt (chapter 11).

Within a single machine, the hardware can actually enforce the meaning of an address and prevent certain kinds of misuse. The operating system doesn't need to prove its identity and its privileges to the programs that it is supporting, because it controls every aspect of the physical machine where it runs. (This total control is part of what makes it challenging to write a hypervisor for virtualizing the machine, as we mentioned in chapter 12.) In contrast, there is nothing in a network message that prevents the misuse or abuse of addressing information. The receiving operating system does not control any aspect of how the sender operates. Any machine can construct any message that it wants to, including intentional frauds and forgeries intended to deceive the recipient.

Recall that each remote communicating party is autonomous. Even if our local machine is secure, the remote machine may be subverted or controlled by an attacker. A remote communicating party is also distant—and therefore not subject to physical controls or inspections like the ones possible on a local machine. As a result of autonomy and distance, the receiver cannot rely on the local operating system or the physical hardware to enforce trust relationships. Instead, trust mechanisms in a distributed system depend on two parts:

1. The receiver has to make sure that the messages received are really coming from a specific party, not an impostor.
2. The receiver has to make sure that the specific party is actually one that it wants to trust.

It's important to keep in mind that both parts are crucial, and that neither part on its own solves the other problem:

• If messages are invulnerable to interception or tampering, but we don't know whether we're communicating with the right party, we could easily have a high-quality channel directly to the attacker.
• If we're highly confident that we are communicating with the right party, but our messages are subject to interception or tampering, then it's easy for an attacker to rearrange the conversation.

Secrets Are the Solution

Since we can't depend on hardware mechanisms, how can we have any kind of trust enforcement in a distributed system? In a distributed system, trust depends on secrets. It is possible to determine that a message is really from the right party, but they have to include some information that is known only to you and them.

The *sender* and *receiver* are collectively the *defenders*. The sender is trying to send a message to the receiver despite the efforts of the *attacker*. The defenders succeed if three conditions are all true:

1. the receiver receives the sender's message;
2. the receiver understands that received message identically to how it was sent; and
3. the attacker does not understand the message (possibly because the attacker never sees it).

The defenders fail whenever one or more of these conditions is not true. So it's a failure if the receiver never gets a message; or if the receiver gets a wrong version of the sender's message because of the attacker's efforts; or if the attacker can read the message.

The message as originally produced by the sender and ultimately consumed by the receiver is called *plaintext*. The plaintext is the original form of the message, before anyone has done any "secrecy work" on it. The plaintext is also the final form of the message, after all of the transformations have been performed. In contrast to the plaintext, the message in its protected, hidden form is called *ciphertext*.

These terms—attacker, defender, plaintext, and ciphertext—give us the vocabulary to talk more carefully about some of the different ways to protect information.

To support secrecy, we want to somehow have problems that are expensive for attackers but cheap for defenders. Fortunately, it turns out that there are many different kinds of problems where finding the solution is hard, but checking a possible solution is easy.

For example, if we are given a large collection of cities and distances between them, it's hard to come up with an itinerary that goes through all the cities and is the shortest possible—there are so many choices, and it's not obvious which one is right. But it's easy if we have a current "best" solution to see whether a new proposed solution is better: we just check whether the new solution is shorter and whether it still goes through all the cities.

Something of the same spirit is involved in secrecy mechanisms. The attacker has to do a lot of work (ideally, an infeasible amount of work)—as in the problem of finding the shortest possible route. Meanwhile, the defender has only a modest amount of work—as in checking a new possible route.

Steganography

The first possibility we consider is a situation where the defenders are sneaky and hide even the existence of the information. In such an arrangement, the defenders (sender and receiver) are trying to conceal their roles, as well as the existence of the ciphertext. The sender might physically conceal the message, or embed it in some other, more innocent-looking information. All of these kinds of games go by the technical term of *steganography*, or "concealed writing."

What does it mean to conceal the information? Consider the possibilities of secret messaging via junk mail delivery. Most households receive a postal delivery each day, and among the letters and bills are items that are advertisements or solicitations of various kinds. These are intended to grab attention, but they are frequently ignored or discarded. The junk mail itself is a carrier of visible information, although it is not considered very high-value information (thus the term "junk" is applied). But consider the possibility of the postal service conveying numeric information secretly via junk mail. It would be easy to convey a number between zero and five each day by supplying or suppressing pieces of junk mail, so that the number of pieces of junk mail delivered corresponds to the number being signaled. Of course, this example leaves open the question of what we would want to signal in this way, but it does convey the essence of how we could hide information inside another communication mechanism.

There are two primary drawbacks to this sneaky approach. The first problem is that it depends on the defenders having shared understanding. So it won't work between defenders who have never met before, and it can't readily adapt to a situation in which the scheme needs to be changed (perhaps because an attacker has discovered it). The other problem is that being sneaky implies low data rates. The more information you need to convey, the harder it is to hide its existence. By analogy, we can think of the problem that old-school spies could have when using microdots—tiny micrographic photo-reductions of graphical information. It might be easy for a spy to hide one microdot containing a small set of plans, perhaps by pasting it under a postage stamp or sneaking it under the jewel of a ring. But if you want to communicate a whole encyclopedia, and it turns into 500 microdots, suddenly it's much harder to avoid discovery.

Cryptography

Instead of hiding the existence of the message, the opposite extreme is to use some very well-known technique to obscure the content of the message. In this approach the ciphertext is readily available to the attacker, but its form is nevertheless unintelligible. The technical term for this approach is *cryptography*. There is some kind of "machinery" for transforming between plaintext and ciphertext, usually a program but sometimes a hardware/software combination. Whereas steganography tried to hide the existence of the message entirely, cryptography allows much more to be known. Apart from the plaintext itself, the only item kept away from the attacker is the secret used to drive the transformation from plaintext to ciphertext. That transformation-driving secret is called a *key*.

Usually a good key will be a random string of bits. The length of the key is determined by the encryption scheme, and in general a longer key corresponds to stronger (harder to attack) encryption. Unfortunately, keys for sensible-quality encryption are already much longer than people can remember (anywhere from 128 to 512 bits, at this writing). Keys of that length in turn require some kind of key-management system so that people can generate, store, and supply these long keys as required without needing to write them down or otherwise disclose them. Typically, the key-management system encrypts the key using a shorter password that is possible for a person to remember (this is a sort of recursive use of encryption!). Users employ a short password to send or receive encrypted data, but there is an intermediate step in which they have supplied a longer key that is used for the real encryption/decryption task.

One drawback to all of this machination is that each step, and each new level of complexity, offers another opportunity for attack. There is both a human system and a technical system involved in trust; often attackers succeed not by breaking the sophisticated mathematics of an encryption system, but simply by stealing or guessing passwords from careless users.

"Security through Obscurity"

As we have noted, a sensible implementation of cryptography assumes that the attacker already knows how the encryption machinery works. However, we should also mention another less wise implementation possibility: sometimes people advocate using a *secret* technique to transform the message, instead of a well-known technique. Intuitively, it seems like a secret technique should be even better protection than using a well-known technique; but this is one of those places where intuition is misleading. Although it's common for people to convince themselves that this approach is a good idea, it's not.

Why not? In practice, it's hard to limit knowledge of implementation techniques to only the two communicating parties. It's particularly hard to limit this knowledge if many users share the implementation: for example, in widely used operating systems and applications. In such cases, the supposedly secret implementation is unlikely to really be secret; instead, it's likely to be exposed in the worst-possible way, in which attackers know everything about it, but defenders are in the dark about its potential vulnerabilities.

In contrast, if defenders use a publicly known mechanism, then much less needs to be kept secret. Indeed, only the keys themselves need to be well-guarded. Both attackers and defenders have equal access to analyzing the implementation, which increases the likelihood that weaknesses will be identified and fixed by the defenders.

The overall approach of using secret implementations is sometimes summarized as "security by obscurity." It's important to be aware that this is a derisive slogan, not a desirable condition. If you encounter someone who is touting their use of security through obscurity, run away!

In the rest of the chapter, we'll focus instead on the right kind of solution: publicly known encryption systems, where the only secrets are keys.

Shared Secrets and One-Time Pads

If the encrypted message is readily available, and the mechanism is well known, then the only thing protecting the data is the cost of undoing the encryption. In general, the only advantage of the defenders is knowledge of the secret key. The attackers may well be able to use more computers, and they may also be willing to spend a long time in attacking a particular message. In a properly functioning encryption system, it is very easy for the defenders to encrypt and decrypt messages because they have the necessary key(s), but it is essentially impossible for an attacker to do likewise.

So far we've assumed that the defenders share secret keys. For thousands of years, the sharing of secret keys was a requirement for encryption to work. One of the most important—and possibly surprising—aspects of the computer age is that it led to an entirely different approach to secret communication.

First, let's understand the older approach and its limitations. There is a kind of "chicken-and-egg" problem for shared-secret communication: it's possible to have very secure communication between the defenders, but only if they can somehow first establish secure communication (oops!).

In shared-secret communication, the best security comes from using a *one-time pad*. Think of a one-time pad as a notepad where each sheet has a key printed on it. The communicating parties start with identical one-time pads. When communicating, they use the one-time pad for each new message by tearing off the top sheet (with the last-used key) and then using the key printed on the revealed sheet to send the new message. Of course, a software implementation doesn't use pads of paper or tear anything off. Instead, the "pad" is just a series of different keys, each used only once and then discarded. Because no key is ever reused, it doesn't matter if the attackers collect the encrypted messages and try to find common patterns. The attackers won't find any common patterns related to the keys that were used, because each message was encrypted with a different key—one from each "page" of the one-time pad. As long as the defenders can keep their use of the keys synchronized, and they change keys more frequently than attackers can analyze their traffic, this is an essentially unbreakable scheme. In particular, when the keys are truly random numbers and are the same length as the text being sent, then it's provably impossible to break the code.

But there are two serious problems with a one-time pad:

1. If the defenders fall out of sync, communication breaks down. Such a problem can happen if a defender loses their one-time pad, or has lost track of which key they should be using. For example, if you start to encrypt a message but then change your mind, you really should "go back"—perhaps paste the page back on that you tore off. This is particularly hard to get right if the reason you didn't finish encrypting the message is that your machine crashed.

2. The scheme isn't relevant for parties that are *never* able to establish a secure connection by some other means. If we imagine that the defenders meet in person, they can arrange to use identical pads and then they "only" have the synchronization problem. But that doesn't help defenders who are physically far away from each other and unable to meet in person. They can use some other secret communication technique, but that won't be as secure as a one-time pad.

It's not OK to transmit the one-time pad via an insecure technique. Unless the one-time pad is communicated securely, an attacker may have also intercepted the one-time pad. A one-time pad that might be known by the attacker is of little value to the defenders.

Key Exchange

A notable step forward came with the idea of key exchange (a computer scientist would call it Diffie-Hellman-Merkle key exchange, after the inventors). At the end of a key exchange, two parties end up knowing the same shared secret, and no one else knows it. In terms of what the defenders know vs. what the attacker knows, that result can be as good as a one-time pad. But in contrast to a one-time pad, key exchange happens by public interactions: the two defenders don't need to already have a secure channel. So key exchange gets us partway out of the chicken-and-egg problem of needing secrecy before we can have secrecy.

The underlying mechanism, as with most aspects of cryptography, is mathematical, but we can understand the principles in terms of paint mixing. Mixing two colors of paint together is easy, but separating a mixed paint into its original component colors is hard. If we mix the same proportions of three paint colors together, it doesn't matter the order in which we do the mixing: the color will end up the same.

Let's assume that Alice has a secret color a. Correspondingly, Bob has a secret color b. There is a single public color P chosen by some arbitrary method for this particular exchange. P is publicly visible, and so known to the attacker. Here's how key exchange works in terms of paint mixing:

1. Bob and Alice each mix their secret color with the public color, so Alice produces a mixture of $(a+P)$ while Bob produces a mixture of $(b+P)$.

2. Next, each party provides that mixture to the other party. That doesn't disclose the secret color of either party, because it's visible only in the

mixture. Alice winds up holding the $(b+P)$ mixture received from Bob, while Bob winds up holding the $(a+P)$ mixture from Alice. They're each holding a mixture containing the other party's secret color.

3. Finally, they each mix in their own secret color to the mixture received. Alice winds up with $(b+P+a)$, while Bob has $(a+P+b)$. We know those are the same mixture, and thus the same color. Alice and Bob now have a shared secret but have never revealed their unique secret colors.

Even if the attacker mixes together everything he or she has seen in different combinations, the shared secret color can't be constructed. The attacker will always have too much P. Because separating paint is hard, it doesn't even matter that the attacker knows that's the problem.

Key exchange is a neat trick, but unfortunately it doesn't address the question of how Alice and Bob know that they are communicating with the right party. As previously noted, we don't really want to work out a shared secret with an attacker, and there's nothing about key exchange that lets Alice know that "her Bob" is the intended Bob.

Public Key

A group of computer science researchers revolutionized the practice of secret-keeping with two related inventions. The first is *public-key cryptography*. (The second is the *key distribution center*, which we'll take up in the next chapter.)

Public-key cryptography changes the nature of the key in secret communication. In the shared-secret cryptography that we described in the previous sections, the key is secret and known *only* to the two communicating parties.

Figure 23.1 shows how a key works for shared-secret cryptography between two defenders, with an attacker shown below. The practical challenge in these systems is that the two defenders have to find a way to share the secret key while still keeping it from the attacker. Although it is possible to be quite ingenious about this, there is an intrinsic problem: since the defenders have to share, that sharing might be subverted to also share the same data with an attacker.

Public-key cryptography changes the structure of the sharing that's needed. In public-key cryptography, the key is no longer secret; instead, it's *partly public* and *partly secret*, with the secret part known only by *one* party.

Figure 23.2 shows the exact same defenders and the exact same attacker, but now using a public-key system. The keys have become quite a bit more

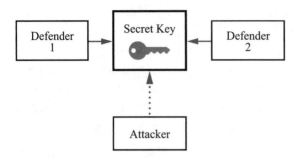

Figure 23.1
Key in shared-secret cryptography.

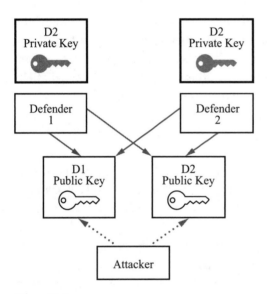

Figure 23.2
Keys in public-key cryptography.

complicated: where there used to be a single key, there are now four. However, the sharing situation has become quite a bit easier. There are two public keys, freely known to all. The defenders don't care if the attacker has the public keys. There are also two private keys that are completely unshared—in the diagram they are "locked away" in heavy boxes. Because the defenders don't need to share these private keys with each other, those keys are much easier to defend against the efforts of the attacker to find them.

In contrast to a public-key system, a shared-secret system has the problem that the key must be shared with "only the right people." A public-key system does away with that problem entirely. In a public-key system, a key can be public and shared with absolutely anyone else; or a key can be private and shared with absolutely no one else.

It's easy to see that key management would be easier in a public-key system. However, we don't yet know how such a system can work. The keys come in public/private pairs. The two parts of the pair have a mathematical relationship that is "easy to check but hard to generate." Recall that our plan here is to exploit that difference to protect secrets by ensuring that the defenders get the easy task while the attackers have the hard task.

Multiplying and Factoring

To get a flavor of the math involved, we'll look at multiplying and factoring. These operations are opposites (what a mathematician would call *inverses*). Everyone learns in elementary school that multiplication combines two or more numbers into a single result. Meanwhile, factoring reverses that operation, dividing a single number into two or more numbers that can be combined via multiplication to yield the original single number.

You probably learned in elementary mathematics that a *prime* number is one that does not allow even division except by itself and 1. So, for example, 2, 3, 5, 7, and 11 are some examples of prime numbers, while 4, 6, 8, 9, and 10 are not. The numbers in the second group are not prime because 4 has 2 as a factor; 6 has 2 and 3 as factors; 8 has 2 as a factor; 9 has 3 as a factor; and finally, 10 has 2 and 5 as factors.

Assume now that we are given a larger number—say, 920,639—and asked to produce two prime factors. It's a hard problem to solve by hand. It's not obvious to most people what its factors are, and it's very tedious to start trying different possibilities to figure it out. However, if we are given the two numbers 929 and 991 and asked to check whether they work, that is a relatively easy problem to solve. We simply perform the multiplication (929×991) and confirm that the result is 920,639. We might look at that multiplication problem and say that's not easy—but it's *much* easier than the factoring problem. Even with pencil and paper, it's only a few straightforward steps to multiply two given three-digit numbers together; it's much more daunting (and many more steps) to determine the prime factors of a six-digit number. Multiplication effectively discards information about the original prime factors, and that information is hard to recover. If you don't already know what the prime factors are, it's a hard process to figure them out.

Messages via Multiplication

So multiplying is easier than factoring—so what? This particular trio of numbers (929; 991; and 920,639) is not actually useful for keeping secrets. All of the numbers would have to be much larger for a comparable level of difficulty when using computers, because computers are so much faster at arithmetic operations than people are. Fortunately, each time we make a number just one bit larger we're doubling the size of number that can be represented—and repeated doubling quickly makes numbers really big, as we learned earlier with the chessboard story (chapter 6). Even if the numbers get to be incomprehensibly huge, the principles are the same.

A more significant problem with our discussion so far is that even though we've pointed out a difference in effort between multiplication and factoring, we haven't really explained how to exploit that difference when there is an actual message involved. To remedy that deficiency, let's work through an example of transmitting a message in this scheme. Keep in mind that this is emphatically *not* a real public-key scheme—we're just trying to capture some of the flavor of multiplication vs. factoring in the context of transmitting information.

Suppose that our "message" is a number. Let's first look at how Alice sends the value 49 to Bob. To use the scheme for sending information, each defender has one of the small numbers and also knows the big number. Let's assume that Alice's small number is 929 while Bob's small number is 991. To transmit 49, Alice multiplies $49 \times 929 = 45521$. Our "ciphertext" 45521 doesn't look very much like the original "plaintext" 49, so in a very crude way the encryption seems to be effective.

On the receiving side, Bob multiplies the received message by 991 and divides the result by 920,639. $45521 \times 991 = 45,111,311 / 920,639 = 49$, so Bob successfully recovers Alice's message.

Now Bob wants to send back the number 81. Bob multiplies 81×991 to get 80271. That ciphertext 80271 again doesn't resemble the plaintext 81; nor does it resemble the previous ciphertext transmitted from Alice to Bob.

On the receiving side Alice (who was the previous sender of 49) multiplies the received message by 929 and divides by 920,639. $80271 \times 929 =$

74,571,759 / 920,639 = 81, so again the receiver successfully recovers the sender's message.

An attacker watching this interaction sees only 45521 in one direction and 80271 in the other direction, as well as possibly knowing the "public key" 920639. Those numbers don't have any obvious relationship. The defenders do a single multiplication followed by a single division, both with numbers they already know. Meanwhile, any attacker can only proceed by trial and error to figure out the missing numbers so that it all works out. The attacker's task can be made much harder by making the numbers bigger, and by using a more sophisticated operation than a single multiplication.

This simple scheme takes advantage of a handy property of multiplication, which you probably know but might take for granted. It doesn't matter whether we multiply 929×991 or the other way around. In fact, when we have three numbers multiplied together, it doesn't matter in which order we multiply them; we still get the same result.

This example of factoring vs. multiplication is just providing an intuition of how we can build encryption with "one-way" functions: operations that are easy to carry out but hard to reverse. For our purposes, what matters is only that the right kind of math exists. We don't need to be able to construct these things ourselves. We just need to understand that they exist, we can use them, and they aren't magic—even though their properties are quite amazing. With public-key encryption, we are exploiting specific properties of particular mathematical "materials."

Proving Identity Remotely

We'll assume for now that we can somehow get the right keys in the right places. With that assumption, public-key cryptography does a nice job of giving the easy work to defenders and the hard work to attackers. After we look at how a public-key system works when we just assume that everyone has the right keys, chapter 24 will explain how to get the keys in the right places.

Let's assume that Alice wants to communicate with Bob using public-key cryptography. Both Alice and Bob have key pairs, which each consist of a private key and a public key. Alice keeps her private key to herself, but can freely share the matching public key. Likewise, Bob never shares his private key, but can freely distribute the matching public key.

Because we're assuming that we can get all the right keys in the right places, Alice has Bob's public key, and Bob has Alice's public key. The main problem we are ignoring for the moment is how Alice knows that her "Bob public key" is *really* the public key for the Bob she wants to communicate with; we are simply assuming that she has somehow found the right key. Likewise for the reverse case, we are simply assuming that Bob somehow possesses the right public key for the Alice of interest.

With this configuration, suppose that Bob receives a message from Alice that says she'd like to set up a secure communication channel. How can Bob know that the message is really from Alice? He really can't, at least not yet. But Bob can challenge the sender of the message to prove that they are really Alice. How can he do that? By having that sender demonstrate that they have Alice's private key. One way to do that would be to just ask for Alice's private key—but that would be foolish for two reasons: first, if Alice shares her private key with Bob it isn't private anymore; and second, Bob can't tell from looking at it whether it's Alice's private key or not. The only way that Bob can verify that it's really Alice's private key is by seeing if it's the matching key to Alice's public key—which Bob already has.

That is, verifying Alice's identity is not so much a matter of what Alice's private key *is* but more a matter of what the key can *do*. With that insight, it becomes apparent that Alice can prove her identity by responding to a challenge from Bob: essentially Bob says, "encrypt this!" and Alice responds. If Alice's response is one that only Alice could construct, then Bob knows he's dealing with the real Alice.

Figure 23.3 illustrates the stages of the exchange. In the first part, Bob is sending Alice the challenge "?" and asking her to respond with an encrypted version.

In the next part, Alice has constructed an obscuring "container" around the challenge, using her private key. In the third part, she sends this encrypted challenge back to Bob.

After receiving the encrypted challenge, Bob decrypts it in the fourth part. In the fifth part, Bob is applying Alice's public key to the encrypted "package" he received from Alice. Finally, in the last part, Bob applies Alice's public key to the encrypted reply, revealing that it contains "?"—which Bob knows is what he sent to Alice.

Correctly encrypting the challenge so that it's decrypted by Alice's public key must mean that it was encrypted by Alice's private key. Whoever can do that must be Alice (at least as far as we can tell from public-key cryptography).

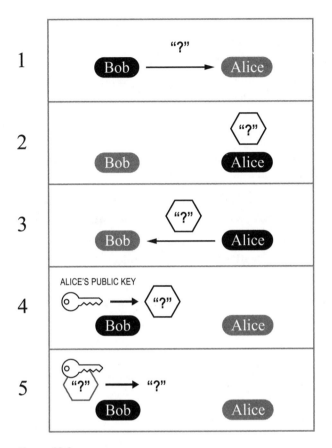

Figure 23.3
Alice proves her identity to Bob.

If some attacker Eve were trying to pretend to be Alice but didn't have Alice's private key, Eve would not be able to construct an encrypted package that behaves the right way. Applying Alice's public key to Eve's fake package would either yield an answer other than "?" or would fail.

What should Bob ask Alice to encrypt? It should be something that an attacker wouldn't be able to guess, so choosing a large number at random should work. So Bob chooses a random number, then both remembers it and sends it to Alice. When (if?) a reply comes back, Bob uses Alice's public key to decrypt it; if the decrypted value matches what he sent to Alice, then Bob can be pretty sure that the other party really is Alice. Because of the mathematics of public-key cryptography, we're pretty sure that the only likely way to get the right kind of reply is to actually use Alice's private key.

So if Bob gets the right kind of reply, that most likely means that someone with Alice's private key did the relatively easy work to produce it.

The short summary, then, is that this scheme lets Bob be sure that Alice is the party with whom he's communicating. It's worth noting some footnotes or disclaimers to that broad claim:

• There is a small chance that someone without Alice's private key did the very hard work to produce the right kind of reply.
• There is also a small chance that Alice lost control of her private key, so that someone else is replying.

Those two unlikely issues are not easily fixed, so we'll just have to live with them. However, there is one additional weakness in this first simple scheme that is fixable: if Bob and Alice have had many previous conversations, it's a little too easy for an attacker to take advantage of that. We'll fix that weakness in the next chapter.

24 Secure Channel, Key Distribution, and Certificates

In the previous chapter, we were considering how Bob can determine whether he's really communicating with Alice. Although Alice initiated the communication by sending a message to Bob, she has the mirror-image problem: she doesn't (yet) know that she's really talking with Bob. She knows that she's sending messages to Bob's address, but let's be paranoid for a minute. What if an attacker is intercepting those messages and sending back the attacker's version of the replies? Is there a way to rule out that possibility?

In the previous chapter, we saw how Bob can test Alice's identity. Alice can use the same approach, asking Bob to encrypt a random number. Alice remembers her choice of random number, and compares it to Bob's reply. So Alice's "hello, I'd like to talk" message needs to contain a little additional information. That initiating message includes a random number for Bob to encrypt using his private key and send back to Alice in his "OK" reply. Alice decrypts alleged-Bob's reply using real-Bob's public key and compares it to the number that she sent. If it matches, she can be pretty sure that the real Bob really encrypted it.

In this chapter we will outline the full recipe for Alice and Bob to communicate securely. To do that, we need to introduce some abbreviations. Although these details help illuminate the issues that need to be covered to make communication secure, you can skip them without missing the main point. So if the recipes and notation start to seem unhelpful, feel free to skip on to the section about "Key Distribution Center (KDC)."

When we write

$[X]y$

that means the plaintext X encrypted with the key y. We can also write the reverse operation, as

$\{Z\}a$

meaning the ciphertext Z decrypted with the key a. Notice that encryption hides information and uses square brackets while decryption exposes information and uses curly brackets.

We'll also use these abbreviations:

• B for Bob's public key
• b for Bob's private (secret) key

Using these abbreviations, we can say that we ought to be able to get any message X back after we encrypt with public-key and decrypt with secret-key:

$\{[X]B\}b=X$

It all works likewise for the reversed situation. We get the same message X back after we encrypt with secret-key and decrypt with public-key:

$\{[X]b\}B=X$

As you can see, these lines can quickly look impressively complex, but the actual transformations are not hard to understand.

With these abbreviations to assist, here's the seven-step outline for how the mutual identity-verification works so far:

1. *Alice sends*: Alice sends a request to talk to Bob, including a random number *Na* that she remembers. (The "*a*" in "*Na*" is for "Alice.")
2. *Bob replies:* Bob sends a reply to Alice. His reply includes Alice's number encrypted by his private key: [*Na*]*b*. He also sends a random number *Nb* that he remembers. (The "*b*" in "*Nb*" is for "Bob.")
3. *Alice decodes:* The message as received by Alice consists of an obscure element X (unintelligible due to Bob's encryption) as well as the random number *Nb*. Alice uses Bob's public key on the obscure element X, which we could write as $\{X\}B$. That decrypts what Bob encrypted because $\{X\}B=\{[Na]b\}B$, and we know from our preceding "equations" that $\{[Na]b\}B=Na$.
4. *Alice knows:* Since Alice recovers *Na* and this number matches the one that she sent, she now knows that this message really came from Bob.
5. *Alice replies:* Alice replies to Bob including Bob's number encrypted by her private key: [*Nb*]*a*.
6. *Bob decodes:* The message as received by Bob consists of an obscure element Y (unintelligible due to Alice's encryption). Bob uses Alice's public key on the obscure element Y, which we could write as $\{Y\}A$. That decrypts what

Alice encrypted because $\{Y\}A = \{[Nb]a\}A$, and we know from our "equations" above that $\{[Nb]a\}A = Nb$.

7. *Bob knows:* Since Bob recovers Nb and this number matches the one that he sent, he now knows that this message really came from Alice.

This is not the whole scheme we will end up using. We're going to add a further refinement. But it's already enough to get a flavor of how this works.

Why Is This Worthwhile?

It is reasonable to think this scheme is already a crazily complicated way of communicating, and we should step back to remember why it's worth bothering. Despite operating in an anarchic world of data communication where anyone can pretend to be anyone else, we are nevertheless quite close to having a scheme that lets us be sure that we're not being cheated. Considering that this approach lets us go from a zero-trust free-for-all to a high degree of confidence that we're talking to the right party, this is not such a bad deal. There are two remaining problems. First, this scheme is not quite strong enough yet to keep from being fooled by bad guys; and second, this scheme depends on Alice knowing Bob's public key B and Bob knowing Alice's public key A. We'll fix the first problem in the next section, and after that we'll fix the second problem by explaining key distribution.

Before we proceed, it's also worth reexamining the foundation of the security we're achieving, so we can understand what might go wrong. The security of this communication scheme depends on random numbers, public-key math, and secrecy of private keys. Let's consider each of those elements in turn.

Random numbers: Alice and Bob both need to use random numbers that are not easily guessed. For example, if Alice has a really bad random-number generator that always picks 42, it's easy for an attacker to reuse a previous Bob answer to substitute themselves for Bob. Alice simply won't be able to tell the difference. Both Alice and Bob need to have random-number generators that are good: unpredictable, nonrepeating.

Public-key math: The public and private keys must have certain properties, specifically

• the public key easily decrypts what is encrypted by the private key and vice versa;

• the private key is not easily derived from the public key; and
• the plaintext is not easily derived from a ciphertext in the absence of a matching key.

If any of these properties is missing, then we can't expect to achieve secure communication with the scheme we outlined.

Secrecy of private keys: When using a public-key scheme, "identity" is no more and no less than the use of a particular private key. If Alice lets someone else use her private key, that someone will appear completely identical to the "real" Alice. Indeed, from a cryptographic perspective that other person *is* the real Alice. Accordingly, we have to keep in mind that the scheme actually determines whether parties possess particular private keys—not any other concept of identity or authority.

Secure Channel, Refined

Now, let's refine our system to fix one problem we mentioned. In this fix, we still assume that Alice and Bob magically have each other's public keys. In the next section, we'll show how to solve that key-distribution problem.

The refinement we now add is to hide the random numbers that Alice and Bob are using to challenge each other. Alice and Bob don't want to show a possible attacker any more information than they have to. For example, it's possible that a randomly chosen number will (purely by chance) coincide with a number that one party sent previously—it's unlikely, but possible. We need to be concerned about an attacker who is watching and recording everything. Such an attacker might take advantage of any repetition: When the attacker sees a previously used number sent as a challenge, the attacker may be able to substitute a previously recorded response to that challenge and thereby hijack the conversation.

The fix is easy enough. Instead of simply sending a random number that the attacker could read, the sender should encrypt the random number before sending it. How should the sender encrypt the random number? Ideally, it should be encrypted in a way so that only the recipient can read it. We can achieve that if both parties send their random-number challenge encrypted by the *other* party's public key. In fact, each side will encrypt the entire message containing the random number (including the response to the other party's challenge). The result is that an attacker can't see any other elements of the conversation.

With those changes, here's how the conversation works. It's basically the same structure as before, but the steps have become a little more elaborate, and there are now eight of them:

1. *Alice sends:* Alice sends a request to talk to Bob, including a random number Na that she remembers. Alice encrypts the request before sending it, using Bob's public key. So what Alice sends is $[Na]B$.

2. *Bob decodes:* Bob receives the obscured information, which we'll call Q, and decrypts it with his private key: $\{Q\}b$. Because $Q=[Na]B$, this is the same as $\{[Na]B\}b$; and we know that $\{[Na]B\}b=Na$. Bob has now extracted Na, which is Alice's randomly chosen challenge.

3. *Bob replies:* Bob sends a reply to Alice. His reply includes Alice's same number Na, but now reencrypted using Bob's private key: $[Na]b$. Bob also sends a random number Nb that he remembers. Bob's reply thus contains two data items: the reply to Alice's original challenge, and Bob's new challenge to purported-Alice. Bob encrypts both elements, using Alice's public key: $[[Na]b, Nb]A$. Notice the nested item: it's the number Na that Alice sent originally. It has one "inner layer" of encryption to demonstrate that it was sent from Bob, and an "outer layer" of encryption to protect it from being read by anyone except Alice.

4. *Alice decodes:* Alice receives the obscured information, which we'll call R. She decrypts it with her private key: $\{R\}a$. We know (because we saw Bob encrypt it) that R consists of some stuff (that we'll call S) encrypted by A: $[S]A$. Accordingly, when Alice decrypts it, $\{[S]A\}a=S$, she recovers whatever stuff S was originally encrypted. There are two items in S. The second item is simply a number (in fact, it's Nb), but the first item is at this point just another obscure object that we'll call T. So now Alice has some obscure object T, and she knows Bob's challenge number Nb. Alice knows that T is Bob's response to her challenge. Alice then uses Bob's public key and decrypts the part that Bob encrypted: $\{T\}B=\{[Na]b\}B=Na$. Through this process she recovers Na.

5. *Alice knows:* Since the number Na matches the one she previously sent in step 1, she now knows that this message came from Bob. We could say that Bob has met her challenge.

6. *Alice replies:* Alice replies to Bob's challenge by including Bob's number Nb that she extracted in step 4. Alice encrypts that number using her private key: $[Nb]a$. This step of encryption is needed so that Bob will know the message came from Alice. Then to protect it from being read en route, she

hides that result with another layer of encryption using Bob's public key: [[Nb]a]B. This second layer of encryption ensures that no one except Bob can read Alice's response to Bob's challenge.

7. *Bob decodes:* Bob receives an obscure object, which we'll call U. He decrypts it using his private key: {U}b = {[V]B}b = V. So he extracts another obscure object, which we'll call V, as Alice's response. Bob then uses Alice's public key and decrypts Alice's response V: {V}A = {[Nb]a}A = Nb.

8. *Bob knows:* Bob has now recovered Nb; since this number matches the one he originally sent in step 3, he now knows that this message really came from Alice. We can say that Alice has also met Bob's challenge.

That might seem like a lot of steps with a lot of complexity—and it is—but let's keep in mind what it accomplishes. If we assume for a moment that all the mathematical constraints related to public-key systems work out, and that Alice and Bob have each other's public keys, this exchange means that Alice and Bob can set up a secure channel to each other: they each know that the other party is the one they want to talk to, and they know that *no one else* can see what they are discussing. That's pretty impressive. And remember, for all the history of secret codes in all of civilization before the late twentieth century, this particular result was impossible!

Key Distribution Center (KDC)

The eight-step conversation we have outlined lets the parties set up a secure channel, assuming that Alice already had Bob's public key (and vice versa). At some level that assumption is not much better than assuming that Alice and Bob each have the same one-time pad, unknown to anyone else. It's an assumption that allows for great security, but it seems hard or impossible to accomplish if you don't already have great security.

So in some respects the most impressive part of public-key cryptography is not the message exchange itself, but the key distribution. How can you get an authentic public key for someone whose public key you don't already have?

Conceptualiy, it's pretty simple to solve the problem of trustworthy distribution of public keys. We assume that there's a key distribution center (KDC) that establishes individual trust relationships with individual key holders (see figure 24.1). The KDC knows who Alice is and who Bob is, and knows both of their public keys; in addition, both Alice and Bob know the KDC and know its public key.

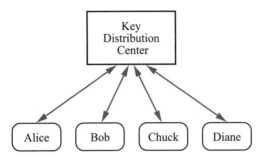

Figure 24.1
A key distribution center (KDC).

Alice and Bob don't need to know each other (or all the many other parties who each have an individual relationship with the KDC). The one relationship each has with the KDC is sufficient for Alice and Bob to get each other's public keys, even though they may not know or trust each other initially.

You might be wondering, why doesn't Alice just contact Bob and ask for his public key? That can work in some special cases, but in general it doesn't get us past that frustrating chicken-and-egg problem: how do you know it's really the right Bob if you have never contacted him before? In general, you will be depending on some mutual acquaintance whom you already trust to introduce you or to confirm that you have the right person. The KDC takes that same idea and makes it a simple general mechanism.

We start with Alice and the KDC knowing each other's public keys by some reliable mechanism. That mechanism most likely involves some kind of non-computer, non-network interaction, probably completely unrelated to public-key cryptography. For example, Alice might go to a local office of the KDC organization and speak to an employee of that organization, presenting some physical evidence of her identity. Similarly, Bob and the KDC know each other's public keys, again perhaps via a "real-world" interaction.

So the KDC knows Alice's public key and Bob's public key. In addition, Alice and Bob both know the KDC's public key. However, Alice and Bob don't know each other's public key. What we want is that Alice and Bob should be able to learn each other's public keys in a way that is not vulnerable to an attacker.

Fortunately, we already know how to establish a secure channel between two parties who know each other's public keys, as we developed in the previous section. So Alice simply establishes a secure channel to the KDC and asks for Bob's public key. The use of a secure channel means that Alice knows she's talking to the KDC, and the KDC knows it's talking to Alice. Accordingly, when Alice asks the KDC for Bob's public key, she can trust that the data she receives is actually Bob's public key (as known to the KDC), not some attacker's substitute.

Likewise, when Bob wants Alice's public key, he can simply ask the KDC over a secure channel. Since Bob knows he's talking to the KDC and trusts the KDC, he can be sure that he's getting Alice's public key and not some other key.

This seems like a pretty easy solution to the problem, and it just reuses what we previously developed to perform secure communication. So what justifies our previous claim that this function was impossible without an important invention?

Scaling up Key Distribution

The KDC we're describing works at small scale, but has some problems if we try to scale it up. It's not clear how to have a simple system where anyone can find the key of anyone else they might want to reach. Likewise, it's not clear it's feasible—or even desirable—for everyone in the world to have a trust relationship with one single KDC. So while this simple system is a good starting point for thinking about how we can get secure communication in general, the scheme we've presented isn't very practical.

To get a more practical system, we want to solve the key-distribution problem without depending on a single central source of knowledge. We notice that the KDC is serving two roles: it links names with public keys, and it is the trusted source of those linkages. We can instead think of these as two distinct functions: we can have one mechanism that links names with public keys and another mechanism that establishes which of those linkages is trustworthy.

Accordingly, we will make two major changes from the simple KDC approach:

1. Instead of having the KDC distribute the public keys over secure connections, we wrap each public key in a *certificate* signed by the KDC. A certificate simply links a name to a public key. Because the signatures can't be forged, we know that the linkage is a valid one, at least to the extent that we trust the signer. We explain more about certificates in the next section.

2. We organize the signing of certificates into hierarchies of *certificate authorities* (CAs). A CA is composed of both a technical mechanism that performs the signing, and a human process that determines which certificates to sign or not sign. Each CA is testifying to the trustworthiness of certificates it signs. We explain more about CAs later in the chapter.

With these changes, we have the essential elements of the commonly used internet trust infrastructure.

Certificates

Each certificate links a specific name to a specific public key, in a way that we can check easily. Certificates are useful because they are *signed*. Without signatures, it would be easy to substitute different names or keys in the certificate, and we would have no reason to trust the linkage between name and key. But a signed certificate makes a package: name, key, and signature are tied together so that any tampering will be detectable. For the moment we'll just assume that signatures are possible and consider why they allow a better solution; then we'll look a little more closely at how they work.

A signed certificate is what it is—its merit (or lack of merit) is not determined by who gave it to us. In this "inherent trust" approach, a certificate works like cash: it doesn't matter whether we receive a $20 bill from someone we trust or someone we distrust—as long as it's a real $20 bill, it's still valuable and useful. Likewise, a properly signed certificate provides a trusted linkage between name and key, regardless of who gives us the certificate. The signature, not the source, is what determines trustworthiness.

Using certificates is a significant improvement over the KDC as we first presented it, because that first KDC required secure connections to the particular single central service. Now, instead of trying to build a single highly available central service as a KDC, we can think of having a "sea" of duplicate certificates available from many different servers. Those servers don't need to worry about secure channels. In fact, they don't even need to take special steps to protect the certificates, because the certificates have built-in mechanisms to detect tampering. An attacker can't keep us from learning the right public key by taking down the KDC service, because there may be many possible alternative sources for a copy of the relevant certificate.

Cryptography for Integrity

Signatures are different from the secret-keeping we've considered previously. We were previously using cryptographic techniques for *secrecy*, but with signatures, we're using cryptographic techniques for *integrity*. Using cryptographic techniques but not trying to hide data can seem weird, so let's look at a non-cryptographic example of a signature to be sure we have that clear.

Consider playing chess against an opponent you don't trust. You need to leave the room. Especially if you aren't a very good chess player, you probably won't notice if your opponent moves a piece or two into positions that help the opponent. Even if you do notice, it might be hard to make the case that the opponent is cheating. In this situation you can take a quick digital photograph of the board (probably using your mobile phone) as a kind of signature. The board is not hidden, and it's still vulnerable to manipulation by the untrustworthy opponent. But now there's a clear mechanism to verify that things are unchanged, by comparing the board with the photo. If the photo and board don't match, then we know the opponent has changed the board.

Cryptographic signing works a little differently from this conceptual "photographic signing." As used for certificates, signing combines a chunk of data with a private key to produce a signature block. The signature and the data together are "signed data."

In figure 24.2, the signed data has an appended block of some additional bits that were computed by the signing mechanism. The signing mechanism computed those bits by somehow combining the original data with the private key. The signed data (original data + block) can be checked to ensure that no tampering has occurred, as we will shortly see.

In figure 24.3, we're checking the signed data by using the public key. The computation either says the signed data is OK (the attached block is the one that matches the original data and private key) or says that something is wrong:

• the signature doesn't match the data, or
• the public key doesn't match the private key.

Notice that we don't necessarily know *exactly* what's wrong—we can just tell that something is not right.

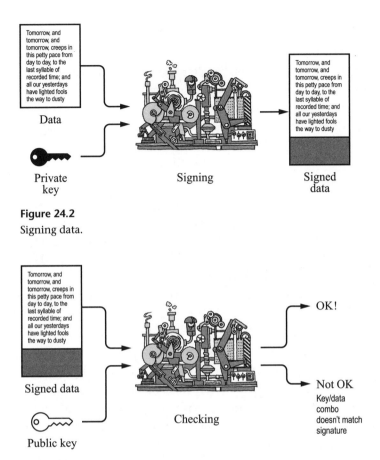

Figure 24.2
Signing data.

Figure 24.3
Checking the validity of signed data.

What are the necessary properties for this kind of signing and validation?

1. The signature block has to be *obscure*, so the attacker can't easily tell how to change it to match a change in the signed data. The only way to produce a valid signature for changed data must be to sign it again with the relevant key. Again, this obscurity of the signature does not mean that we're hiding the original data. For signing purposes, it's fine to leave the original data as unchanged plaintext; signing just provides another (checkable) element that goes with that original data.

2. The signature block also has to be *sensitive*, so that even the tiniest change to the original data (one bit flipped) produces a different value for the

signature block. This requirement means that even the smallest change to the signed data "breaks" the signature.

As with other aspects of public-key cryptography, these requirements can seem like unreasonable demands. But marvelously, there are mathematical mechanisms with the right properties. Once again, we won't try to explain how or why signatures work mathematically; we'll just take advantage of their properties.

Signed Certificates

Signatures let us distinguish between good and bad certificates. Let's assume that we have a certificate in hand that we've somehow found or received. (Recall at this stage that we're still assuming that everyone knows the KDC's public key somehow. In a later section we'll get rid of that dependence on a single KDC.) For that certificate to be authentic, it must have been signed by the KDC.

So we can make a certificate that links a name to a public key, have the KDC sign that certificate, and then make as many copies of that certificate as we like. Every one of the certificates is equally valid and equally useful for the purpose of learning the public key linked to a name. Anyone who has a copy of the certificate no longer needs to contact the KDC to get the public key linked to that name. We can distribute and share name/key pairs without requiring the KDC to be involved—we have eliminated the need for the KDC to be some kind of super service that's always available and always correct.

Revocation

Unfortunately, there is a new drawback that comes along with this new benefit. With all these certificates potentially floating around, it's somewhere between hard and impossible to undo a name/key linkage. For example, suppose that Dennis realizes that his private key has been compromised—a bad guy has stolen it, or Dennis is just not sure any more whether someone might have a copy of it. Meanwhile Alice may well have a certificate, duly signed by the KDC, binding the name "Dennis" to what is now the wrong public key. Dennis really doesn't want Alice to trust that public key to protect interactions with him, because some attacker may use the corresponding (compromised) private key to pretend to be Dennis.

What can Dennis do to improve the situation? He can certainly get a new pair of corresponding private and public keys, replacing the old bad ones. And Dennis can certainly get the KDC to sign a new certificate that binds "Dennis" to the new correct public key. But there's not much that Dennis can do about the old bad certificate that Alice is using. After all, Dennis and Alice may not know each other at all before Alice attempts to contact Dennis via the information in the certificate—that is a part of what we wanted to enable with a certificate-based system.

What we see here is the problem of *revocation*. A certificate establishes a linkage between a name and a public key in a way that can't be tampered with, but it's hard to correct that linkage—for example, if there has been a security breach or even if there's something more innocent that changed the name/key linkage, like a reconfiguration or upgrade.

Given that a certificate is a freely distributable, freestanding object, how can we eliminate old obsolete certificates? One answer is to have a certificate revocation list (CRL). Entities wanting to invalidate a certificate add it to the CRL, and entities using certificates then check the CRL to see if the certificate has been revoked. Although this works in principle, in practice a CRL has rarely been successful. In some ways the CRL is the KDC all over again: we have to have a trusted source for the CRL to ensure that our certificates aren't undercut by an attacker, and unfortunately, it's hard to scale up that kind of service.

In practice, the scope of certificates is limited primarily by expiration—that is, each certificate is valid only until a particular date and time, after which it is no longer trustworthy. Organizations can trade off the expense of more frequent renewal and replacement of expired certificates vs. the longer time of exposure after a security breach with less frequent renewal and replacement.

Unfortunately, the expiration mechanism is clumsy. All too often, the expiration of a batch of certificates requires a flurry of pointless bookkeeping work to replace them. Meanwhile, people often continue to use certificates beyond their stated expiration dates. In most people's experience, an expired certificate is usually an innocent housekeeping oversight—an annoyance rather than a bona fide security problem.

Certificate Authorities (CAs)

In the previous section, we used certificates to get away from the need to inter-act with a single KDC service, but we still used a single KDC as the basis for all the signatures. As we mentioned previously, the other half of the solution is to allow more than one entity to sign certificates. In computer science terms, we move from a single certificate authority (CA) to having multiple CAs.

Any CA can sign a certificate, but a certificate signed by an unknown or untrusted CA is no better than an unsigned one. If we look back at the two previous KDC schemes (without certificates, then with certificates), we can say that the single, central KDC was the single common trusted entity in both schemes. Every user has to trust the KDC, and as a result every user can trust any certificate signed by the KDC. There are two different ways of moving from a single CA to multiple CAs, and they are both useful in practical sys-tems. One approach is to have multiple independent sources of trust, and the other approach is to delegate trust.

Root CAs and Hierarchies

If we consider multiple independent sources of trust, then we shift from talk-ing about the single KDC to talking about *root CAs*. A root CA plays much the same role that the single KDC did in our earlier explanation: It is a trusted entity, with the trust relationship established by some mechanism unrelated to signing and certificates. A root CA signing certificates is a little like a sov-ereign country issuing passports. Although you might well be prepared to accept a lot of different passports, you won't want to accept just anything that claims to be a passport. Passports from France and Germany are prob-ably OK, but a passport from Upper Voltonia probably isn't.

How do you know the public key of a root CA? You find it in a "self-signed" certificate from that same root CA. Some of those root CA cer-tificates are actually built into browsers so that your browser can easily validate certificates signed by those popular root CAs. If you choose to trust a root CA that isn't already built into your browser, you can manually add its certificate to your browser. And just as it's possible to add certificates to indicate that you trust the corresponding CAs as root CAs, it's typically also possible to do the reverse—remove certificates if the user or organization chooses not to trust some or all of those corresponding CAs.

Having multiple independent root CAs offers one kind of scale: multiple diverse unrelated entities that we would expect to fail independently. But the use of multiple root CAs doesn't really address the other scaling question: how to support a larger, more reliable workload of signing for a particular single CA. Rather than requiring the single CA to do all signing work, we put mechanisms in place that allow the delegation of signing work, in a *hierarchy of trust*. This approach is like a sovereign country allowing multiple offices and embassies to issue its passports. The authority all eventually hinges on the root, but the root doesn't have to do all of the work. In a hierarchy of trust, a well-known CA can sign a certificate that names another CA. So now a CA is not just providing reassurance about the name/key binding for a communicating party like Alice or Bob: it's also potentially providing reassurance about the name/key binding for another CA.

So now suppose that we encounter a certificate from an unknown CA. If the unknown CA's certificate is signed by a known (and trusted) CA, the known CA is indicating that the unknown CA can itself be trusted. The trust hierarchy has many of the same merits that we already saw when we looked at DNS (chapter 15) and when we looked at making better servers (chapter 20). In particular, in the same way that DNS let names be "owned" by subordinate directories, a trust hierarchy lets certificate signing be "owned" by subordinate CAs. Just as we don't want to try to implement a global search service or a global name service with a single server, we don't want to implement a global signing service with a single server. Instead, we gain capacity, fault-tolerance, and responsiveness by allowing the signing to take place at multiple, separately administered, globally distributed CAs.

In such a hierarchical system, checking on a single name/key correspondence may well require checking a sequence of certificates. If we don't already know and trust the CA signing a particular certificate, we shift to examining that CA's certificate. If we don't know the CA that signed that first CA's certificate, we shift to examining the second CA's certificate. We follow a chain of certificates until we either find a CA that we trust or we reach the end of the chain.

If we encounter a CA that we trust, then we can believe the name/key binding in the first certificate considered. However, we might end this process by finding that there is no CA in the certificate's chain that we trust. If we follow the whole chain to the root CA without finding a CA we trust, we have no basis for believing that the name/key binding is correct. We also don't know for sure that it's wrong. Nor do we know that there's an attack or an attacker. Failing to find a trusted CA is a problem, but not necessarily a cause for alarm; we just don't know whether the key in that first certificate is trustworthy.

Trust Problems

We previously mentioned that there are both technical and nontechnical (human) aspects to trust systems. That's still true—and a potential source of vulnerability—regardless of whether we use certificate hierarchies and multiple CAs. In particular, we need to be aware that a person or organization can choose to accept a certificate that later turns out to be bogus: the certificate appears to be valid, and in narrow technical terms is completely fine. Nevertheless, something in the trust system has broken down. For example, if an attacker successfully commits fraud in the process of obtaining a certificate from a CA, the legitimate signature of that CA won't somehow overcome the fraudulent information in the certificate.

For a concrete example, assume that attacker Eve has convinced a legitimate CA to issue her a private/public key pair, and that same CA has issued a certificate that ties Eve's public key to Alice's name. Now anyone who relies on that certificate believes that they are interacting with Alice, but they are actually interacting with Eve. There is nothing wrong with the certificates or keys that would allow an automatic warning of potential harm, even though this is clearly a bad situation. Even when certificates appear to be working correctly, communicating parties need to be alert for other possible signs of attacks or misbehavior.

An even worse problem is that an entire CA—not just one certificate—can turn out to be bogus. Why is that worse? Because, as we just learned, trusting a CA implies trusting *all* of the certificates signed by it: that's what a trust hierarchy means. So trusting a bogus CA not only means accepting everything directly signed by that CA; it also means accepting all of the certificates signed by any other CAs to which the bogus CA delegated trust.

What causes a CA to fail in this way? Unfortunately, even a legitimate CA making good-faith efforts can have these kinds of problems. For example, some CAs have suffered security lapses and lost control of their private keys. If an attacker controls a CA's private key, then everyone trusting that CA is vulnerable to apparently good but actually fake certificates.

It's worth underscoring that "everyone trusting them" includes *everyone* interacting with the signed certificates. There's an obvious harm for the users whose certificates that turn out to not be very convincing, but there's also a subtler harm for anyone who is trying to validate a certificate. Many users of a certificate are *only* seeking to determine if it is correct; as we've noted, part of the attraction of a certificate scheme is that such validation can be performed locally, without needing to contact the issuer. These "ordinary users" of certificates may not see themselves as customers of a particular CA, and indeed have no business relationship with that CA. However, they are just as vulnerable to the subversion of a CA as the people who obtained certificates. Anyone who pays a CA for signing certificates is clearly harmed when the CA endorsement turns out to be dubious—but so is everyone using any certificate that came from the problematic CA.

We already saw that there is no effective way to recall bad certificates. Accordingly, we can see that the first trust failure of a CA is also, in some ways, its last: a CA that has been compromised cannot really be repaired. Since we know from previous chapters that failures do occur in systems, it's unfortunate that the CAs are so fragile; and doubly unfortunate that CA failure affects so many parties, many of whom are not even known to the CA. This alarming fragility is somewhat mitigated by the presence of multiple independent root CAs, which we expect to fail independently. However, that is not especially comforting. If you are personally affected by one of these trust failures, you are unlikely to feel much better knowing that most other parts of the internet are unaffected.

25 Bitcoin Goals

It has been famously observed that money is the root of all evil, so it seems apt to wind up our examination of attackers and defenders by looking at a kind of money. In particular, we'll look at Bitcoin. In this chapter we start by looking at money more generally to understand what's hard about a system like Bitcoin. In the next chapter, we look at the mechanisms in Bitcoin that solve those problems, as well as examining some associated limitations.

Ledgers

Let's start our exploration of money with a really simple case: Alice is paying $2 to Bob. Presumably the payment is in exchange for some goods or service, but we're only concerned here with the payment. They can use paper currency, the familiar pieces of paper printed in green and black ink by the U.S. government. For example, Alice can hand two one-dollar bills to Bob. Let's say she starts with $6 and Bob starts with $5. Then she takes $2 to give to Bob, reducing her total to $4. After Bob adds the $2 to his pile, Alice has $4 and Bob has $7.

There are many circumstances where paper currency is inconvenient. When a large amount of money is involved, no one wants to be handling large stacks of bills. Similarly, if Alice and Bob are far away from each other, handing over pieces of paper is physically impossible.

Instead of handling pieces of paper, we can accomplish the same effect through various kinds of recordkeeping. For example, Alice and Bob can write entries in a shared book. A book that's used in this way is typically called a *ledger*. Figure 25.1 shows the same starting state as the one we described previously, but now Alice's and Bob's money piles are recorded in a ledger.

Alice: $6
Bob: $5

Alice

Bob

Figure 25.1
Alice and Bob and ledger, starting state.

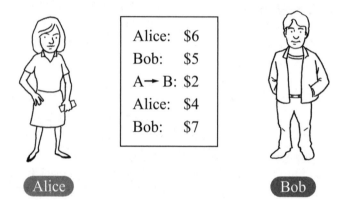

Alice

Bob

Figure 25.2
Alice and Bob and ledger, final state.

Figure 25.2 shows the same final state that we described previously, but using an updated ledger instead of handing over dollar bills.

Notice that these ledger entries are themselves the payments—not just the record of payments that took place in some other way. Once we see that the payment can just be an updated record instead of handing over pieces of paper, it's easier to see how payments can happen even if Alice and Bob are far apart.

It might seem a little weird to think about using a ledger this way to replace cash payments. But a similar kind of recordkeeping happens if Alice and

Bob hold accounts at the same bank, and they perform transfers between their accounts. Instead of writing in the shared book, they instead trust the shared bank to keep accurate records of their holdings. Of course, a modern bank doesn't use a ledger book to keep those accounts; instead, it stores and handles the necessary data using computers.

For most people in economically developed countries, there's nothing new or surprising in what we've described so far. There are also many variations and elaborations possible with different parties in the middle. There may be more than one bank involved, and there are specialized interbank payment systems with well-known brands like Visa or MasterCard, as well as various more obscure payment entities like check clearinghouses.

However, it sometimes surprises people that this kind of recordkeeping represents the majority of money. There are two main ways that people use money: to store something valuable for possible future use, or to pay someone in exchange for goods or services. When experts look at the money that is "at rest" and being used primarily as stored value, most of it turns out to be in bank accounts and investment accounts of various kinds. Likewise, when experts look at money that is "in motion" and being used for payments, most of it is actually in transaction records: checks, electronic payments, charge cards, credit cards, debit cards, and the like. So in any realistic assessment, modern money is just bookkeeping.

As we think about computer systems and money, we may find ourselves considering philosophical questions like "What is digital money?" or "How does money function in the network age?" To answer, it's helpful to keep in mind that in some important ways money is *already* digital. Even before we start to consider Bitcoin or another exotic-seeming new system, we can see that in the modern world most money exists only in the form of computerized records.

Special Roles vs. Ordinary Participants

We can analyze the bank-transfer approach in a little more detail. We've seen that there is a special role: the *bookkeeper* (probably a bank) keeps the accounts of how much money each person has. The bookkeeper role may involve more than one person or organization, but for simplicity we'll talk about it as a single party.

There is also a second special role: the *guarantor* (probably the U.S. Federal Reserve) underpins the value of the currency in use. Again, the guarantor role may involve more than one person or organization, but for simplicity we'll also talk about it as a single party.

Apart from these two special trusted parties, there are the ordinary parties who transfer money among themselves. For want of a better term, we'll call them *participants*. The essence of Bitcoin is building a system that allows the participants to transfer money without having any special trusted parties.

To see what's required to eliminate the special parties, let's first consider each of them in turn.

Bookkeeper

The bookkeeper tracks the changes made by each participant. All participants must trust the bookkeeper. In addition, the bookkeeper must always be available to record whatever changes a participant wants to make. What happens if the bookkeeper disappears or doesn't function? In that situation, the participants don't know what their balances are. Participants have to make do with their last best guess of their holdings. If they want to do something with that money—buy, sell, transfer—they have to find a way to do it without the bookkeeper. In the worst case, all the money may be gone—there may be no way to prove one's ownership of the money without the bookkeeper.

In practice, banks in most developed countries have deposit insurance to protect against this worst-case scenario of losing your money—at least up to a certain amount of money per account holder. But even if we believe we are protected against the total loss of our money, we may nevertheless be uncomfortable with what this worst case shows. There is a hazard that comes with trusting the bookkeeper: the system fails catastrophically if the bookkeeper is actually faulty or malicious. There is a potential for a *bookkeeper's* poor behavior to impair your ability to use *your* money.

Guarantor

Now let's turn to the other special party, the guarantor. Whereas the bookkeeper tracks balances in dollar terms, the guarantor controls what a dollar means. We previously asked what happens to participants if the bookkeeper fails; now let's ask, what happens if the guarantor fails?

Sometimes such a failure occurs because the guaranteeing government ceases to exist, such as happened to South Vietnam in 1975 at the end of the war between North Vietnam and South Vietnam. At other times, the guaranteeing government is still sovereign, but has spectacularly mismanaged the currency. The most striking example of such mismanagement is when a currency has severe *inflation*. Inflation is the rate at which money is losing its value—or, equivalently, the rate at which prices are increasing.

Although there is disagreement among economists about the "right" level of inflation, all parties agree that high inflation is bad. A number of countries have experienced *hyperinflation*, with a recent example being Zimbabwe. Its annual inflation rate increased from an uncomfortable 7 percent in 1980 to the last official rate of more than 231 *million* percent in 2008, which in turn prompted the printing of 100-trillion-dollar banknotes (yes, each individual banknote was worth 100 trillion Zimbabwe dollars!). Eventually the Zimbabwean currency was abandoned and foreign currencies used instead.

Although few people anticipate a situation in which the U.S. Federal Reserve acts as poorly as the Zimbabwe government did, there are people who are skeptical of the Federal Reserve's competence and good intentions. The potential for poor performance by the guarantor is a little like the potential for misbehavior by the bookkeeper—unlikely, but with severe consequences if it does occur.

Bitcoin

The Bitcoin system supports payments among distributed participants without any special roles. There is no need for a bookkeeper to maintain a ledger. Instead, the participants collectively implement a shared distributed ledger. There is likewise no need for a guarantor to regulate the issuance of currency; instead, the participants collectively implement a unit of value called a bitcoin.

(Notice that the usual custom is to use the capitalized term "Bitcoin" to refer to the system architecture, as in "With Bitcoin, there's no central bank." Meanwhile, lower-case "bitcoin" refers to the unit of value, as in "Joe just paid me 1.2 bitcoins.")

Bitcoin goes beyond removing the two special trusted roles. There really aren't any trusted entities in Bitcoin; in particular, the participants don't trust each other. In fact, Bitcoin is designed to continue functioning as a reliable trustworthy ledger even when the community of participants includes some members who are trying to cheat or otherwise undermine the system.

Does that mean that Bitcoin is unstoppable and indestructible? No: Bitcoin won't work reliably if *everyone* in the community is attacking it, or even if a majority of the community is trying to subvert it. But the system will give correct results even when some of the participants are not behaving correctly—indeed, even if they are actively undermining the system's operation. Our previous look at fault-tolerance and software failures exposed us to some similar concerns (chapter 17), but the mechanisms in Bitcoin will prove to be quite different from what we've seen before.

Bitcoin provides both a distributed shared ledger and a unit of value. In principle, these two constructs are completely unrelated:

• A bank could maintain an ordinary ledger that is denominated in bitcoins. The use of bitcoins doesn't *require* a distributed ledger.
• A group of participants could implement a distributed ledger in which the entries track balances and transfers of dollars. The use of a distributed ledger doesn't require the entries to be denominated in bitcoins.

In practice, the distributed ledger and the unit of value have an intertwined implementation, as we'll see in the next chapter. In our explanation, we'll first consider how to get the distributed ledger to work for a community, without worrying about bitcoins as a unit of value.

Distributed Ledger

A distributed ledger has to work despite failure or misbehavior by some parts of the system. As with any other fault-tolerant system (chapter 16), we know that depending on a single copy of data means that we can't tolerate a loss or failure of that copy. So instead we have to think in terms of multiple copies that somehow cooperate.

We'll work our way to the Bitcoin solution by considering some simpler ways to build a distributed ledger. One initial possibility is that each participant simply keeps a separate copy of the ledger. If we pursue this approach, we also need some mechanism so that all the participants always see the same changes—we don't want to be in a situation where two participants have different ideas about how much money some particular participant has.

It's helpful to return to using the language of "attackers" and "defenders." The correctly functioning participants in the Bitcoin community are defenders, while those that are malfunctioning or actively subverting the system are attackers. The defenders want to achieve these properties:

• Every defender has an identical view of every item in the ledger. We call this the *agreed sequence.*
• The agreed sequence is stable and only changes at one end (we'll refer to the end that changes as the *tail*). Like other logs (chapter 16) it can grow as more entries are added, but old entries are permanent and unaffected by these additions.
• The group of participants can grow or shrink over time; a particular participant can choose whether and when to join or leave. (In a later section, we'll consider the motivations of participants for joining or leaving the group.)
• The group achieves some kind of shared consensus about state changes: in particular, the defenders have to agree on the same result in spite of the attackers actively working against a successful resolution.

Each participant trusts or distrusts other participants equally; unfortunately, the participants are not clearly labeled as "attacker" or "defender."

We have seen this kind of problem before: it's basically Byzantine agreement (agreement with a Byzantine failure model). As we mentioned in chapter 17, Byzantine agreement allows a group of participants to reach a common agreement as long as a substantial majority (typically 2/3 or 3/5) of the participants are behaving correctly. So one high-level way of understanding Bitcoin is that it's a shared, extensible recordkeeping system in which each update is shared with other participants via a kind of Byzantine agreement. (A computer scientist might quibble about this characterization. In a careful comparison, true Byzantine agreement requires a greater fraction of "good" players but also gives a more reliable shared answer. Bitcoin is somewhat looser, supplying a weaker notion of the agreed sequence while allowing a larger fraction of attackers before failing. However, these distinctions aren't especially important for our purposes.) The next chapter looks in somewhat more detail at how to actually build such a system.

26 Bitcoin Mechanisms

In chapter 25 we laid out goals for Bitcoin and summarized it as a shared extensible recordkeeping system for a community of untrusting participants. In this chapter we consider how the system is actually constructed so that it works that way.

Some systems achieve a stable permanent record by using physical irreversibility. For example, archival storage media such as write-once optical disks are designed so they cannot be altered once data is written onto them: there is simply no way to erase or rewrite them. When we describe the consensus view among Bitcoin participants, it's worth noting that its stability is not enforced by any physical mechanism. At the physical level, Bitcoin records can be completely reversible and rewritable—all of the history in the ledger could be changed if a large enough group of attackers performs that attack. The stability of the agreed sequence results from the efforts of the defenders.

What are these efforts of the defenders? Each participant operates independently in making its decisions about whether to join or leave and in deciding what to accept or reject from other participants. A participant has to be prepared to incorporate genuine updates into its local version of the ledger, while rejecting any bogus updates.

Suppose that Charlie is a cheater and Victor is his intended victim. Charlie could insert bogus records showing that he has received money and then send those updates to Victor. An alternative way of committing the same kind of fraud is that Charlie could receive legitimate updates showing that he has spent money, but then suppresses them. Rather than forward them on to Victor, Charlie could delete the records showing that he has spent money.

With either kind of cheating, Charlie can potentially fool Victor. Victor receives updates showing that Charlie has more money than he really has, or fails to receive updates showing Charlie has less money than he claims.

In turn, Victor might be convinced to sell something valuable to Charlie in exchange for that (actually nonexistent) money. We need to find a way to protect Victor from Charlie. We may not have any good way to prevent cheaters from *trying* to fake the log, but we can make sure that they don't succeed.

There are four different aspects of Bitcoin that make life hard for a cheater:

1. Each individual transaction is hard to forge or modify.
2. Adding a new item at the tail end of the sequence is somewhat challenging. Furthermore, the difficulty of modification increases with distance from the tail, so older transactions are harder to change.
3. Participants compete to be allowed to add an update at the tail of the sequence, and cheaters can't be sure that they will win.
4. It's not enough to win the competition to add an update at the tail of the sequence—in addition, most of the community must accept that update.

We'll examine each of these aspects in turn. Let's first consider how to make an individual transaction hard to forge.

Unforgeable Transactions

If each entry in the sequence were actually represented in the way that we showed in the earlier diagram, such as "Alice: $6," then it would be easy to forge entries. If we saw some updated state such as "Alice: $4," we wouldn't know whether it was a real change or a fake change. It doesn't matter whether the recorded items are balances (as in this example) or changes like "Decrement Alice's account by $2" or transfers like "Move $2 from Alice's account to Bob's account." The problem isn't in the form of the record, it's that we have no idea whether to believe it or not.

Fortunately, we already know a way to protect against spoofing and forgery. We have already seen a similar problem of distinguishing trusted information from untrusted information, when we wanted to distribute public keys (chapter 25). There, we were interested in finding the public key that is linked to a particular name. The hazard that we had to overcome was that an attacker might fake such a linkage and fool us.

The solution there was to use a signed certificate for each name/key pair. The signing establishes both that the information is from a trusted party, and also that the information is unchanged from what the trusted party published. Because of the mathematical properties of the signatures, we are confident that an attacker can't simply substitute different data.

In a similar fashion, Alice can sign a transaction with her private key. That signature allows anyone to check the signed transaction for validity. If it passes the validity check, that means both that

- the signed transaction was really signed by Alice, and also
- it hasn't been altered from what Alice signed.

However, if the signed transaction fails the validity check, it's meaningless; there's no way of knowing whether it wasn't really signed by Alice or whether it was signed by Alice and subsequently altered. But either way, it's not a transaction to use.

In fact, Bitcoin goes a little further than this. Although we can talk about "Alice's public key," the underlying technical reality in Bitcoin is that "Alice" is *identical* to her public/private key pair within the payment system. Anyone who knows Alice's private key essentially *is* Alice. We noted this characteristic when we first looked at public-key cryptography (chapter 24), but it's more noticeable in Bitcoin.

Bitcoin transactions take place between "wallets" that are identified by special addresses. These addresses are derived from public keys, and for our purposes they're basically the same as public keys—it's just inconvenient to use the public keys directly. In contrast to what we saw when we were concerned with certificates, Bitcoin intentionally does not have any means to match people to particular addresses or public keys. This unusual structure is part of why descriptions of Bitcoin sometimes call it "anonymous," which is technically incorrect. Bitcoin indeed does not have any personal names, but the wallet addresses are *pseudonyms*, so using Bitcoin is like publishing articles and books under a pen name. If Bitcoin were really anonymous, there would be a total lack of identifying information, and thus a lack of traceability. In fact, the wallet addresses are identities, and the transactions are easy to trace between those identities. If any wallet address can be tied to a particular person, that person is in turn tied to all of the transactions relating to that wallet.

By analogy, we can imagine a world in which every cash transaction involves recording the serial numbers on the bills being used, with those serial numbers then being posted on websites along with date/time/location information. In such a world, cash transactions would still be anonymous in the sense that the convenience-store clerk wouldn't know your name as you bought a soda but it would be easy for authorities to figure out where money went to or where it came from, in a way that's usually impossible for cash transactions.

A person who is concerned about Bitcoin traceability can use multiple addresses in an effort to reduce their exposure, but it's hard to be sure you've covered your tracks. Investigators have already been successful at learning many interesting patterns of spending among Bitcoin users, and prosecuting criminals based on records of Bitcoin payments.

Unforgeable History

So far we've figured out only how to make each individual item hard to forge, but that doesn't necessarily prevent an attacker from deleting one or more whole items, or reordering the items. Let's next consider how to make the sequence hard to modify. When we first get a copy of the sequence, we may well need to validate every item in it to make sure it's all OK; but we don't want to revalidate every individual item in the sequence every time we read or modify the sequence. Instead, we want something that is cheaper to check.

One possible solution is to use a digital signature that covers the whole log. Figure 26.1 shows a single signature protecting a two-item log. Such a signature means that not even one bit of either item can be changed without breaking the matching signature.

We can then add an item and protect the new three-item log with a new signature (figure 26.2).

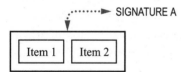

Figure 26.1
Whole-log signature, two-item log.

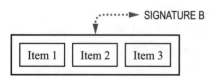

Figure 26.2
Whole-log signature, three-item log.

Although the new signature ensures that the three signed items are not changed subsequently, the transition from a two-item list to a three-item list was essentially unprotected: There's nothing stopping the substitution or alteration of item 1 or item 2 after signature A is removed and before signature B is applied. Figure 26.3 shows the problem.

At the top of the diagram, we have the two-item sequence, and we want to add a third item. In the second line, we have to remove signature A to

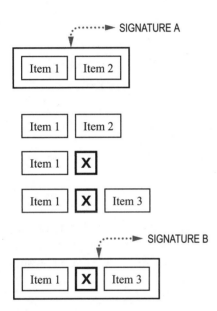

Figure 26.3
Altering the log while it's unprotected.

add the third item—just adding in the third item would break the existing signature, which isn't what we want. But while the signature is absent, an attacker replaces item 2 with X. We then add in our item 3 and sign the three-item sequence, even though the second item was corrupted.

The signature scheme here clearly isn't working correctly, because removing and replacing the signature left a vulnerability. So we'd instead prefer a scheme in which we sign an item once and then leave the signature alone.

What about signing the whole log all over again every time an item is added?

Figure 26.4 shows a one-item log and its associated signature. Figure 26.5 shows a two-item log and its associated signature.

Figure 26.4
Nested signatures, one-item log.

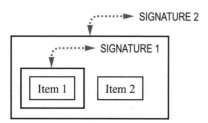

Figure 26.5
Nested signatures, two-item log.

The second item is just appended to the first item with its signature, and the whole pile is then signed.

In principle, this looks like a success. In practice, there will be problems if each change has to sign the whole log again. The log just keeps getting longer, and there is always some per-bit cost for any signing mechanism; so the cost of signing the whole log just keeps growing. A potential hazard is that the system can eventually get to a point where it takes a long time just to read all the bits that need to be signed, without even considering the time it takes to actually do the signing computation as well. A successful long-running system sows the seeds of its own failure; as the number of bits grows, the system becomes ever slower. We don't really want to build a "success disaster" system, where successful operation of the system guarantees that it just gets slower and slower over time. So we'd prefer to build a system where the cost of signing stays roughly the same, no matter how long the log is.

Fortunately, we don't have to sign the entire log. All that we really need to do is to ensure that there's an unforgeable way of adding in each new entry. We can think about simply chaining together two entries:

1. the signature of the last entry, and
2. the new entry.

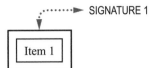

Figure 26.6
Chained signatures, one-item log.

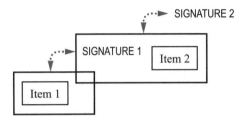

Figure 26.7
Chained signatures, two-item log.

Recall that computing a signature over some piece of data means that the signed piece of data can't be changed by even a single bit. Even a one-bit change will "break" the associated signature—that is, the signature will fail if we test its validity for the changed data. So computing a signature over both the last signature and the new entry means that not even a single bit of either one can be changed.

As with our previous scheme, figure 26.6 shows a single-item log with a corresponding signature. But adding a new element now doesn't involve all of the earlier items. Instead, the new signature only covers the old last signature and the new item (figure 26.7).

Even though the signature doesn't cover the whole log, it still has very similar behavior. In the chain, if even a single bit of item 1 is changed, the corresponding signature breaks.

In figure 26.8, there is a small dot that is different in item 1. As a result, signature 1 no longer matches item 1, as indicated by the large exclamation point.

Fixing such a break requires recomputing the relevant signature. In figure 26.9, we've repaired the mismatch between the modified item 1 and signature 1, by computing a new signature: signature 1'. But changing signature 1 to signature 1' in turn breaks the following signature. In the same diagram,

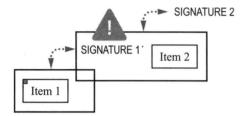

Figure 26.8
Single-bit change in item 1 breaks signature 1.

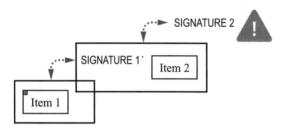

Figure 26.9
Recomputed signature 1 breaks signature 2.

signature 2 has broken (as indicated by the large exclamation point). So changing even a single bit somewhere inside the chain ripples down the chain from there, breaking all of the following signatures. Although it's possible to "fix up" the chain so that it once again contains all correct signatures, such a fix requires recomputing *all* of the chained signatures after the point of the change.

With this chained-signature scheme, we can now have an extensible sequence of items that's hard to forge. Attackers can't simply delete an item, insert an item, or modify an existing item, because any of those changes will break signatures that are expensive to recompute.

Bitcoin Puzzles

The Bitcoin ledger goes a step further than simply chaining entries so they can't be split apart. There are also limits on what kind of an entry can be added. To understand those limits, we can start by thinking about a large collection of Lego blocks, all the same size, but various different colors. The signature mechanism that we've described so far is a little bit like putting blocks together, and using a strong glue to keep them connected. The longer the glue has dried, the harder it is to pry the blocks apart; but we haven't yet had any limitations on what colors can be added in what order. But let's assume that we now have a rule that says the blocks have to go in rainbow order: red, orange, yellow, green, blue, indigo, violet, then red again, orange again, and so on. That means it won't be enough to just have the end of the chain and the glue ready when we want to add a block—we'll also have to find a block that's the right color. If the last block of the chain is green, it doesn't matter if we have lots of red blocks handy; the next block we need has to be blue.

We described this constraint in terms of a well-known fixed sequence of colors. Our next step toward the actual Bitcoin arrangement is to think about a table to let us determine the next color from the current color. For the seven colors of the rainbow, that table may not be necessary if we are pretty good at remembering the colors. But if there were a much larger number of colors and we insisted on particular sequences ("mango" after "fuchsia," say), then we would have to use a table to keep track of what the next allowed color is.

In Bitcoin, there is a similar kind of constraint in terms of what kind of element can follow another one, but it's actually even more complicated than a big table of allowed colors. A Lego block has both "bumps" on top and "hollows" below. A single piece both fits onto the piece before it *and* defines the place where the next piece will fit. In a somewhat similar fashion, in Bitcoin the last element of the sequence is both a solution to the previous puzzle and a new puzzle to be solved. What kind of puzzle is it? In chapter 24, we saw the problem of factoring numbers as an example of a problem that's hard to solve but easy to check. If you or someone you know likes Sudoku puzzles, those also have the same characteristic. The specific puzzle to be solved in extending the Bitcoin ledger is neither a factoring problem nor a Sudoku, but it shares those characteristics: it's mathematical, it's hard to solve, but it's easy to check.

So instead of having a sequence of Lego blocks where each color determines the following color, Bitcoin has a sequence of puzzle solutions where each solution determines the next solution. A rather elegant aspect of Bitcoin is that the puzzle to be solved hinges on the same kind of mathematical characteristics that we already exploit for signatures, but turned "backwards." To understand that, we'll first look inside signatures to examine hash functions.

Hash Functions

A hash function takes an input value and produces a very different output value. It metaphorically "hashes it up." Typically the hashing-up happens by various transformations on the bits of the input value, but we're not going to look any further at exactly how any particular hash function works. Instead, we'll just consider a physical (if crazy) way to build a hash function. Suppose that you have a collection of 1,000 small boxes, each of which has a different output value from 0 to 999 written inside. You take the boxes to some suitable open space like a field or a gymnasium, and you scatter them around and mix them up, so that they are all in random unordered positions. Then you gather them together—still in that random order—and write a sequence of input values from 0 to 999 on the outside of each box. This is now your hash function: to "hash" a number like 72, you just find the box with 72 written on the outside and open it up (to find a value like 381).

This "box-based" hash function is special in two ways: First, the input values have the same range as the output values (both of them run from 0 to 999). Second, every input value maps to a single output value and vice versa. Hashing is actually much more general than this particular field of boxes, but it's not hard to adapt the field-of-boxes metaphor for more general cases. For example, if two or more different input values can hash to the same output value, that just means that a single box might have more than one number written on the outside.

Now consider how this field-of-boxes works if we want to run the hash function in reverse. We won't worry yet about why we would want to do such a thing. We're just looking at how it would work.

Let's say that the goal is to find the input value whose output value is 42. Naturally, we don't just go over to the box labeled 42, because that's an *input* value—we need the *output* value (the one written inside the box) to be 42. Instead, we have to open one box after another until we find the one that has 42 inside. It doesn't much matter whether we open the boxes sequentially or randomly, because we don't have any way of knowing the fastest way of finding the box that contains 42. However, as soon as we find the box that contains 42, we can easily yell out to any others around what the number is on the outside of the box (say, 89). Anyone who's skeptical can easily walk over and pick up the 89 box for themselves and verify that it has 42 inside.

Hashing Data

The actual Bitcoin puzzle is like this reverse hash, but it uses much larger numbers than this example. In fact, the input value for the Bitcoin hash is the chunk of new information that we want to add to the distributed ledger. We don't ordinarily think of a chunk of information—a pile of names, numbers, data structures—as a number. But for any chunk of information in the digital world, we can also look at it as just a string of bits and treat it as a really long number.

So now let's revisit the situation with much bigger numbers and a much bigger hash function. We won't try to sustain the field-of-boxes metaphor, just relying instead on the intuition we've developed about a forward-hash being easy (opening a single box) while a reverse-hash is hard (opening many boxes in the quest for a particular value).

But wait, there's more! We don't just use the chunk of data as the input value to the hash function. The new wrinkle in the Bitcoin puzzle is that the chunk of data we're adding to the ledger has one part that is adjustable. In that place, we can put any number that we want. That means that we can produce a whole series of different numbers to try with the hash function.

With this arrangement, we can produce lots of different numbers. Can we produce any possible number? No. Even with an adjustable part of the chunk, we can't produce every possible number. After all, we do still have some unchanging data in the chunk. The situation with these chunks-that-can-be-numbers is a little like being told that the input values have to be of the form 429XXX387, where each of the X's can be any value from 0 to 9. There's some variability or freedom, but there are also limits. We can produce 429000387 or 429924387 or 429888387, but there's simply no way we can adjust those X's to produce a number like 333333, for example.

Does it matter that we can't produce every possible number? Not really. In our earlier example of running the hash function backward, we were looking for the single value 42. We might be in trouble if we had to find a single output value now, since we know we can't produce every possible input value. Fortunately, that's not an issue for the Bitcoin puzzle. The limits are OK, because we aren't looking for only a single matching value. Instead, we are looking for any number with a particular "shape." When thinking about decimal numbers—not the way the real Bitcoin puzzle works—the rule might be that any number ending in three zeroes is acceptable. So that means we don't care if the number found is 1000, 2000, 10000, or 48290302000—only that it has to have (at least) three zeroes at the end. The real Bitcoin puzzle is like this, but it works in terms of having a certain number of *bits* being zero.

By trying different values in the adjustable part of the chunk, we can produce different input values for the Bitcoin hash function. For each different try, we then treat the chunk as a number and "look inside the corresponding box" (run the hash function) to see if the number inside has enough zeroes at the end. As soon as we have a winner, we can publish the winning chunk—including the "right" value for the adjustable part. Everyone else can readily verify that the winning chunk does indeed achieve the right "shape" value for the hash function.

Because the hash function is intentionally complex and unpredictable, the only way to find the right input is to proceed by trial and error. Once the solution is found, it's obvious to all that it does indeed fit; until it's found, no one knows who will find it first. There are no shortcuts to finding the right solution.

A correctly formed puzzle solution is called a *block*; not surprisingly, the chain of blocks that the participants collectively build is called a *blockchain*.

Moving Time Forward

We've now seen three of the ways that the blockchain is protected against forgery:

• Each wallet-related item in a block is signed to avoid fake transactions.
• A chain of signatures helps ensure that it's hard for an attacker to change any item of the blockchain.
• Extending the chain only by solving an unpredictable puzzle both makes it hard for an attacker to change the chain *and* makes it hard for any attacker to monopolize the process of adding updates to the chain.

These techniques already mean that it would be expensive to forge a different version of the blockchain: it would require recomputing lots of signatures, and again solving lots of trial-and-error puzzles.

However, we still have to be concerned that a well-equipped attacker could invest a lot of time and resources in just such a brute-force approach. We know that the cost of altering the chain increases with every block following the point of change; accordingly, we would expect a brute-force attacker to focus on something that's newly added to the chain. Can the participants discourage such an attack? Yes, thanks to an additional part of the system: The blockchain does not simply sit idle, waiting for new items to be added. Instead, there is an ongoing process whereby participants are *always* trying to add more blocks to the shared chain. The participants are in a perpetual churn of working to lengthen the chain, even if there's no new information to add to the ledger.

Why is it useful to have all this logically unneeded work of chain-lengthening, even if the ledger's content is not otherwise changing? We can see it as imposing a kind of deadline. Suppose that we are given a hard puzzle to solve, and without a deadline it would usually take us a month to solve it. That puzzle becomes harder if we impose a deadline of solving it in an hour or less, even though the puzzle itself is identical. In a roughly similar fashion, if the chain were static, then it might not matter that the chain is expensive to forge—because a determined attacker could choose to spend whatever time was required to forge it. However, there's a deadline because the puzzle keeps changing. The blockchain combines both an expensive-to-forge representation and a "now" that is constantly moving forward. That combination makes it hard to forge a replacement log.

The Crowd Foils Cheating

What if attackers simply assert that they have solved the necessary puzzle when they really haven't? Remember that the puzzle solutions are easy to check, even though the puzzle is hard to solve. Each participant maintains his or her own local view of the chain, with his or her own local decision about whether a block can be added at the end of the chain. A correctly functioning participant (defender) who receives a failed puzzle solution simply ignores it. If most of the community does likewise, then the collective view of the chain is not fooled by the attempt to cheat.

What about the inverse problem, where a cheater ignores a correct solution? The cheater's local view of the chain would no longer match what others have; in particular, the cheater would still be working on solving the problem of adding to the "old" tail of the chain while everyone else has moved on to a new problem. Ignoring a correct solution hurts only the cheater.

Informally, we can argue that successful cheating requires that the cheater(s) have far more computing power than everyone else. With completely dominant computing power, it would be possible to find solutions faster than anyone else. After enough time, it would be possible to build up a completely bogus ledger so that it was the longest chain, and accepted by the wider community. However, if computing power is divided among participants with diverse interests, the overall system will still function properly even if some of those participants try to cheat. Notice that we can also turn that reasoning around to produce a caution: if some participant or group of participants can amass a majority of the available computing power, they will be able to cheat.

Rewards via Mining

As we have noted, the Bitcoin system depends on convincing participants to spend their resources on producing new elements of the blockchain. In fact, it's not enough to just have some participants working on that task— to beat an attacker, the defenders need to ensure that more resources are spent extending the blockchain than any attacker can use. How is that possible? The answer is surprisingly simple: Participants are paid for successfully extending the chain. Every successful addition to the blockchain also produces a small amount of new bitcoins, credited to the participant that successfully solved the relevant puzzle. How do the new bitcoins appear? There's just an entry in the distributed ledger, like any other entry describing a transfer; we can think of it as a reserved entry in each block that is filled in with the identity of the participant, and thus becomes part of the chain if that participant solves the problem first. The process of adding blocks to the chain is often called *mining*.

Let's compare bitcoin mining to gold mining. Mining for bitcoin is like mining for gold in that a lot of effort and machinery are used in the pursuit of unpredictable rewards. In the case of bitcoin mining, all of the effort and machinery is computational—but overall, the analogy still works. Whereas a gold miner is handling a large volume of low-value minerals to find a small volume of gold, a bitcoin miner is handling a large volume of failed puzzle solutions to find a small volume of correct puzzle solutions.

However, the analogy has its limits. A notable contrast to gold mining is that there are no richer or poorer veins of the desired reward. All the bitcoin miners are effectively competing within one single mine, as defined by mathematical properties of the universe. In fact, they're all working at the very same "mine face" within that single mine.

Another notable contrast is that speed is essential to miners—a puzzle solution is only valuable if immediately published, beating all the competitors who are also looking for the next solution. That's not like gold mining, where once you have the gold it's yours regardless of whether anyone else knows about it. In some ways, bitcoin mining is more like staking claims than like mining—if there are competing claims to the same property, the winner is the one who gets the paperwork filed first.

Also in contrast to gold mining, the productivity of bitcoin mining is controlled by an automatic feedback process. When bitcoins are being produced too quickly, mining them becomes harder. When bitcoins are being produced too slowly, mining them becomes easier. The system includes a well-known limit to the number of bitcoins that can ever be mined, so eventually mining will end. Until then, the bitcoin "mine" never gets "worked out" like a gold mine—but it also never hits rich new veins like the ones a gold mine might have.

Pollution and Bitcoin

Although it might sound very clean and environmentally friendly to perform mathematical puzzle-solving at high speed, the ugly reality of fast computing is that it requires energy. Bitcoin miners compete with each other in terms of their ingenuity and engineering for who can most effectively convert energy into new blocks on the blockchain; however, the blockchain itself is indifferent to everything except the mathematics of the puzzle-solving. Accordingly, it's often economically attractive to use lots of cheap energy, rather than being sophisticated about energy usage. At this writing, bitcoin mining is dominated by miners in China, who achieve their advantage primarily through the use of highly polluting (but cheap) coal to generate the electricity used.

Even if we were using energy to provide a direct benefit to people in the form of heat or electricity, increasing the consumption of "bad" energy sources seems like a poor choice. Such a choice of harmful energy sources

seems especially dubious when the growth in pollution and heat generation is simply driving a kind of computational treadmill. Although that
activity might be worthwhile to keep people from cheating on Bitcoin transactions, it doesn't seem like it should be a high priority if it's damaging the
environment.

The Bitcoin system structure is elegant if all miners are using similar
sources of energy, but this "race to the bottom" for the cheapest, nastiest
energy is a serious drawback. It will be interesting to see whether this situation can be improved: perhaps in a future evolution of Bitcoin, or perhaps a
different competing approach to building a distributed ledger.

Mining and Value

The community of miners is not fixed. Instead, each individual participant
is free to join or leave the community of miners at any time. Indeed, if you
are so inclined, you can personally acquire the equipment and knowledge
required to mine bitcoin—part of its appeal is that there are no gatekeepers
to judge your worthiness to join the community. That community is the
engine powering the blockchain, and the community's efforts are an important component of how well the system can defend against cheating. So it's
worth looking a little closer at what prompts a participant to join or leave
the group of miners.

Being a miner means that you have some step-taking machinery at your
disposal, and you choose to perform the mining computations: the puzzle-
solving task that allows an update to be added to the chain. If there are no
other miners, the analysis of rewards vs. effort is easy: the sole miner reaps
all the rewards. As soon as there are any other miners, there are no guarantees of rewards; instead, it's a little like buying lottery tickets.

In a lottery, the odds are arranged so that the players lose on average. Bitcoin miners are more calculating than lottery players—they want to "play"
only when they will win. Each participant "plays" when they expect their
reward to exceed their costs. If any participant expects to lose in this exchange,
they will stop mining. But this simple formulation leaves us with the question of what makes the exchange attractive or unattractive at any particular
point in time. The decision is necessarily a matter of judgment—the exchange
is between the likely cost of "winning" the next block on the chain and the
next expected reward. We could pursue this analysis in some detail, but

we wouldn't really learn anything more about Bitcoin as a system. We can simply wind up our examination of the join-or-leave decision by observing that it's impossible to get it exactly right—between the unpredictability of rewards, the unknown behavior of other players, and the volatile "real-world" value of bitcoins, there's too much noise in the system to make precise reliable rules. It's worth underscoring this point: Although parts of the Bitcoin system are encoded as programs and very mechanical, each participant's decision to mine or stop mining necessarily depends on human judgment.

Bootstrapping Value

Bitcoin links economic incentives to a desired system behavior. The system rewards miners for their work by providing them with bitcoins. This approach is great if you can get it to work, but there is a bootstrapping problem: what makes the reward valuable? A number of Bitcoin variants and derivatives have been created, which shouldn't be surprising—after all, once you realize that it's possible to create a money system without government involvement, why stop at just one? But each such new currency creates again the chicken-and-egg problem that afflicted Bitcoin in its early days: to be valuable, a currency needs to be widely accepted; to be widely accepted, a currency needs to be valuable.

For a concrete example, imagine that Bob wants to create a new currency called Bobcoin. It's easy for Bob to just set up the system and start mining bobcoin, awarding himself bobcoins every time that he extends the blockchain. But the bobcoins don't have any value as long as he's the only one who has them, and it's not clear what anyone else gains from joining with Bob in the Bobcoin world.

These kinds of currencies have intriguing analogies to a startup company. In both cases, there is a step that seems like the creation of something potentially valuable from nothing at all: the mining of coins in one case, the issuance of stock in the other. But in both cases the "something" that's created is best understood as a share of something aspirational.

Why do people accept payment in shares of a startup company? Because they believe it will be worth more in the future; because they believe in the future of the company. Likewise, why would early adopters accept a reward of bitcoins? Because they believed that reward would be worth more in the future.

Bitcoin and Governance

Bitcoin is an ingenious system. However, its origins can prompt some understandable concern. The system was invented and published by "Satoshi Nakomoto." At this writing, no one has satisfactorily connected a real person or group to that name. Since no one knows for sure who invented the scheme, it's hard to judge their motivations. It's entirely possible that there are hidden conflicts of interest or outright cheating that should affect our willingness to use the system.

The Snowden revelations about activities of the U.S. National Security Agency (NSA) included some surprising efforts by the NSA to subvert cryptographic standards. It's entirely conceivable that some actor—not necessarily the NSA, not necessarily any U.S. agency—is doing something similar with Bitcoin. Unfortunately, it's not even clear whether such subversion would be undercutting Bitcoin (to cheat in the future) or whether Bitcoin itself is a big subversion (to avoid a better, less traceable cryptocurrency). These suspicions will necessarily endure as long as the origins of the system remain obscure, and to be fair, there will probably be some concerns about the nature of Bitcoin even if all of its origins and early history are completely revealed.

For partly related reasons, governance of the Bitcoin system is problematic. The problems don't affect the minute-to-minute, day-to-day behavior: the ordinary operations of recording transactions in the blockchain seem to be quite reliable. Despite a variety of attacks and errors, at this writing the Bitcoin system itself is still running. If some participants take actions that cause the state of the system to be split or unclear, the participants with the most computational power eventually win; the ongoing operation of the system resolves the conflict. That part of the Bitcoin experiment can probably be deemed a success.

Although the features that let Bitcoin work are powerful and interesting, they should not be oversold as somehow providing new ways to organize society. Indeed, there is at least anecdotal evidence in the opposite direction: that Bitcoin needs more "political" elements to thrive. Although the day-to-day operation of the system works surprisingly well, there are serious problems whenever that operational system encounters its own design limits or flaws. Bitcoin is not perfect, and sometimes the imperfections become serious obstacles to continued operation of the system. At such a point it becomes apparent that Nakomoto's design did not include any reliable mechanism to choose among competing versions of how the block-chain mechanisms should evolve. We might say that the system's operations work acceptably, but in contrast its "meta-operations" are not adequate. In some ways Bitcoin is like a constitution that does not include an amendment process.

Naturally, it's difficult to establish trust in a system intended for use among mutually untrusting participants. However, experience with Bitcoin suggests that evolving systems inevitably encounter some situations that are difficult to handle without any trust. In certain kinds of decisions, resolution is easier if at least some of the participants trust each other—accepting a temporary loss of control or power, in the expectation that there will be a better eventual result.

Significance of Bitcoin

What is the significance of Bitcoin? The system serves as a useful demonstration that it's possible to build a distributed ledger that works, even when some people are trying to cheat. That demonstration is valuable regardless of how Bitcoin succeeds or fails subsequently. Whether Bitcoin supersedes the payment systems of the world or collapses due to governance failures, it will have been a valuable experiment and will have accomplished more than many people thought was possible when it started.

Bitcoin is potentially important to the world at large. We can see in it the seeds of a next wave of digital revolution. We have seen textual information become digital and then networked. After that, we've seen audio and video became digital and then networked. In Bitcoin we can see ways in which various kinds of financial entities—money, commitments, contracts, and escrow—become digital and then networked.

What if we narrow our interest to the focus of this book? What is Bitcoin's significance as a computational system? Bitcoin comes closer than any other system we've examined to substituting mathematics for trust. That capability of achieving something useful for a group, with others whom you don't know (or perhaps even know and actively distrust) is very interesting. Bitcoin is powered by an intriguing combination of self-interest and mathematics.

27 Looking Back

Congratulations! You've completed your tour. You've seen some aspects of how a single process works. You've seen some of the ways in which multiple processes interact. You've seen some of the ways that failures affect processes and ways that systems can be organized to overcome those failures. Finally, you've seen some aspects of how processes attack or defend.

Let's consider what difference that tour has made to your life. Have you had a life-changing experience? Have you learned skills that make you highly employable? Probably not, although no one will complain if you have. I'll certainly be delighted—let me know of your experience!

Instead, what I think is more likely is that you have a different perspective. You've now seen some things you hadn't seen before and learned of connections between ideas that are new to you. Of course, you could have learned about new ideas and connections from many different books on many different topics—so why would this set of ideas be of particular value?

In considering that question, I ran across this idea from William Gibson. He is responding to the question of whether we'll have computers embedded in our brains:

> I very much doubt that our grandchildren will understand the distinction between that which is a computer and that which isn't. Or, to put it another way, they will not know "computers" as any distinct category of object or function. This, I think, is the logical outcome of genuinely ubiquitous computing: the wired world. [....]
>
> In this world there will be no need for the physical augmentation of the human brain, as the most significant, and quite unthinkably powerful, augmentation will have already taken place postgeographically, via distributed processing.
>
> You won't need smart goo in your brain, because your fridge and your toothbrush will be very smart indeed, enormously smart, and they will be there for you, constantly and always.

I don't know if I necessarily agree with Gibson about the inevitability of this future, but I am hesitant to second-guess him. I encountered his novel *Neuromancer* when I was an undergraduate studying computer science in the early 1980s. At the time I first read his book, my everyday reality was a primitive slog with punched cards and batch computing. Gibson wrote about cyberspace and virtual reality, envisioning a world that is recognizable thirty years later, but that is still futuristic and incompletely realized.

I don't know the future feature set of your smart toothbrush, but I do know something about how its computational mechanisms will likely work. Products come and go, technical concerns go in and out of fashion, but the underlying realities of computation are unchanging. They are properties of the universe, not attributes of the current technology. Understanding those properties of the universe gives us skills to deal with the computational systems in our lives; but more important, it also gives us insights into the broader world of ideas about communication, process, failure, and coordination—all of which affect us in some way every day of our lives.

Index of Metaphors and Examples

Subject Index